LIFE
AND
TIMES
OF
SIR ALEXANDER
TILLOCH
GALT

OSCAR DOUGLAS SKELTON

LIFE
AND
TIMES
OF
SIR ALEXANDER
TILLOCH
GALT

EDITED AND WITH AN INTRODUCTION BY

GUY MacLEAN

The Carleton Library No. 26 / McClelland and Stewart Limited

By permission of Mr. H. H. Skelton and Mrs. A. R. Menzies

Life and Times of Sir Alexander Tilloch Galt was first published in 1920 by the Oxford University Press, Toronto.

The Canadian Publishers

McClelland and Stewart Limited
25 Hollinger Road, Toronto 16

PRINTED AND BOUND IN CANADA
BY
T. H. BEST PRINTING COMPANY LIMITED

THE CARLETON LIBRARY

A series of Canadian reprints and new collections of source material relating to Canada, issued under the editorial supervision of the Institute of Canadian Studies of Carleton University, Ottawa.

CONTENTS

Introduction to
the Carleton Library Edition

The life of Alexander Galt is a history of Canada in the nineteenth century. From the moment he arrived in Lower Canada in 1835 until his death fifty-eight years later, his pursuits paralleled the story of his adopted country. At eighteen he was settling virgin lands in Lower Canada; before he died he was pioneering schemes to open up the West. And in the years between, as businessman, politician, and diplomat, he played a leading role in every new phase in the nation's growth. The biography of such a man required the hand of an historian with a solid grasp of all those social, economic, political, and constitutional forces which were influenced by and had influenced Galt. One such scholar emerged to accept the challenge.

Oscar Douglas Skelton (1878-1941) was a forerunner of modern Canadian historians. Born in Orangeville, Ontario, he was educated at Queen's University where he graduated with first class Honours in Classics. Following two more years of classical studies at Queen's and the University of Chicago, he spent some time as a journalist and as assistant editor of a literary periodical. He returned to Chicago for two years of graduate study in Political Science and Economics, after which he was given an appointment at Queen's where he remained for seventeen years as Professor of Political and Economic Science and subsequently as Dean of the Faculty of Arts.

Skelton was an enormously productive scholar as well as an inspiring teacher. His first book, *Socialism: A Critical Analysis* (1911), attracted the favourable attention of Lenin, and prompted G. D. H. Cole, an acknowledged authority on the subject, to describe it as the best criticism of socialism ever written.[1] His numerous articles appeared with impressive regularity in a variety of journals ranging from the highly academic *Journal of Political Economy* and *American Economic Review* to the more practical *Grain Growers' Guide*.

His contribution to the writing of Canadian history was prodigious. The sheer bulk of his work is in itself awesome. In a ten-year period he published seven, often large and always authoritative, studies: an essay on the general economic history of the Dominion, 1867-1912, which comprised most of volume

[1] G. S. Graham, "Oscar Douglas Skelton," *Canadian Historical Review*, XXII (June, 1941), p. 233.

IX of *Canada and its Provinces* (1914), *The Railway Builders* (1916), *The Day of Sir Wilfrid Laurier* (1916), *The Canadian Dominion* (1919), the *Life and Times of Sir Alexander Tilloch Galt* (1920), and the *Life and Letters of Sir Wilfrid Laurier* (1921). It was an astonishing demonstration of steady industry combined with sound learning, and one which has rarely been equalled in this country.

Skelton was intensely interested in all the important issues of the day, but after the First World War he was particularly concerned with Canada's equivocal position *vis-à-vis* Great Britain. The growth of self-government had brought the colonies internal autonomy but the legal control of foreign policy was still reserved to the Mother Country. In other words, on major issues, there was one foreign policy for all members of the Empire and it was dictated from London. For a state whose national interest did not always coincide with that of Britain, this was an unsatisfactory, even an intolerable, situation. So in 1920 Skelton, keenly aware that within the Empire practice normally outran constitutional form, submitted a solution. In two articles he described an Empire of equal partners bound by a common allegiance to the Crown. Two years later, in an address to the Canadian Club of Ottawa, he emphatically rejected a statement by Lloyd George that the British Foreign Office was the instrument of foreign policy for the Empire. He presented a forceful argument for Canadian control of Canadian foreign policy. "Let us remember," he said, "that as a matter of actual fact we have assumed, and with cumulative rapidity in the last few years, control over the greater part of this field of foreign policy through our own government, and that the path of security, the path of safety, the path of responsibility, the path of honour and of duty toward other nations in the world lies, I think, in following that course to the logical end."[2]

This speech marked the beginning of a new career. Mackenzie King had heard it and was very favourably impressed, noting in his diary: "An excellent address – would make an excellent foundation for Canadian policy on External Affairs and Skelton himself would make an excellent man for that department."[3] Skelton was asked to prepare background infor-

[2] W. A. Mackintosh, "O. D. Skelton," in R. L. McDougall (ed.) *Canada's Past and Present: A Dialogue* (Our Living Tradition, Fifth Series), Toronto, 1965, p. 69. Dr. Mackintosh's essay is found on pp. 59-77 of this volume.

[3] R. MacG. Dawson, *William Lyon Mackenzie King, A Political Biography, 1874-1923* (Toronto, 1958), p. 454.

mation for the Imperial Conference of 1923 and to accompany King to London.[4] And in the next year, with some misgivings, he accepted the invitation to join the Department of External Affairs as Counsellor. He succeeded Sir Joseph Pope as Under-Secretary of State for External Affairs in 1925.

Skelton exerted a very great influence on Canadian foreign policy in the years that followed. Inheriting a department of three officers, he built it into one of the world's most respected diplomatic services. He was the trusted adviser not only of King, but of Meighen and Bennett as well. An unobtrusive confidant of three prime ministers, he helped to guide Canada to full nationhood and, as an architect of the Commonwealth, assisted in establishing the principles which have grouped a host of emergent nations into a unique family of states.

At the time of his death Skelton enjoyed an immense prestige as the man who, more than any other in his time, created Canadian foreign policy and the machinery to execute it.[5] Recently, however, there have been signs of a reassessment of his role as a policy-maker and, as is always the case with a forceful and influential public figure, controversy will no doubt continue. But until the diplomatic records are open to scholarly examination, it is too soon to pass judgment.[6] In the meantime we may safely assume that, whatever the revision, the portrait of a dedicated and extraordinarily capable public servant will endure.

Certainly Skelton's stature as an historian remains undiminished. If voluminous writings are the only criterion of a scholar's worth, then Skelton's prolific pen alone should secure him an honoured place among Canadian historians. His significance, however, may be measured not only by the number of

[4] King drew on the assistance of Skelton because the Department of External Affairs had a tiny establishment of three officers, two of whom were elderly, and the third a man whom King suspected of Conservative leanings. In 1922 he described the department as a "Tory hive" (James Eayrs, *The Art of the Possible: Government and Foreign Policy in Canada* [Toronto, 1961], p. 39).

[5] G. S. Graham, *op. cit.*, p. 234.

[6] For some recent references to Skelton and Canadian foreign policy, see: Bruce Hutchison, *The Incredible Canadian* (Toronto, 1952), p. 250; James Eayrs, *In Defence of Canada* (Toronto, 1964), pp. 11, 24; Vincent Massey, *What's Past is Prologue: The Memoirs of the Right Honourable Vincent Massey* (Toronto, 1963), pp. 134-35; H. Blair Neatby, *William Lyon Mackenzie King: The Lonely Heights, 1924-1932* (Toronto, 1963), p. 35; C. P. Stacey, review of Vincent Massey, *What's Past is Prologue* in the *Canadian Historical Review*, XLV (December, 1964), pp. 322-23.

books he wrote, but also by the methods he employed in writing them. For he was part of the revolution which took place in historical scholarship about the time of the First World War.

Nineteenth-century writing in Canadian history was largely the hobby of amateurs – antiquarians, journalists and lawyers who were content to chronicle political events. They were preoccupied with two particular periods: the conquest of French Canada and the achievement of responsible government. Equally important themes, such as the coming of Confederation, they virtually ignored. They rarely ventured into the fields of economic and social history, a deficiency which struck Skelton as deplorable. "It never occurred to me before," he wrote to Adam Shortt, "how completely and absolutely and inexcusably wanting all the histories of Canada are on the side of trade and commerce and industrial life generally."[7] Trained in modern techniques, he endeavoured to break with the traditional approach and to set forth the underlying economic and social factors which determine the course of politics.

The *Life and Times of Sir Alexander Tilloch Galt* is a classic example of Skelton's approach put into practice. It describes a man whose interests were as sweeping as the country itself: a politician who helped create it, a businessman who made it economically viable, and a statesman who blazed new trails in its diplomacy. The biographer content to write this life from speeches would have given but a fleeting glimpse of a restless giant. Skelton, hindered by the paucity of previous historical research, set about the immense task of compressing within one volume a history of Canada and the life story of one of its principal figures. The wonder was, to paraphrase Samuel Johnson, not that he did it well, but that he did it at all.

Not surprisingly, the end result was a massive volume. Interspersed through the personal narrative were large chunks of general history. These produce a patch-work effect and make tedious reading today. This unhappy form was dictated by Skelton's assumption that most of his readers would have only a vague knowledge of the period and might, therefore, miss the full impact of Galt's genuine creativity. These segments really detract from the main story and for that reason have been largely eliminated from this reprint of *Galt*. When first written, however, they shed light on many hitherto neglected but forma-

[7] Kenneth N. Windsor, "Historical Writing in Canada to 1920," *Literary History of Canada* (Toronto, 1965), p. 235.

tive phases of Canadian history. Thus Skelton broke new ground which subsequent scholarship has cultivated intensively. As will be gathered from the footnotes prepared for this new edition, his descriptions of land settlement, railway building, party politics, Canadian-American relations and imperial problems have long since ceased to be definitive. This fact should in no way lessen one's admiration of the work of an incisive intellect in interpreting detail and fitting it into a broad integrated pattern.

Skelton was not a stylist of prose. His books have neither the graceful artistry of a Creighton nor the sharp wit of an Underhill. Nevertheless, his writing was fluent and lucid, very often concealing from the casual reader his close-knit reasoning and imaginative skill. Embedded in his work are frequent flashes of insight which laboriously researched monographs have merely served to confirm.

This is not to say that Skelton's biography of Galt is without its faults. Although he deprecated his predecessors' neglect of economic history and made a conscious effort to compensate for it, his interests remained focused on the formal development of institutions and the achievement of self-government. Great portions of the original edition of the book are devoted to accounts of Galt's encounters with scheming Englishmen bent on frustrating the steady Canadian advance toward full autonomy. Sometimes the assiduous pursuit of this theme managed to bring to light events of immense importance. For example, Skelton properly attached great significance to Galt's "declaration of independence" in 1859 when he confidently affirmed the right of Canadians to impose a duty on British imports despite the loud protests of British manufacturers and a rebuke by the British government. This was a turning point in the history of imperial relations, making possible the effective control of the self-governing colonies over their own trade and tariff policies. Obsession with imperial relations, however, diverted Skelton's attention from another predominant theme of Canadian history, the influence of geography.

The state of Canada has been moulded by its geography. Early trade routes ran east and west from the Saskatchewan valley and through the Great Lakes–St. Lawrence system to the sea. Over this vast natural system of communication the staple products of the hinterland moved to the large cities of the East. Men of imagination perceived that the natural pattern might be sustained by acts of will. Galt was one of the very first to see that ribbons of steel could reinforce the old commercial empire of the St. Lawrence. Fully six years before the Charlottetown Conference he was proposing to superimpose a political structure, Confederation, upon the geographical skeleton. Political union of the colonies, canals and railways all became part of a single grand design to impose a nation upon the inherent facts of geography. It is within the context of this design that Galt's perceptive genius emerges.

Skelton accorded Galt full recognition as the prophet who called for a federation of the colonies as early as 1858, but inexplicably he failed to note that Galt, as much as any man, made it a practical reality. The representatives of Nova Scotia, New Brunswick and Prince Edward Island at the Charlottetown Conference were initially sceptical about the larger union which the Canadians had come to propose. They feared that the Maritimes stood to suffer financially. If their suspicions had not been overcome, the conference might have dissolved and with it the project of Confederation. Only one man among the Canadians was capable of convincing the Maritimers that they had nothing to fear.[8] Galt may not have been as able a politician as some of his colleagues from Canada but he had a quick, clever mind, able to devise arrangements capable of circumventing the most stubborn opposition. Here was a challenge worthy of his mettle.

On the second day of the discussions Galt outlined the financial implications of union. With sweeping generalities substantiated with pertinent facts and figures, he drew for the delegates an exciting vision of a nation stretching from sea to sea. The plan of national development, he argued, could only become a reality if the central government possessed unlimited powers of taxation. He brought forth an ingenious scheme of debt allowances which convinced the Maritime delegates of the practicability of federation. At luncheon aboard the *Queen Victoria* immediately following his speech, enthusiastic expressions of general approval were heard for the first time. Once the hurdle of Maritime hostility had been cleared, the delegates could sit down to hammer out the shape of union.

A successful biographer must have a curiosity about people and the skill to evoke his subject's presence. When we have finished reading Skelton's life of Galt, we know a great deal about a Maker of Canada, a Father of Confederation, a Diplomat; but somehow Galt is missing. It is as if we had been given a

[8] Donald Creighton, *The Road to Confederation, The Emergence of Canada: 1863-1867* (Toronto, 1964), pp. 114-116.

formal portrait of an institution rather than a man. Propriety seemed to restrain Skelton from probing beneath the surface to discover what motivated this dynamic, volatile, infectiously enthusiastic person. There is little about Galt's private life, his family, his wealth, his appearance and habits. We can only regret that Skelton, who had the full co-operation of Galt's son, did not inquire after those intimate details which, though they may be incidental, make a figure out of the past come to life. It is the make-up of Galt that is intriguing. What did he want of life? What drove him in relentless pursuit of money? What interest did politics really have for him? Was the *Globe* near the truth when it wrote: "He has not the courage of a mouse, nor has he the sense of right and desire for the people's good. . . . He is a jobber at heart; the benefit of the people is his last thought in considering a public question."? Certainly, as we follow Galt's career, the suspicion grows that to him politics was distasteful but necessary. It was to further the interests of the British American Land Company that he went into politics in the first place. In 1849 he was a strong supporter of union with the United States, resenting what he thought was a British betrayal of Lower Canadian merchants. Thirty years later he advocated closer imperial unity in the hope that it would lead to preferential treatment for Canadian produce in British markets. The prospect of wider horizons for business expansion inspired him to take up the cause of Confederation. The need for more profitable negotiation of trade treaties prompted him to fight for Canadian diplomatic independence. Behind the political achievements there was always the hard-headed, pragmatic Scot, ready to promote an idea when it served his interests. Skelton judiciously presented the accomplishments with scarcely an inquisitive glance at the motives behind them. A more personal biography will some day reveal a character far more complex than the one portrayed by Skelton.

Skelton set out to write a general history of the period as well as a biography of Galt. The background material which might have been necessary in 1920 is now familiar to most educated Canadians and for that reason has largely been omitted from this abridgement. The omissions, which are always indicated by ellipses, amount to about one-third of the original text. Chapters 1, 16 and 18 have been deleted and the chapters in this Carleton Library edition renumbered. Chapter 1, "John Galt and the Canada Company," and Chapter 2 in the original edition have been combined as Chapter 1 of this edition; Chapters 16, "The Halifax Commission," and 17 have been combined and renumbered as Chapter 15; and Chapters 18, "The Northwestern Enterprises," and 19 now form Chapter 16. At appropriate points brief connecting passages have been inserted and marked by the symbol ~. Quotation marks in these connecting passages indicate material taken from Dr. Skelton's text. In a few places explanatory material has been introduced by the use of square brackets. Skelton's system of footnoting was inconsistent and most of the original references have been dropped. Several exceptionally pertinent ones (indicated by asterisks) have been included among the editor's notes at the end of the volume.

GUY MACLEAN
Dalhousie University
November, 1965

Preface to the Original Edition

Few among the makers of Canada have played so varied a part in her upbuilding as Alexander Tilloch Galt. There have been statesmen who impressed themselves more spectacularly upon popular memory. There have been businessmen who have since carried through greater projects of industrial development. There have, however, been few men in our annals who combined in such a degree eminence both in political and in commercial life.

No man did more, if any did as much, to achieve Confederation. While he declined the highest office in his country's gift, Galt was for many years foremost in party council and in parliamentary struggle. Few finance ministers have combined his large grasp of public affairs, his power of bringing order out of chaos, and his lucidity of expression. He was our first and is still our foremost diplomatist. In the shaping of opinion upon the future political relations of his country he took a changing but always reasoned and always influential part. Yet he never could bring himself to make politics his sole or dominant interest. In the opening of the Eastern Townships to settlement, in the early railroad development of Canada, and in the first great projects of joint stock company enterprise, he displayed unusual financial capacity and power of handling men, while in his latest years his energy and optimism found an outlet in enterprises for developing the land and mining resources of the far west.

Throughout the formative period of our national history, Galt played a part of lasting significance to the Canada and the Canadians of after days. The forces that shaped the life and destiny of the Canada of the days before Confederation, and the new Canada of the first years after, are nowhere more fully displayed than in his manifold interests and achievements. In presenting this story of his life, it is hoped to give some picture of the times in which he worked, and particularly of the political experiments worked out under the Union of the two Canadas.

It is a pleasant duty to acknowledge the kindness of Mr. Elliott Galt in placing his father's private papers unreservedly at the writer's disposal.

O. D. SKELTON
Kingston, Canada, 1919

1: The British American Land Company

John Galt, agent for the Canada Company; backwoods settlements and sensitive governors; the break with the Company; last days in London; the call of Canada; the British American Land Company; Alexander Galt and the Company's policy; Galt as Commissioner; the success of his policy.

~ The career of Alexander Tilloch Galt cannot be properly understood without reference to that of his father, John Galt. In temperament and in ability the younger Galt resembled his father, "with just sufficient variation to turn the dreamer into the doer."

John Galt was born in Irvine, Ayrshire, in 1779. After an apprenticeship in the Greenock Customs House, he moved, in 1804, to London where he engaged in several unsuccessful business enterprises. He studied law at Lincoln's Inn, but was never called to the Bar. A new and more eventful period in his life began when he sailed on a trip through the Mediterranean, during which time he travelled briefly with Lord Byron. Upon reaching Turkey it suddenly occurred to him that here was a base for an evasion of the Napoleonic blockade. He negotiated with a Glasgow firm and, by circumventing Turkish red tape, managed to organize the shipment of British manufactures through the Balkans into Hungary and Germany.

Following Napoleon's defeat at Waterloo, Galt turned to literature. He wrote travel books, biographical studies, and several novels. Most of his work is best forgotten, but *Annals of the Parish*, published in 1821, enjoyed a deserved success. A lively description of Scottish life, it has been compared favourably with the best of Sir Walter Scott's novels.[1]

In the year that *Annals of the Parish* appeared, Galt was appointed agent in London for residents of Upper Canada who were seeking redress from the British government for damage suffered during the War of 1812. He pressed his clients' claims successfully and the British government agreed to make partial compensation. At the same time, they argued that the government of Upper Canada should provide the remainder. Unfortunately, the Upper Canadian government had few sources of revenue and was unable to assume this unexpected obligation. Encouraged by the prospect of winning his clients' case, Galt saw a plan whereby Upper Canada could raise a large sum of money quickly through development of the Crown Reserves in the province. When the colony had been settled, large tracts of choice land had been reserved to the Crown in order to provide a stable revenue in the future. A similar reservation had been made for the support of the Protestant clergy. In this way about one-third of the land of the colony had been reserved from settlement. Galt proposed that some of both Reserves be sold to a private company for development and that the income thus obtained from the sale be used to meet the claims of his clients.[2]

He interested a number of London merchants in the project and became the main instrument in the founding of a great colonizing organization. The Canada Land Company, which was set up in 1824 with Galt as secretary and resident manager, acquired vast tracts of land in Upper Canada at very favourable prices. On a grant of one million unsurveyed and largely unexplored acres near Lake Huron, Galt proceeded to lay the foundations of an extensive colony. It was the most important single attempt at settlement in the history of Upper Canada; Guelph, Goderich, and many other towns of Western Ontario are his monument.

The Canada Land Company prospered under Galt's management, but unfortunately he incurred the enmity of Sir Peregrine Maitland, the Lieutenant-Governor of Upper Canada. Maitland unjustly suspected him of sympathizing with the radical party of the colony, led by William Lyon Mackenzie, and complained of his alleged political activities to the Colonial Office, which, in turn, passed the reports on to the Company's directors. In 1829, having been accused of political interference and financial extravagance, Galt was summarily dismissed.

A financially ruined man, Galt returned to England and resumed his literary pursuits.* He produced a large number of insignificant books on a variety of subjects, and was briefly editor of a London newspaper. But unable to relinquish his interest in North America, and hopeful of recouping his earlier losses, John Galt took a leading part in the formation of the British American Land Company for the purchase and development of Crown lands in the Eastern Townships of Lower Canada. Before he was able to pursue the new project actively, he suffered a paralytic stroke and spent his remaining years in

* Skelton failed to note that John Galt served some time in debtors' prison following his return to England. It is interesting to speculate as to whether or not this fact was of any influence in shaping Alexander Galt's fervent ambition to make money.

the painful compilation of an autobiography until his death in 1839. "His work lived after him, and to the land of his chief interest he gave his three sons to carry on the work he had been compelled to abandon."

Alexander was the youngest of John Galt's three sons. The eldest, John, entered the service of the Canada Company and died at a relatively early age. Thomas also was employed with the Canada Company before studying law. He became a very successful lawyer and a Queen's Counsel. In 1869 he was appointed a puisne judge of the Court of Common Pleas of Ontario and became Chief Justice in 1887. He was knighted in the following year. ~

Alexander Tilloch Galt was born in Chelsea, London, September 6, 1817. Of his early boyhood there are few records: happy the boys that have no history. It was largely for the sake of his growing family that his father removed in 1823 from London to Eskgrove, near Edinburgh. Five years later came the great adventure: John Galt, looking forward to years of successful work as the Canada Company's Commissioner, had sent for his family to join him. The prospect was hailed with delight by the three boys, who talked all day and dreamed all night of bears and Indians and forest trails. The slow journey across the Atlantic, the honours showered upon the famous author and his family in New York, the journey by steamboat and barge up the Hudson and the Erie Canal to Lockport, were all sources of keen delight to the expectant youngsters. A halt was made at Burlington Bay, but early in the summer Mrs. Galt went on to the Priory in Guelph, while the three boys were sent to the school of Mr. Braithwaite, in Chambly, Lower Canada. Two years later they were recalled to join their father in England, and it seemed that the brief Canadian episode was over.

In London the chief associations and interests of the family were literary, and for a time it appeared probable that it would be the man of letters rather than the man of business in John Galt who would live again in his sons. Tom and Aleck wrote in 1830, when one was fifteen and the other thirteen, the tale which appears, scarcely revised, in *Bogle Corbett*, and the younger boy, a year or two later, had the honour of seeing a story all his own appearing in *Fraser's Magazine*, then in the full flush of its success. But these first flights were not continued. Opportunities for business careers developed, and all three sons seized them. The literary facility and the power of lucid, straightforward narrative which Alexander inherited stood him in good stead in both his commercial and his political career, but it never tempted him to make literature an end in itself. It was to be business and politics, not business and literature, which were to divide the interest of the younger Galt.

Early in March, 1835, Alexander Galt sailed for Quebec, to take up his work in the head office of the new Land Company at Sherbrooke.

From the outset his fortunes were closely linked with those of the Eastern Townships, the vast undeveloped territory which lay between the St. Lawrence and the American border and between the Richelieu and the Chaudière. They were the field of the operations of the Land Company in which his business training began and his first success was achieved. It was with the object of developing the Townships that he was induced to take up the building of the St. Lawrence and Atlantic Railroad, and thus entered upon his railroad career. And it was also the interests of the Township and of the Company which first led him into politics, as it was the limitations of the Townships field which throughout shaped his political career. . . .

~ French settlement in Canada had been confined largely to the banks of the St. Lawrence and its tributaries. When British rule began in Quebec, seigneuries were dotted along the river banks, but a few miles beyond the land was a wilderness. The British attempted to encourage settlement but with little success. Crown and Clergy Reserves were allocated and hundreds of thousands of acres were given to those who had fled from the American Revolution or had fought in the War of 1812. Many who received grants subsequently sold them to speculators who eventually acquired large estates. Most of the large proprietors did not live on these estates and some lived outside the province altogether. The land in large areas of Lower Canada consequently lay unsettled and unproductive.

The British Land Company was organized in 1833 to undertake a settlement venture in Lower Canada similar to that carried out by the Canada Company in Upper Canada.[3] The Company secured a grant of over 800,000 acres and in subsequent purchases acquired another 400,000 acres. The land was situated in the Eastern Townships, in the counties of Sherbrooke, Shefford, and Stanstead, and in the southeast corner of the province between Lake Megantic and the St. Francis

River. The coming of the Company was welcomed by the English-speaking settlers in the Townships, but was bitterly opposed by the French representatives in the Legislative Assembly. The French feared they would be swamped by a new influx of English settlers.

The Company began operations in 1835, proceeding to open up roads, to build warehouses, mills, and wharves, and to attract settlers. The results in the next few years were not encouraging. The better class of English immigrant was frightened off by the rebellion in 1837, many settlers failed to meet their obligations, and some of the agents proved to be inefficient or dishonest. By 1838 the Company was in financial difficulty and was forced to ask for a suspension of interest on loans. ~

In all the ups and down of the Company's affairs and in the political excitement of these years, young Galt had been a watchful but quiet observer. He mastered thoroughly the routine tasks assigned him, laying a solid basis for that grasp of commercial forms and insight into intricate financial relations which always impressed his fellows. In 1840, he was given his first independent commission, the task of collecting from the St. Francis settlers the long overdue debts for the provisions advanced on their first settlement. His report to the Commissioner soon made it clear that the young man of twenty-three had a power of going direct to the heart of a difficulty, a fertility of resource, and a quiet assurance of power which marked him out as the only man who could save the situation for the Company.

After reporting the arrangements made to cancel or renew the provision obligations, Galt proceeded to review the whole situation in the St. Francis district and to suggest changes in the Company's policy. Sales had practically ceased, reaching less than £1,000 the preceding year; and now a tax on wild lands was threatened, which, even at a half penny per acre, would amount to £2,500 a year. As for the sales already made and the settlements effected, Galt drew a dark but not exaggerated picture. The bulk of the settlers secured had been "brought up under the English poor laws," and had little veracity or adaptability. The expenditure of a great amount of capital in making roads, bridges, and mills, and in introducing and supporting these pauper immigrants, had brought about a hectic prosperity, followed by a sweeping reaction. Many of the immigrants were gone and their debts with them; more would follow; few who remained could meet their pressing obligations to the Company. The roads made at such vast outlay were falling into ruin; many were actually impassable – grown up with bushes four feet high. Victoria, on which so many thousands of pounds had been spent, was deserted by all but one family. The saw mill was idle. At Gould the storehouses were falling to ruins. At Robinson only four families remained, including the agent; the tavern keeper had departed in despair, the blacksmith's forge was silent, the grist mills on which over £1,000 had been spent were in bad order, the pearl ashery in ruins.

For the future, the young observer calmly recommended a complete change in the directors' policy, as to both men and methods. There could be no doubt in the mind of any person acquainted with settling in the woods that British pauper immigrants were helpless when left to their own unaided judgment. To give a new settlement a fair chance, a large proportion of the pioneers should be Americans or Anglo-Canadians; many of this class were now in the Townships, anxious to push on somewhere. Some had means, others none, but any able-bodied man going with nothing but his axe into the woods would make a more valuable settler than nineteen out of twenty of those already in St. Francis. Further, the methods of payment should be changed. The present practice of requiring the settler to pay one-fifth of the purchase price down, and the balance in rapid instalments, deprived him of funds badly needed for the support of his family and the cultivation of his land. Instead, the Company should adopt a still more extensive credit system, throwing open their lands to any who appeared likely settlers, at the current value, interest only to be paid for a certain number of years, and thereafter the principal in easy instalments. Incidentally, this would mean that the Company would turn a large area of land liable to the proposed wild land tax into a revenue-producing asset.

As for the present settlers, the only means of saving the Company's interests was to take payment for land and services in labour, and apply this labour to the building of public works accepted by the government as part of the purchase price, and of grist mills and asheries at Gould, which was much better adapted than Victoria as headquarters of the district. The final recommendation in this sweeping review was that in view of the emergency and of the numerous daily calls requiring prompt decision, it was essential that the Commissioner should be given a free hand: the Court of Directors must by this time have learned that the Company's interests would be safe in his discretion.

The report did not lead to immediate results. Before deciding on the best method of carrying on the Company's affairs, the directors had to decide whether they would go on at all. Negotiations were opened for the resumption of the whole or part of the lands acquired from the Crown, while alternative proposals for relief from interest or postponement of instalments were pressed both in London and in Kingston.

It was clear by this time that the business of a land company was far from being the certain and speedy road to wealth it had seemed. Land could indeed be bought for three or four shillings an acre, but it was not land in England, but land in the heart of an American wilderness, requiring time and patience and ability to develop. Millions of acres in Upper Canada and in the states of the middle west were being thrown on the same bargain counter. Costly roads must be built and maintained, to take the settlers in and bring their produce out. Unexpected political disturbances and racial jealousies must be faced. The cumulative attraction, to prospective immigrants, of friends established in the western sections must be overcome. Values would rise in time, but in time interest on the capital invested would also mount and the cost of the establishment would eat into possible profits. If increment of value was to be secured, it would have to be earned.

Matters went from bad to worse. In 1841, only 400 of the 28,000 immigrants who landed at Quebec could be diverted to the whole Eastern Townships. The sale of land was under 1,500 acres and did not even meet the cost of the Canadian establishment. A new calamity was threatened in the imposition of a tax of a penny an acre upon all wild lands, by the newly created Municipal Council of the County of Sherbrooke, a tax more than double current receipts. The only gleam of relief came in the consent of the government to take back 511,000 acres, much of which had been surveyed and rendered accessible.

In this crisis, late in 1842, the young clerk whose report, forwarded by the Commissioner to the Directors, had shown such a confident grasp of the situation, was summoned to London. He laid before the Court a full analysis of its various undertakings, and repeated the remedies suggested, with others which later experience had shown necessary: as for British emigrants, canvass them before sailing, not at Quebec or Montreal; seek Americans and French Canadians, who were now showing a disposition to settle in the Townships; accept payment from settlers in labour and especially in produce; sell wild lands on long credit, for the present; obtain improved farms for sale to settlers with capital by making arrangements with the present settlers to take over their holdings when required, paying them in money, wild land and cancelled debts; throw no more money into the lake at Port St. Francis; endeavour to bring manufacturers to Sherbrooke and help them to utilize the Company's mill sites there available; give the Commissioner more independent discretion; let him endeavour to take the place in the Eastern Townships which the extent of the Company's interests warranted, and lead rather than be driven in such matters as the imposition of taxes and the expenditure of receipts. In a separate memorandum, on which no action was taken, Galt proposed to take over from the Company its Sherbrooke holdings, in which £27,500 currency had been invested and on which no return was being secured. He offered to pay £25,000 on five to ten years' credit, secured by a mortgage and by the assignment of his whole salary.

Leaving the Directors to consider this extensive programme, he paid a lengthy visit to Scotland with his mother, renewing old acquantances and old memories. By September, 1843, the Court had concluded that if the Company was to go on, it must be largely on the lines Galt suggested and under his control. He was appointed Secretary, and instructed to return to Canada, where his first task would be to carry on negotiations with the government as to further resumption of unproductive lands and annulment of the wild land tax. In these proceedings he was to consult the Commissioner, but this instruction was largely for form's sake, as the Court had already determined to give the Secretary still further promotion if his plans succeeded.

The new Secretary lost no time in returning to Canada. After a brief conference with the Commissioner he posted on to Kingston, the seat of government. How he fared in his first experience of practical politics, how he found the Company's influence at Court rather less than nothing, how he bargained with the Governor-General, Sir Charles Metcalfe, for mutual support, will be seen later. It need only be said here that he soon realized that resumption of the lands was out of the question and that it would be difficult to induce the provincial legislature either to restrict the general powers of the new municipal bodies or to overrule the specific exercise of their power complained of. The sudden break-up of the ministry and the approaching general election put definite action at Kingston out of the question. Galt turned to Sherbrooke and began to sound the Municipal Council and especially its leading spirit, Samuel Brooks, local manager of the City Bank, as to the possibility of a compromise. Meanwhile the system of long credit sales had been put into operation, and had already led to a large increase both in the price and the quantity of land sold. The purchasers were chiefly residents of the Townships, many of them squatters on the land they bought, and French Canadians from the seigneuries. This first instalment of the new policy was promising success. It appeared that the tide had turned. When Galt again crossed to London to report, in February, 1844, he received his reward by being appointed Commissioner.

In undertaking the task of restoring the Company's desperate fortunes, the new Commissioner promised to finance future operations without further calls upon the shareholders. In return he stipulated a free hand and a reasonable length of time to prove the success or failure of his plans. This confidence the Court of Directors freely gave and loyally continued. Throughout the period of Galt's service as Commissioner he enjoyed the personal friendship and official backing of the leading shareholders of the Company, and found the connection thus formed of much value in later financial enterprises.

Galt's first task was to avert the crushing burden of taxation imposed by the Sherbrooke Council. He admitted at once that some measure of taxation was just and imperative, both to secure revenue and to compel development. He protested, however, that the rate of a penny an acre levied was far in excess of that required for the works in view, and that it made no distinction between good land and bad, land near and land remote, or between absentee proprietors who had received their land free and done nothing to develop it, and the Land Company, which had paid for its holdings and had poured out thousands in betterments. The Council itself had recognized the unfairness of the tax by making no determined effort to collect it in any of the three years it had been levied. . . .

In lieu of this tax he urged an assessment upon all real property, improved and unimproved, according to the value, and offered to advance the Council £2,000 to set the work in motion. As a result of this negotiation and the influence of the minor proprietors, the tax was not collected, but constructive

measures halted, pending the reconstruction of the whole municipal machinery. In 1845 the District Councils were abolished
and township authorities with no power to collect such taxes
established in their place. Two years later county municipalities
were again set up, and in 1848 the Sherbrooke Council once
more proposed to collect arrears of taxes. Once more the
Commissioner succeeded in averting this blow and henceforth
the Company's lands bore only a moderate tax burden.

Galt now turned to the vital problem of attracting settlers.
From the formation of the Company the United Kingdom had
been looked to as the natural source of immigration, but hope
had been repeatedly deferred. The campaign was now carried
on more vigorously, though the personal canvass in the British
Isles which Galt suggested was not undertaken. In preparing
information for intending colonists Galt was unusually frank
and plain spoken, and his expressions of opinion on settlement
have therefore a value unusual in immigration literature either
of governments or of private enterprises. He warned all comers
that Canada was a land of hard work, a land where in six
months a farmer or labourer must earn the bulk of his support
for the whole year. "A settlement in the backwoods of Canada,"
he continued, "however romantic and pleasing may be the
accounts generally published of it, has nothing but stern
reality and hardship connected with it. Alone in the woods in
his log cabin with his family, tired with his day's work, and
knowing that the morrow brings but the same toil, the emigrant
will find but few of his fancies realized. Instead of the certain
and luxuriant crop he has looked to as assured, he may find that
either his own unskilfulness, the quality of the seed, or the
premature severity of the season, has reduced his harvest within
a narrow compass. His cattle may die or he and his family may
be afflicted with sickness. An observation of seven years and an
intimate acquaintance with most of the new settlements of the
Eastern Townships, has satisfied the writer that for the first
years the emigrant to succeed must work as hard and suffer
perhaps greater privations than if he remained in Great Britain,
but he has throughout the consciousness that he is working for
himself and that while meantime he does not want for food, he
will soon be possessed of the same comforts and enjoy the same
independence as his older neighbours around him."

He distinguished three classes of immigrants. In the first
class were the men of capital, perhaps £750 to £3,000. They

were the most likely to become disappointed with the country, since they usually invested the bulk of their means at once in land and buildings and stock, lived comparatively lavishly, depended on hired labour, and either knew nothing of farming or had learnt it in a country where land was dear and labour cheap, and were unwilling to unlearn. When in a few years they looked about and saw men whom they had at first employed in a situation superior to their own, they too often decided that "Canada is a very good country for a labouring man but not for a gentleman." They would do much better to bank their money and live in comfort in one of the villages in the Townships until they had acquired experience, or else to start in a modest way. The labouring man, again, often dreamed that the rise to independence would be much more rapid and wages higher than the facts warranted. "Unfortunately," he continued, "but few labourers on their arrival in Canada consider what their position was in the land of their birth, and instead of being grateful to Providence and their fellow-men for the improved prospects afforded them, they are difficult to please and quite insatiable in their demands. The writer has known instances where thirty shillings a month and board has been refused by men who preferred begging their way around the public works, where they expected higher wages. The labouring man who seeks a home in Canada should be satisfied to be secured with his family from want in the first instance, and in the course of a very short time opportunity is never wanting for an industrious honest man of this class to better his condition." It was, however, the middle class, the small farmers and mechanics with sufficient means to support their families for about eighteen months, until the land gave returns, who were best advised in emigrating. With £80 or £90 such a settler could make a good start, and soon achieve not wealth, which few found, but independence, and opportunity for his children after him: "the real object can be readily obtained, that of an independent home, subject to the curse of original sin, but the possessor must work hard for its enjoyment."

Advice such as this gave little ground for complaint of being lured to Canada by false pretences. It was supplemented by literature of a more conventional and optimistic kind, but neither frank words nor glowing prospectuses could divert to the Townships any large number of British immigrants. The fact was that in the British Isles Lower Canada meant French-speaking Canada: its climate was reputed more severe, and its means of communication much more backward than was the case in Upper Canada or Illinois. While tens of thousands passed on to the fertile English-speaking west, and thousands halted in Montreal, hundreds trickled into the Townships.

There was more hope of settlement by farmers already in the province or in the adjoining states, swarming to new scenes. A goodly number of these men were secured, but the source of supply was limited and the growth slow. Soon the lure of Ohio and Illinois called the Vermonter, when the Erie Canal and the railroad made western travel easy, and he ceased to push northward.

It became clear that the Company must look more and more to the very men whose representatives had for years bitterly attacked it and all its ways – the French Canadians. One great barrier to their incursion had been the unwillingness of the Catholic clergy to see their flocks settling upon any land held in free and common socage, since by the Quebec Act of 1774 it had been provided that French law and custom, including the right of the priest to tax and tithe, extended only to lands held under seigniorial tenure. By an ordinance of 1839, however, confirmed by an Act of the Canadian Legislature in 1849, permission was given to the church authorities to set up parishes beyond the old bounds. With the parish system, it was held, went the tithing power. At the same time that this barrier was removed, the growing tide of emigrants to the New England states was stirring clerical and nationalist leaders to realize the need of making the swarms from the seigneuries settle within the province. Thus the Company found their new efforts met more than half way. Additional French-speaking agents were appointed, and, solicited or unsolicited, a steady stream of sturdy habitants began to pour in. A special impetus was given to the movement in 1848 by the conclusion of an agreement between the Company and the newly organized Association for the Establishment of French Canadians in the Eastern Townships. The Association agreed to encourage approved French-Canadian settlers to settle in the Township of Roxton, and later in Ely, Stukely, and Oxford, and, with the assistance of the Bishop of Montreal, to build a church and school and provide a mission priest. The Company engaged to provide land on long terms, to build roads and mills – "in short, to accomplish all that has hitherto been the duty of the Seigneur without exacting from the settler the obnoxious conditions which apply to lands in the (French) Canadian parishes."

The Commissioner who in 1848 offered his French-Canadian compatriot "a settlement in the Eastern Townships where
he will retain all the advantages of his native parish, his
language, his clergy, and his social habits, without one of the
restrictions which there curb his industry and enterprise," little
thought that before the century ended the Eastern Townships
would be overwhelmingly French-speaking.

The terms of sale experimentally adopted in 1843 were
continued. No payment on purchase was required; for the first
ten years interest only was paid, and then the principal was paid
off in four equal annual instalments. This was long credit, and
it could not have profited the Company if it had not been for
the high prices set upon land, before 1843. Writing the Court
of Directors in 1850, Galt declared: "It must be borne in mind
that the sales made of the Company's property have been at a
price enormously greater than their real cash value, a result
almost entirely produced by our long credit and partially by
our system of produce payments. By these two points combined
the Company have not merely had a monopoly of sales but at
their own prices. Lands equally good have been sold for 3/-
and 3/6 an acre cash when our sales were made at 10/- and
12/6 (currency)." From some points of view these terms
might seem excessive, but they evidently suited the circumstances of the purchasers, since practically no wild land was
sold by the Company before the change was made nor by other
proprietors during the later period. In any event, to charge
$2.00 and $2.50 an acre, for good Townships land, could
hardly constitute extortion. The fact recorded in the same
report, that it had not been necessary to bring a lawsuit against
a single purchaser since 1843, made clear the considerateness
of the policy adopted.

The produce system to which the Commissioner refers in his
1850 report was another outstanding feature of the new regime.
Settlers were allowed to make payment in grain or stock,
preferably young cattle, and while this entailed much additional
work upon the agents, it met admirably the circumstances of
settlers who lived far from markets and were short of ready
cash. Galt was able to say with truth that he was carrying on
the most extensive system of barter known in the western world.
The scheme bore a curious resemblance to one of John Galt's
proposals for the Canada Company territory, but seems to have
been suggested rather by observation of customs on the seigneuries. It was a temporary measure, gradually abandoned as the

growth of transportation and banking facilities made such a primitive survival unnecessary.

In pursuance of his policy of active development, Galt pushed on the building of roads as far as the cash on hand or the labour services due permitted, and built or aided the building of mills and stores and asheries in Township centres. Sherbrooke, where the Company had early acquired practically all the available water powers and some 1,500 acres of adjoining land, he regarded as potentially the most valuable part of the whole estate, though bringing in no return for the time. He urged that the only way to make the large investment productive was to put in still more capital, developing the water powers and making advances to manufacturers who could lease or later purchase the mill-sites. This was done, out of the proceeds of land sales, and the growth which followed justified the policy, though one experiment, the establishment of a cotton factory in which the Company took an interest, resulted in a loss. Later, in 1853, when the mineral wealth of the Townships began to arouse attention, Galt organized a subsidiary company, the British American Mining Association, which had a chequered career in its pursuit of gold and copper, and finally resold to the parent company, in 1866, the bulk of the lands it had purchased.

The chief enterprise in which Galt embarked for the development alike of the Townships and of the Company's estate was, of course, the building of the St. Lawrence and Atlantic Railroad, but the record of this undertaking must be deferred to a later chapter.

For twelve years Galt directed the policy of the British American Land Company. Then growing business interests and political engagements made it difficult to give the detailed attention its affairs demanded. The directors pressed him to remain, and for the last year, 1855, he arranged to give only a general oversight, with an Assistant-Commissioner, Mr. R. W. Heneker, to carry on the routine work. Even this partial release proved insufficient, however, and with the close of the year he resigned his post, Mr. Heneker succeeding.

The results of this stewardship may be summed up briefly. They amply justified the confidence which the young Commissioner had felt in his own powers, and the confidence which the Court of Directors had freely given. From annual sales of fifteen hundred acres, the average during Galt's term increased to twelve thousand. When he took charge, practically the whole of the Company's investment was unproductive; when he retired, the revenue-bearing mortgages held equalled the book value of the remaining wild lands. The actual value of the real estate alone had come to equal the whole capital, leaving over £100,000 mortgage credits to the good. With all this improvement in conditions, it was not until 1851 that actual cash returns warranted the payment of a dividend, but from that year till Galt's retirement it was not again passed. The very year after he withdrew the Company found itself unable to declare a dividend and not until ten years had gone was it resumed. With the gradual reduction of its holdings, the activities of the Company were lessened, but it is still in existence.

The credit of this achievement did not rest entirely with the Commissioner. The Company shared in the prosperity or the stagnation of the whole country, and each year that passed increased the value of the lessening land. Yet the experience of the Company both before and after Galt's Commissionership made it clear how much depended upon the personal factor. Opportunities might be frittered away, profits eaten up by loose management. There was need of decision and sound judgment if the happy skirts of chance were to be seized, and fortunately they were at hand. The Directors said no more than bare truth when in 1856 they declared that the retiring Commissioner had by his able management "changed the position of the Company from one of almost helpless insolvency to that of a valuable and remunerative undertaking."

2: Galt and the Coming of the Railway

Canada in the forties; canal and railway; the rivalry of Boston
and Portland; promoting the St. Lawrence and Atlantic; the first
Canadian appeal for English capital; the failure: Galt takes hold.

In the closing forties Canada entered upon its first great
railway era.[1] For a decade, in the words of Sir Allan MacNab,
railways became our politics. They dominated public interest
and private speculation. At the close of the era Canada was
vastly different from what it had been at the outset. Not only
were the ends of the great struggling province bound together,
and winter's six months' ban upon intercourse with the outer
world removed, but new experience had been attained in
organizing joint stock companies. The flow of capital from
London had been started. New possibilities of sudden wealth
by railway promotion or land speculation opened up before
the sober plodding provincials. The all too intimate connection
between railways and politics which has ever since been a
distinguishing feature of Canadian life had begun. The nation-
building possibilities of the railway were becoming manifest to
the eye of faith. The province definitely emerged from the
pioneer stage and became an organic part of the great world of
commerce and finance.

In this development A. T. Galt took a varied but always
prominent part. Alike in the promotion, the financing, and the
construction of railways, his skill and tact and optimistic
courage found fitting opportunity. He was the representative
railway figure of the decade, and a survey of his activities
enables us to realize in some measure the changes in Canada's
industrial life. . . .

~ Backward methods of transportation were a serious
handicap in the development of the Canadian economy in the
1840's. The system of roads was totally inadequate to the needs
of the population. A vigorous policy of canal construction was
begun immediately after the union of 1841 but, even when the
St. Lawrence canals were finished, they provided only a partial
solution to the problem of transport, since they were available
for only a part of the year, and served a limited area. In Montreal it was hoped that the canal system would divert an increasing volume of the trade which flowed southeast through New
York by way of the Erie Canal and the Hudson River.

The hopes proved overly optimistic; nine-tenths of the trade from the west by way of the lakes continued to pass through New York. On the eastern seaboard of the United States, the chief rival of New York for the developing trade of the western interior was Boston. New York had gained a clear advantage over its competitor by the building of the Erie Canal. Although Boston had already tapped the canal at Albany, the possibility of a still more ambitious stroke was obvious; a railway from Montreal to Boston would give the New England port direct access to the canal system of the St. Lawrence and the heart of the western states. Such a rail connection would be of immense benefit to the Eastern Townships which desperately needed better communications. The rivers of the area were closed during the winter months and in any case were poorly adapted to navigation. Clearly the interests of Montreal, Boston and the Eastern Townships should have coincided.

When first approached by the Boston promoters of the proposed railway, Montreal business circles were unenthusiastic. Aside from the fact that the large amounts of capital required for the scheme were not readily available in Montreal, merchants there were confident that the recently completed canal system, combined with the preferential duties provided by Great Britain, would be sufficient to make the St. Lawrence port the great distribution centre of the interior. They saw no necessity for the construction of hundreds of miles of railway to reach the New England coast. ∼

The seed planted by the Boston missioners fell on stony ground in Montreal, but in fertile soil in Sherbrooke. In February, 1843, a meeting of the inhabitants of the St. Francis district was held at Sherbrooke, and the proposed railway heartily commended to the attention not only of the British, Canadian and United States governments, but also, with unconscious prophecy, to "the Philanthropist and the Patriot." Galt was absent in England at the time but on his return and his appointment as Commissioner of the Land Company, he threw himself into the project with enthusiasm and energy. He recognized its supreme importance, not only for the Townships generally but for the Land Company in particular. He became chairman of a provisional committee, composed of B. Pomeroy, Edward Hale, Samuel Brooks, John Moore, J. McConnell, and George S. Browne, visited Boston and interviewed the leading railway men, and prepared a modest prospectus or "Statistical

Information relative to the proposed Rail Road from Montreal to Boston via the Eastern Townships." But to no avail. Boston's efforts were distracted by the rivalries of different companies and different routes, and Montreal remained aloof.

Her aloofness suddenly ended. Hitherto the practice of importing goods in bond over foreign soil had been unknown in America, but in 1845 a Drawback or Bonding bill was passed at Washington. In the interest of United States ports and railways it permitted free passage in bond to Canadian imports or exports. At once Montreal saw its monopoly threatened. Canada West would import its British wares by New York, or Boston, particularly during the months when the St. Lawrence was sealed with ice. The establishment in 1840 of the Cunard line of steamers, plying between Liverpool and Boston, and heavily subsidized by the British government, had already tended to make Boston a distributing point for the province, and the new measure would hasten this development. Montreal must itself seek railway communication to the sea, if it was not to be side-tracked for six months of the year.

At the same time a rival claimant appeared for the choice of Atlantic terminus. Portland, a sleepy little town in Maine, threatened with the loss of what population and trade it had by the irresistible attraction of Boston, had yet two assets of importance, one a good harbour, the most northerly on the United States coast, and the other the enthusiasm of John A. Poor. Poor, a young lawyer practising at Bangor, had early become fired with enthusiasm for railway-building. In 1843 he made public two schemes which had a lasting influence on the railway progress, not only of Maine, but of the British provinces on either border. The first was for a road from Montreal to Portland, which would be much shorter than any possible route to Boston, and the second for a road from Portland to Halifax which would connect with the New England and New York railways and make Halifax the landing place of all passengers, mails and fast freight between England and North America, with Portland an important secondary distributing centre. Galt and his Sherbrooke friends soon decided to throw in their lot with Portland rather than with Boston, mainly because it was becoming apparent that if Boston won, a southerly route by Burlington and Lake Champlain, thence northward, would be chosen, and the Eastern Townships left out in the cold. In endeavouring to bring the merchants of Montreal to this view,

Galt formed many lasting business connections and personal friendships which were to lead him a decade later to make Montreal his home. His efforts were earnestly backed by Poor, who early in 1845 made a five-day journey up from Portland through a north-east blizzard and turned the scale by a fervent address to the Board of Trade. A spectacular element in the contest between Portland and Boston was introduced by a race arranged by Poor and the Boston agents. An English ship was shortly to arrive at Portland and to proceed at once to Boston; it was agreed that an express should start from each port immediately upon arrival, Portland being favoured by distance, Boston by its partially completed railways. The Portland agents stationed relays of teams from five to fifteen miles apart, and marked out the road by evergreens stuck in the snow. They had the triumph of seeing a coach and six arrive in Montreal twelve hours ahead of its Boston rival; the 280 miles had been covered in 20 hours.

Whether moved by this victory or by more prosaic arguments, the Canadian legislature in March, 1845, incorporated the St. Lawrence and Atlantic Railroad Company, with power to build to the New Hampshire border, there to join the Atlantic and St. Lawrence, running to Portland, and chartered by Maine and New Hampshire. Its capital was put at £600,000, Halifax currency, or $2,400,000. Maximum rates – five pounds per ton for freight and thirty shillings per passenger for the whole 125 miles to the border, and proportionate rates for shorter distances – were named, and it was provided that half of any surplus profits over 12 per cent were to go to the province. A provisional committee was struck, including Peter McGill, William Molson, George Moffatt and John Torrance, prominent among Montreal merchants, John Fotheringham of the City Bank, A. N. Morin, then in parliament and later to be joint premier, Samuel Brooks and Edward Hale, members for Sherbrooke town and county, A. T. Galt, and others.

The terminus chosen and the charter secured, the next step was to obtain the capital. The provisional directors expected to be able to raise the whole amount from private sources, partly in Montreal and the Townships, but mainly in England. They had little doubt as to the large profits to be reaped once the road was built, but realized that it might be difficult to persuade outside capitalists to take their own rosy view of the possibilities of this undertaking in a remote and obscure province. Accordingly they determined to seek government assistance, not a subsidy, but a bond guarantee of 3 per cent for twenty years on the estimated cost, £500,000. Accordingly, in March, 1845, the provisional committee waited upon the Draper-Viger cabinet, Galt acting as chief spokesman. They found little welcome. The finances of the province were not flourishing. The canal programme absorbed all surplus revenue. In any event, the ministers, as Galt had feared, . . . looked upon the support of the Eastern Townships members as secure for Metcalfe and themselves whatever happened, and were not disposed to make unnecessary concessions to keep them in line. Galt himself was not *persona grata* with several of the members, partly because he was gradually becoming more moderate in his political sympathies, more distrustful of the extreme Compact party, and partly because of a not unnatural jealousy which the official representatives of the Townships felt of the influence and energy displayed by the young Commissioner. It was not surprising, therefore, that no guarantee was forthcoming.

Failing government backing, the provisional committee were compelled to rely on the merits of the plan or their own skill as prospectus writers. In bringing the investment before the Canadian public, provincial hopes and local fears alike were appealed to. The railway was "to be considered as the completion of the Canadian efforts to obtain the trade of the West," and the only means of averting the disastrous blow to the important interests of Montreal that would come "by diverting the supply of Western Canada to New York and Boston." The settlement of the Eastern Townships and the development of large local traffic were also emphasized. With all this persuasiveness, the total subscriptions in Montreal and the Townships amounted to only £100,000 currency, or one-sixth of the capital required.

To secure the remainder, the committee determined to send Galt to London, and accordingly he spent the summer of 1845 learning the ways of the English investor. The St. Lawrence and Atlantic was the first Canadian enterprise to appeal for English capital.

The time seemed propitious. England was in the grip of the Hudson railway mania. After the Liverpool and Manchester was opened in 1830, railway development proceeded steadily and soundly. In 1840 about 1300 miles had been constructed. The extortionate price set on land by the great proprietors, and

the heavy cost of getting a bill through parliament had prevented more rapid expansion. After 1840 the pace quickened.
George Hudson, a merchant of York, who had been successful
in promoting a local road, embarked on wider schemes and
soon became a power in the land. The influence which the
landed proprietors had brought to bear upon Parliament to
block railway proposals was now exerted to carry the bill of any
and every company which had seats at its board and gold to
fling for its right of way. The capital which Parliament authorized railway companies to raise was, in 1842-3, £4,500,000; in
1845, £60,000,000. In two days Hudson obtained approval of
forty bills involving the expenditure of £10 million. The scrip
of a company which stood at £4 a share went up to £40 three
or four days after he joined the directorate. In a single week in
1845, in three newspapers, eighty-nine new schemes were announced, requiring £84 million capital. And still the issues
poured forth. Every hotel in London was jammed with the
witnesses brought down by counsel for rival lines, and the committee rooms and lobby of the House of Commons presented a
scene such as they never witnessed before or since.

Galt reached London when this pandemonium was at its
height. He was not without influential friends in Lombard
Street. The shareholders and directors of the Land Company
included many men prominent in finance, Edward Ellice,
Alexander Gillespie, Robert McCalmont, and others, and both
because of the Company's interest in the upbuilding of the
Townships and their confidence in the judgment of the Commissioner, they gave the plan their sanction and went on the
London committee. The London prospectus dwelt on the support already given in the colony and the possibilities of through
and local traffic. It estimated the cost at £450,000 stg., the
income at £80,000, and the expenses at £30,000. It is interesting to note, in view of the contrary emphasis in the Grand
Trunk prospectus eight years later, the contrast made between
English and American railways, "the former, from their vast
preliminary expenses, costly land outlays, double tracks and
extensive establishments costing about £30,000 a mile, while
the latter, with single tracks, do not average over £5,000 per
mile and are worked very much cheaper, thus affording the
capitalist a good return in the one case from an amount of
traffic that would subject him to ruinous loss in the other."

On the whole, it was a modest claim compared to the
hundreds of glowing forecasts which appeared in rival columns

in August, 1845. Yet it did not pass unheeded. The bulk of the capital was subscribed at once and small deposits paid down. The young financier and his fellow-directors in Montreal were delighted. Other Canadian railway promoters awoke to the possibilities of tapping this great reservoir, and Allan MacNab journeyed over at once to endeavour to duplicate for the Great Western Galt's success, though without avail. The long procession of Canadian railway magnates, actual and potential, to London had begun.

The rejoicings did not last long. The flood of speculation on which the Canadian offering had been floated so easily, was already ebbing. The disclosure of Hudson's fraud in the Eastern Railway project hastened a collapse. Thousands of scrip holders were ruined in the smash. Those who could still draw back hastened to do so. The St. Lawrence and Atlantic suffered with the rest. Its English subscribers refused to pay up the calls and endeavoured to recover their deposits.

The building of the road seemed further away than ever. When Galt returned to Canada, he found the committee uncertain whether to go on. His own vote was for pressing forward. Blissfully unaware of the difficulties of financing and building a railway in a pioneer country, the majority of the committee came to the same conclusion, and in April, 1846, the definite organization was affected. George Moffatt, Member of Parliament for Montreal, was elected president, and the directors included A. N. Morin, John Torrance, Thomas Stayner, Peter McGill, Samuel Brooks and A. T. Galt.

Under an able engineer, A. C. Morton, surveys were at once begun. Sectional rivalries and the hilly nature of the border country presented equal difficulties. Stanstead and Sherbrooke each sought the line, the one claiming a shorter route, the other offering a junction with a later road running to Quebec and perhaps to Halifax. With similar rivalries rampant on the Maine side of the border, the two boards found much difficulty in agreeing on the junction point; in fact, it was not until 1851 that this was definitely settled. Trial locations by way of Sherbrooke made it seem probable that a line about 126 miles long could be secured, the cost now being estimated at £850,000 currency, or $3,400,000.

By wide canvassing, the stock subscribed in Canada was increased to £200,000; about £35,000 remained uncancelled in London, and the contractors for the first section, from Longueuil to the River Richelieu, took the same amount of stock in part payment. But it was soon found that subscribing was one thing and paying another. Little was secured from London even after lawsuits established the stockholders' liability. Montreal subscribers were hard hit by the commercial depression following the repeal of the Corn Laws, and incidentally, of the preference which Canada-milled flour had enjoyed in Britain. In time, however, the bulk of these subscriptions was paid up.

The Township shareholders, for whom Galt was mainly held responsible, had even less ready money. As late as October, 1849, Galt found it necessary to send an urgent circular to the great majority of the Townships men, in which he declared:

I am aware that the want of money in this district, and the fact that the outlay on the Railroad was not taking place amongst us, have operated prejudicially on the ability of the Township stockholders to make their payments; but now that the work is actually in progress to speedy completion, I have pledged myself to the Directors that there will be no backwardness here, and I rely on the good faith of the people of this district to enable me to fulfil my assurances. In my past exertions on behalf of the Railroad, I have been supported by the conviction that I could depend on the hearty co-operation of every resident in the Townships, and great will be my disappointment if my present appeal be not responded to by the immediate and earnest endeavour of every stockholder here to fulfil his engagements.

This appeal had its effect, and, tardily, the long overdue calls were paid. To facilitate matters, subscribers were allowed to make payments in kind, delivering meat or flour or butter and eggs to the construction gangs along the route, at a fixed schedule of prices. The line was drawn, however, when one of the Sherbrooke shareholders, himself a director, wished to turn in a farm as payment on his subscription. Indignant at the refusal, the director at once resigned.

Even if all stock subscribed had been paid up, the Company's capital would still have fallen far short of the estimated cost. It was next determined to attempt to float a loan in England, in the hope that bonds would appeal more strongly than speculative shares. Again the financial capacity and personal tact of the young Commissioner were recognized, and late in December, 1846, the Board authorized him to proceed to England and endeavour to sell a £500,000 issue of bonds. With the

Oregon difficulty threatening war in America, and railway enterprises still suffering from the reaction from Hudsonism, London declined even to nibble at the opportunity, and Galt returned empty-handed.

These resources failing, the directors turned to the quarter which was to prove for two generations to come the last and often the first hope of the railway promoter – the state. The prospects of securing government aid were more favourable than they had been some years before. The canal system which had absorbed all the funds and all the attention of the province was practically completed. The constitutional struggles which had marked the past quarter century were nearly over, and men were glad to turn to other issues. Politicians of the Hincks and Macdonald type were taking the place of the Baldwins and Lafontaines. In Canada West an influential group, headed by Sir Allan MacNab, were equally anxious to secure government backing for the Great Western project, and they joined forces with the Montreal backers of the St. Lawrence and Atlantic.

During 1848 the government gave no sign of aid, though a Committee of the House, with MacNab as Chairman, recommended guaranteeing the stock of these two roads. Construction was pushed slowly along with existing resources, and on December 7 the road was opened to St. Hyacinthe, thirty miles from Longueuil. Then Montreal underwent an experience which brought home to all the necessity of a winter outlet to the sea. During the fall and early winter the canals had poured into Montreal and Quebec, as usual, the growing stock of western produce, to be shipped across the ocean as soon as the ice broke up in the spring. The winter was scarcely begun when prices in the English markets began to fall, and for nearly six months the Canadian merchants were compelled to sit idly by while every post brought word of still further decreases. The losses that resulted in this single winter were estimated at half the cost of building the railroad through to the winter port of Portland.

Early in February, 1849, George Etienne Cartier presented another petition from the St. Lawrence and Atlantic directors, emphasizing the need of railways to supplement the canal system in securing for Canadian routes and Canadian ports their fair share of the trade of the West. Every United States city on the Atlantic seaboard was backing a railway designed to give it as great a proportion as possible of this growing traffic. Canada must not be behindhand.

Finally in April, 1849, Francis Hincks, Inspector-General in the Baldwin-Lafontaine ministry, brought down a measure based upon a suggestion of the St. Lawrence directors. He proposed that whenever any railroad over seventy-five miles long had been half built from private resources, the government would guarantee the interest, not to exceed 6 per cent, on an issue of bonds equal to half the total cost of the road. The province would be protected by a first lien on the whole road. MacNab, though leading the Opposition of the day, hastened to second the resolutions, and the first step in the policy of state aid to railways was speedily taken.

The horizon brightened, but not all the clouds had yet lifted. It was still necessary to find funds to build thirty-three miles to Melbourne or Richmond, before the Company would be entitled to call upon the province for aid for the second half. To make matters worse, during the summer of 1849, serious mismanagement of the Company's finances came to light. The history of Canadian corporations had fitly begun by a striking instance of directors failing to direct. Under the management of a faithless secretary, a debt of £50,000 had accumulated of whose existence the directors knew nothing! Vigorous measures were needed to save the situation. Galt, who had hitherto taken little part in the detailed management, was pressed by his fellow-directors to come to Montreal and take control. The Land Company were reluctant to give up part of his services but agreed rather than lose them altogether. Accordingly A. N. Morin, the existing president, who was too much preoccupied with politics to give the railroad's affairs due thought, resigned late in 1849, and Galt was elected in his stead. He was not yet prepared to make Montreal his headquarters, but more and more the railroad and other metropolitan affairs drew him away from Sherbrooke.

With the assistance of John Young – politician, promoter, businessman, eager advocate of canal and railway and of a St. Lawrence bridge – Galt soon brought order out of chaos. The city of Montreal had already agreed to aid the road by taking £125,000 preferential stock, giving its bonds in exchange. Now the Land Company and the Seminary of St. Sulpice were each induced to take bonds to the amount of £25,000. To bridge the remaining gap, a contract was made with Black, Wood and Company, of Pennsylvania, who had built part of the Canadian line, and were to build all the Maine portion, by which they undertook to build the whole road. The price per mile agreed upon was £6,550, or $26,200. This was a somewhat high figure for an only moderately well-built road, but it was only a nominal price. The contractors agreed to accept part of their pay in stock which was at a discount of 15 or 20 per cent, and the rest in provincial bonds, when secured. The transaction practically meant that the government's half of the road was sufficiently increased in cost to recompense the contractor for the shortage on the first half.

There were still some difficult corners to turn, days when the City Bank or the Commercial or the British North America would decline to advance a few hundred pounds to meet pressing local debts, days when the procrastination of the contractors or their demands for extra payment strained patience to the utmost. Eventually the Company took the contract from Black, Wood & Co. and completed it by day-work, under the efficient supervision of the new Chief Engineer, Casimir S. Gzowski. But the worst was over. The second section of the road, from St. Hyacinthe to Richmond, was opened in October, 1851, and the third section, from Richmond to Sherbrooke, in September, 1852. The latter event was made the occasion of a great celebration, with the Governor-General and nearly all the members of the provincial parliament in attendance.

Meanwhile the Maine Company, the Atlantic and St. Lawrence, had been facing much the same difficulties. The city of Portland had come to its aid by taking $1,500,000 of bonds, and an equal amount was sold privately, together with a few thousand shares of stock. The state of Maine, however, unlike the province of Canada, was barred by its constitution from giving any aid to railways or other private enterprises, so that the American promoters reached the end of their tether sooner than the Canadians. It was accordingly arranged in 1851 that the Canadian Company should build sixteen miles beyond the border to Island Pond, Vermont. For this purpose a special issue of bonds at 7 per cent was made, and floated in London by the President.

Before the road to Portland was completed, new enterprises had been set on foot which dwarfed it in importance and diverted the interest of its chief officials. The vision of a great Main Trunk line binding all the British North American colonies, running from Halifax to Quebec and on through Montreal and Toronto to the western boundary at the Detroit River, had seized the imagination of leading men in all parts of the scattered colonies. Foremost in conceiving and in executing the first part of this greater project, the Grand Trunk Railway of Canada, was A. T. Galt.

3: The Building of the Grand Trunk

The railway era; the rivalry of the United States; Howe and the Intercolonial; Canadian plans for the Grand Trunk; Hincks and the English contractors; the struggle for the contract; the amalgamation; the building of the road; Gzowski and Company: later years; the balance sheet of the Grand Trunk.

The fifties form the first great railway era in Canada's history. In 1850 there were only sixty-six miles of railway in all the British North American colonies; in 1860 there were two thousand and sixty-five. At the beginning of that period the only roads in operation or actively projected were short and as yet unconnected fragments, for the most part portage roads between the leading waterways. At the close Canada possessed the longest railway in the world under single management – the Main or Grand Trunk Railway, running from the Great Lakes to the sea.[1]

As has been seen, the experience derived in the building of the St. Lawrence and Atlantic deeply influenced later developments. In spite of the difficulties and dangers encountered, in spite of the narrow escapes from bankruptcy and complete cessation of work, the men most closely concerned in its management were fired with ambition to attempt yet greater tasks. They had learned how to finance and how to build a railway, how to secure the help of the British investor and of the provincial government, and how to bargain with contractors and hold them to the bargain. Their appeals to the province for aid had led to the introduction of the bond guarantee policy, and had definitely turned the thoughts of government and of public alike from canals to railways.

When the road to Portland was first projected, it was assumed that Montreal, or rather Longueuil, on the south shore of the St. Lawrence opposite Montreal, would remain the western terminus. The products of the interior were to come down by river and canal, and to seek a further market direct by sea from Montreal or by the new road to Portland and beyond. The railway could supplement river and canal, but could not compete with them in carrying bulky products.

This assumption was soon rudely shattered. The United States ports and railways to the south were not content to let

Montreal win so easily a commanding share of the trade of the golden west. Every important port on the Atlantic was striving to become the outlet of the growing western traffic. Baltimore and Philadelphia pushed railways west to the Ohio country. New York supplemented the Erie Canal by the Erie Railway, and piece by piece put through the road to Buffalo later known as the New York Central. Boston tapped the same stream by its Western road to Albany. Still more threatening to Montreal interests was the Ogdensburg Railway, which ran from Ogdensburg on the St. Lawrence, just south of the Canadian border, to Lake Champlain, where it was to connect with roads to Boston and New York. If all the expectations of its builders were fulfilled, this road would secure every ton of ocean-bound traffic that had filtered past Buffalo and other western points, and Montreal would see the whole stream of western trade deflected to the south.

This wide activity, and especially the competition of the Ogdensburg road, soon convinced Montreal interests, and not least the men behind the St. Lawrence and Atlantic, that a further step must now be taken. It was not enough to supplement river and canal; they must now be paralleled and rivalled by the railway. Late in 1850 a public meeting was held in Montreal, and a committee appointed to consider the possibility of building a road to Prescott or Kingston. Galt and Young were members of this committee, and equally active were two men whose future was to be closely linked with Galt's, Luther Hamilton Holton and David Lewis Macpherson. A preliminary survey was made by C. S. Gzowski, and later a more detailed survey by T. C. Keefer; the municipalities along the line were interested, and in 1851 a charter was sought from the legislature.

The men who came together in this railway enterprise were all destined to achieve a place of distinction in the life of Canada. Equally notable was the experience upon which their interest and confidence in the new undertaking were based. They were not mere promoters, seizing an opportunity in a field in which they had no personal experience and in which they did not expect to continue. Each had had training of a kind eminently desirable for the founders of a great railway project. David L. Macpherson was a young Scot who had come to Canada in 1833 to enter the Montreal forwarding firm of Macpherson, Crane & Co., in which his brother was senior partner; by 1842 he had himself become a partner. Luther H. Holton, of Upper Canada birth and New England ancestry, had entered the same field, and was junior partner in the Montreal firm of Hooker, Holton & Co. Both these firms were active and enterprising, and in their vessels and wagons they carried on a large part of the transportation work of the province to which the railway was to fall heir. Casimir S. Gzowski had had an experience more picturesque and varied but equally helpful for his present task. Born at St. Petersburg in 1813, the son of a Polish nobleman in the Russian military service, he had taken a course in military engineering and then entered the Russian army. When the Polish insurrection of 1830 broke out, young Gzowski threw himself into his country's cause and faced in turn treachery, defeat, wounds, imprisonment and exile. He escaped across the Atlantic, landed in New York without knowing a word of English, and in six years had qualified himself for admission to the bar. After a brief practice he returned to his earlier field of engineering, and in 1841, on coming to Canada, he was appointed to a post in the provincial Department of Public Works which he filled with ability until his appointment to the St. Lawrence and Atlantic. It was a notable group.*. . .

~ The railway situation became complicated when Joseph Howe succeeded in attracting considerable support for the Intercolonial railway project which would connect Halifax and Saint John with Quebec and Montreal, and eventually with Toronto and the western border of Canada. Early proposals for this railway included a route from Nova Scotia diagonally across New Brunswick to Canada. Another suggestion was for a connection from Nova Scotia through southern New Brunswick to Portland, Maine, where it would join with the eastern terminus of the St. Lawrence and Atlantic railway. A third alternative was a line which would follow closely the northern coast of New Brunswick, thus avoiding the American border completely, and from the military point of view be the soundest of the three.

Howe, flushed with his constitutional triumphs, became the

---

* It was, indeed, a notable group. It was also a very rich one, composed of men who, thanks to the first railway "boom," had done very well. See A. R. M. Lower, *Colony to Nation* (Toronto, 1946), p. 285; and R. G. Trotter, *Canadian Federation, Its Origins and Achievements* (London, 1924), p. 167. Skelton's somewhat bland description of them as "not mere promoters" may be accurate, but in view of the evidence it is difficult to avoid reaching the conclusion that they were *primarily* promoters.

leading advocate of an Intercolonial railway in one form or another. His personal preference was for the line from Nova Scotia to Maine via southern New Brunswick. It could be built quickly and cheaply, and could be complemented by a more direct northern connection between Halifax and Quebec later. He went to London to enlist the financial support of the British government and returned with what he thought was an Imperial guarantee to back the southern line to Maine. On the basis of this "understanding," he negotiated successfully with the New Brunswick and Canadian governments concerning their share in the costs of construction. The Canadian government undertook to see that a continuous railway system from Quebec to the western border of the province would be completed. The key to the enormous project, however, was the financial support expected from the British government. Suddenly the Colonial Office announced that it would underwrite the northern New Brunswick route only and declared that any line which passed close to the American border was unacceptable for military reasons. Since the New Brunswick government was unwilling to accept the northern route alone, the whole project collapsed.

Francis Hincks, the Inspector-General (Finance Minister) in the Canadian government, quickly sought to avoid having the rail link between Quebec and western Canada fail merely because it had been part of the greater Intercolonial scheme. He had been impressed by the glowing proposals of C. D. Archibald, an agent of the English contracting firm of Peto, Brassey, Jackson and Betts, which had built railways all over the world. Early in 1852 he reached an agreement with this firm to organize the Grand Trunk Company, which would construct a line between Montreal and Hamilton. This decision contravened the interests of Galt and his colleagues who already had a charter to build between Montreal and Hamilton. While the negotiations over the Intercolonial were going on, this charter had been suspended but, when the Intercolonial scheme was abandoned, the Montreal and Kingston charter came into force. ~

Galt was in London at the time, on St. Lawrence and Atlantic business, and Hincks at once endeavoured to allay his natural opposition to this calm attempt to ignore all that had been done in Canada and override the rights of the Canadian promoters. Hincks contended that "no Canada company could be established that would be able to finance the road," and that the incidental advantages of the bargain he had just made were so great that "even if we pay a little too much it will be to our interest to do so." He hoped, therefore, that Galt would see his way to co-operate. But Galt declined the cool request, and protested against this sudden and unwarranted shift of policy.

From London the scene changed to Quebec, when the provincial parliament assembled in August, 1852. Hincks and Jackson, who accompanied him to Canada, seem to have concluded that the simplest method to pursue was to obtain control of the existing charters. Accordingly, on August 7, a royal proclamation was issued, bringing into force the suspended Montreal and Kingston and Kingston and Toronto companies. Stock books for the former company were opened shortly afterwards, but a week later, on August 23, when Jackson was preparing to subscribe a controlling share of the stock, the Canadian promoters forestalled him by subscribing every farthing of the £600,000 capital authorized, in the following proportions: –

J. Torrance	Montreal,	20 shares,	£500
William Molson	Montreal,	20 shares,	500
John Rose	Montreal,	20 shares,	500
H. N. Jones	Montreal,	20 shares,	500
G. E. Jacques	Montreal,	20 shares,	500
William MacDougall	Montreal,	20 shares,	500
Thomas Galt, per attorney A. T. Galt,	Toronto,	20 shares,	500
A. T. Galt	Sherbrooke,	7,940 shares,	£198,500
L. H. Holton	Montreal,	7,960 shares,	199,000
D. L. Macpherson	Montreal,	7,960 shares,	199,000

By a preliminary agreement each of the main subscribers bound himself not to transfer any of the stock without the express written authority of the other two. Directors were at once appointed, an engineering department organized, a 10 per cent call paid in, and the government called upon to sanction the location of the roads.

This stroke compelled a change of tactics upon Hincks' and Jackson's part. A bill was introduced to charter a new company, the Grand Trunk Railway of Canada, to run from Montreal to Toronto – the Great Western having meanwhile acquired the charter for the Toronto-Hamilton link, thus making it necessary to accept Toronto rather than Hamilton as the western terminus. The capital authorized amounted to £16,000, currency, a mile. Holton as President and Galt as Vice-President of the Montreal and Kingston, protested against this attempt to override them and a battle royal began before the Railway Committee.

Hincks used all his influence to push the Jackson contract through, and Jackson himself displayed all the powers of a railroad lobbyist in a degree rare even in America. He talked of millions as the awed provincials talked of thousands, and claimed that he and his fellow-contractors possessed a power of "open sesame" in the London money markets. So great were their resources that the provincial guarantee was merely a form; in the act as finally passed a solemn clause was actually inserted permitting them to renounce this aid – for why should they consent to pay 6 per cent on the provincial debentures exchanged for the company's bonds, when London was overflowing with money unable to find investment at 3 per cent? Such arguments dazzled the legislators, but the promoters were not content with merely dazzling the eyes; they made assurance doubly sure by filling their pockets where it was advisable. A well-known contractor of the day, who had come from Pennsylvania a few years earlier to take a contract on the Welland Canal, and had stayed to become the first boss in Canadian politics, lent his influence for an interest in the contract, which he soon wisely commuted for a cash sum of £12,000 sterling.

For public consumption other arguments were stressed. No Canadian company could hope to secure in Canada a tithe of the capital needed, and could not borrow in London on terms half as favourable as could the English promoters – especially if the latter blocked their efforts. The subscription of the Montreal and Kingston stock, by Holton, Galt and Macpherson, was denounced as a sham and its legality questioned on account of their preliminary agreement. The fact that New Brunswick and Nova Scotia were making contracts with the same English firm, and that they had also secured contracts for the Quebec and Richmond, made it desirable to give them the control of the western sections as well. Uniformity of management and a standard of construction far above that usual on American roads, permitting a saving of 15 or 20 per cent in operation, would thus be secured.

On the other hand, Holton and Galt vigorously asserted that there was no occasion to bring in these London wizards. Of the five sections into which the Grand Trunk line from

Quebec to Windsor might be divided, two, the St. Lawrence and Atlantic and the Great Western, were under construction, a contract had been made for a third, the Quebec and Richmond, and they themselves stood ready to complete the Montreal and Kingston section. The Kingston-Toronto link would doubtless also be begun shortly. So far as the Montreal and Kingston road was concerned, they anticipated no insuperable difficulty in financing its construction. True, they did not intend to retain all the stock they had subscribed, but would keep it until a fair bargain had been assured. Between the provincial guarantee, subscriptions by every municipality but one along the line, and especially substantial aid by Montreal, and partial payment of the contractors in stock, they had no doubt they could secure the funds required.* They believed, further, that they could build the road for a third or more less than the English contractors. Already three tenders had been submitted from responsible contractors, one of them the contractor for the Ogdensburg road. They were prepared to receive a tender from Jackson and his partners, and, if it was lowest, to award them the contract. What more could fairly or honestly be asked? The interest of the province was certainly identical with the interest of the company in getting the work done at the least possible cost, and this could not be attained by a "sham company formed merely to homologate a foregone bargain with outside contractors."

"The railway policy of the country was settled," Holton and Galt declared before the Committee, "and important sections of the Grand Trunk line in course of construction long before Mr. Jackson was heard of in connection with our railroads. The action of the government in proclaiming the charter was alone wanting to secure a vigorous commencement of the remaining sections. That action had hardly been taken, when it is all at once discovered that nothing can be done without Mr. Jackson, and it is accordingly proposed that our previous legislation be reversed, our established policy abrogated, and existing charters cancelled, in order to meet the views and secure the

* Skelton implies that Galt and his partners would have been able to raise sufficient capital in Canada and that the roads could have been built under Canadian control. On this point there would appear to be some doubt. Glazebrook, for example, is not so sure as Skelton and prefers to suspend judgment: "Whether or not the Montreal financiers could have found enough capital must remain an open question" G. P. deT. Glazebrook, *A History of Transportation in Canada* [Carleton Library, 1964] I, 162; see also A. W. Currie, *The Grand Trunk Railway of Canada* [Toronto, 1957], p. 11.

services of that gentleman. . . . Is the instrumentality of Mr. Jackson and his associates so essential for procuring loans of English capital that they shall be paid from 30 to 50 per cent over the cash value of their work, merely for the facilities they are supposed to possess as money brokers, or is it pretended that a little knot of railway jobbers hold the key of the great money market of the world?"

Both Holton and Galt protested strongly against the assumption that mere colonists could not carry through the undertaking. In words that bear the mark of Holton's impetuousness rather than Galt's tact, they protested against being asked to withdraw in favour of "strangers and foreigners." "We feel strongly on this subject," they continued, "not merely from our direct interest, but because, as colonists, we desire to see the public men of this country promoting provincial enterprise. We desire to see the standard of self-reliance raised. We deny the inferiority of our resources. We assert that a permanent injury is done by repressing every effort to act for ourselves, and we repudiate most solemnly the necessity for calling in foreign aid, to do that which we are amply able to do ourselves." Here was a declaration of financial independence in words which foreshadow the declaration of industrial independence that was made half a dozen years later with the establishment of the Cayley-Galt tariff.

They were careful to discriminate. It was outside control, not outside capital, to which they objected. "It is argued that because the Montreal and Kingston Railway Company do not consider the employment of Mr. Jackson *on his own terms* essential to the construction of our great line of railroads, they are therefore opposed to the introduction of English capital into the country. Nothing could be more unfounded, more unjust. It is admitted on all hands that it is not only desirable but absolutely necessary that English or foreign capital should be obtained for the construction of all our great public works. The question is mainly one of instrumentalities. . . . There can be no doubt that a great leading thoroughfare, such as our Trunk Line is designed to be, would be managed more in consonance with the wants, the habits and the whole genius of our people, by a local company than by any association of speculators residing abroad, having no interest in the Company beyond the punctual receipt of the largest dividends that can be wrung from it. . . . We can construct a railroad in less time, for about one-half the declared capital, and with a smaller amount of aid than the parties applying for the charter in question. Our enterprise, if it fail, will not be burdened with the complaints of the confiding and ruined shareholders in England. If we succeed we shall still be connected with the work, we shall always stand open to the criticism and rebuke of the public, and our profits will be those derived fairly and honestly from the correct appreciation by us of a vast public work, and by an economical and judicious application of the resources at our command in constructing it."

In these shrewd and prophetic words, Holton and Galt made plain the weakest spot in the Jackson offer. The company applying for the new charter was merely a creature of the contractors. Its shareholders and managers were not yet in existence. From this domination of the company by the contractors many of the most serious difficulties of the construction period were to spring. But that was not all. Apparently Hincks and those who thought with him considered that all troubles would be over when the railroad was built. How it was to be operated did not trouble them. Holton and Galt, with shrewder foresight, realized the difficulty of efficient and satisfactory operation of a great Canadian railway by capitalists three thousand miles away, and for fifty years the experience of the Grand Trunk was to prove that they were absolutely right.

In making this and other criticisms they did not assume to be acting solely as disinterested patriots. They fought for their own prestige and pockets, but at the same time they had the interest of Montreal and the whole province at heart. This they proved by making in September an offer to withdraw, seeking nothing for themselves but the repayment of survey costs, on condition that in the agreement with Jackson certain stipulations in the provincial interest should be inserted – limitation of the guarantee and of the total issue of securities, control by the government over future management, and particularly the construction of a railway bridge across the St. Lawrence at Montreal. It seemed likely for a time that this offer would be accepted, but Holton and Galt soon became convinced that Hincks was not playing fair, and withdrew it, continuing their opposition to the new company.

Opposition appeared vain. The government was definitely committed to the Jackson agreement. The Governor-General, Lord Elgin, gave it his blessing. The rank and file of the legislators felt it would be quixotic to refuse the offer of these great capitalists. Some members of Parliament stood by Galt and Holton, including George Brown and the member for Kingston,

John A. Macdonald, but Hincks had the majority both in House and in Committee and all seemed over. Jackson sailed for home, assured of a charter and contract not only for the Montreal-Toronto section, but for a part of the Canadian end of the Intercolonial, from Quebec to Trois Pistoles.

But Galt had still a trump card to play. As president of the St. Lawrence and Atlantic he proposed to that company to amalgamate with the Montreal and Kingston, a proposal which the directors at once accepted. This assured strong Montreal support and gave control of an essential link in the Main Trunk Line. Alarmed at this stroke, Hincks telegraphed to Galt asking him to go down to Quebec again, stating that proceedings in the Bill would be stayed until his arrival. In the discussion which followed, Hincks stated that if opposition were withdrawn to the Grand Trunk — Jackson's road — he would urge that it should amalgamate with the St. Lawrence and Atlantic, and, further, that it should build the bridge across the St. Lawrence to connect both roads, and thus fulfil a project of which Montreal long had dreamed. The proposal meant that Galt and Holton must give up their own personal interest in the road, but the odds were against them in any case. Their opposition had already led Jackson to reduce his demands for aid from a guarantee of bonds equal to half the cost, whatever that might be, to a guarantee of £3,000, currency, a mile. If the new company had such command of millions as was assumed, its co-operation would help the St. Lawrence and Atlantic, which was still in need of funds for the last strokes, and the building of the bridge would certainly be a boon to Montreal. Accordingly all opposition was withdrawn. The Grand Trunk Railway of Canada was incorporated to build from Montreal to Toronto. It had a capital of £3 million stg., and was given a provincial guarantee of £3,000 currency a mile. At the same time the Grand Trunk Railway of Canada East was incorporated, chartered to build from Point Levis, opposite Quebec, to the New Brunswick border, and was promised a provincial guarantee of £3,000 a mile as far as Trois Pistoles, and a subsidy of a million acres of land for the further extension. The legislature completed its work by an Amalgamation Act, repealing the charters of the Montreal and Kingston and the Kingston and Toronto, and enabling any railway forming part of the main trunk line to unite with any other such company, or, as a later amendment provided, with any company whose line joined or intersected the main trunk line. In token of reconciliation,

Holton and Galt were named directors of the Grand Trunk of Canada, but they never took their seats and resigned before the amalgamation was effected. All was ready for the London market.

Meanwhile Galt and his associates had become interested in railways from a different angle. Holton, Macpherson, Gzowski and Galt had now united to form the contracting firm of Gzowski and Company. It was a well-balanced and well-rounded partnership. Galt was the negotiator and diplomat of the combination, Holton took care of the detailed financing, Macpherson supervised the general administration, and Gzowski the actual work of construction. The first important contract which they secured was to build the Toronto and Guelph Railway, which later received power to extend to Sarnia. No provincial aid had been given, but Toronto and other municipalities had subscribed liberally to the stock, and as the road was to run through a rich and promising district, it was believed that its bonds could be floated at no great discount. Construction was begun in the summer of 1852. Galt was empowered by the railway company to go to London and aid its London agent, Alexander Gillespie, and Mr. Franks, the President of the Canada Company, through whose lands the road would run, in placing the bonds. The St. Lawrence and Atlantic and the Maine road, the Atlantic and St. Lawrence, which it was also proposed to amalgamate, put their interests in his hands at the same time. When he sailed for England in December, 1852, accordingly, he had a threefold task to perform.

The negotiations for amalgamation and the settlement of the details of proposed financing occupied nearly four months. The chief parties concerned were: Hon. John Ross, Solicitor-General for Canada, who, at the nomination of the contractors, was to be president of the amalgamated company; Samuel Peto, the financial member of the contracting firm; George Carr Glyn, of Glyn, Mills and Co., and Thomas Baring, of Baring Brothers and Co., who were London financial agents for the province and also bankers for the new company; and A. T. Galt, acting for the Portland and Sarnia roads. Others took a minor part, including Messrs. Rhodes, Forsyth and Pemberton, of Quebec, directors of the Grand Trunk, and A. M. Ross, chief engineer of the new road. Galt soon came to form a much higher and more cordial estimate of the other members of the Brassey firm than the experience in Canada of Jackson's "bluff and bluster" methods had made seem possible, and his intercourse with Messrs. Glyn and Baring led to a lifelong friendship and a valuable financial connection.

Little difficulty was experienced in coming to terms as to the Portland road, since the need of a winter outlet to the sea was clear. It was agreed to offer the shareholders of the St. Lawrence and Atlantic equivalent shares in the new company, and to lease the Maine section in perpetuity at a rental of 6 per cent upon its cost. As the shares of both roads were at a large discount, this was a very favourable bargain for Galt's clients.* A bridge was to be built at Montreal to connect the Toronto and Portland roads. Then Liverpool and London interests connected with the Quebec and Richmond and Grand Trunk East urged their inclusion, which was finally agreed to, upon the same terms as given to the St. Lawrence. Galt protested against this arrangement, as he rightly considered that the traffic possibilities of these eastern sections were poor, and that their inclusion would lessen the value of the securities received by the St. Lawrence shareholders. He held out, therefore, for a further payment to them of some £75,000, equal to the interest during the period of construction, and as in all the contracts for new work it was being provided that the shareholders were to receive interest during this period, the other parties to the settlement agreed.

The westernmost extension gave more difficulty. If the plan of a Main Trunk line from end to end of the province, under single management, was to be carried out, it had seemed essential to secure control of the Great Western, running from Toronto to Windsor. Negotiations were carried on with the English and Canadian interests who controlled it, but without success. The Great Western demanded what was considered an excessive price, but a more serious obstacle to amalgamation was the close traffic relations between it and the roads in Michigan and New York which it linked together. It would lose much of its best paying traffic if it attempted to divert it from the United States roads to the new Canadian through line. At this juncture Galt and Gillespie proposed that the Toronto and Sarnia be made the western link rather than the Great Western, and this proposal was agreed to, the Grand Trunk simply taking over the charter and obligations of the road.

* This arrangement has been described as "imprudent" on the part of the Grand Trunk. The stock of the St. Lawrence and Atlantic had been selling at discounts of as much as 30 or 40 per cent. The terms offered by the Grand Trunk were so generous that the shares rose nearly to par and some stockholders made quick profits. The liberality of the terms has been attributed, in large measure, to Galt's skill as a bargainer (Currie, *The Grand Trunk Railway*, p. 14).

Still the project grew. Refusing to take as final the decision of the British government as to the Intercolonial road, Hon. John Ross sought out the Duke of Newcastle, Colonial Secretary in the Derby administration, and once more opened negotiations for a guarantee of the remaining sections from the Canadian border through to Halifax. This time more favour was shown, and it appeared probable that an agreement would be reached whereby the British government would not only guarantee a loan for the road from Trois Pistoles to Halifax, but would make such arrangements with the Cunard Steamship Company as would induce it to extend its Halifax service.

Unfortunately once more the cup was dashed from the lips of the provinces by the sea. The war with Russia which loomed up shortly afterwards made the British government withhold its aid. The Intercolonial section of the Grand Trunk was left suspended at Trois Pistoles (in reality, construction stopped at Rivière du Loup, thirty-five miles farther west), and the British mail subsidy to the Cunard line continued to build up Boston rather than Halifax.

Definite contracts were made for all the unbuilt sections of the road. This was done, according to the directors, in order to remove any apprehension upon the part of the shareholders that the capital first authorized would not suffice to complete the undertaking. Six-sevenths of the work fell to the firm of Peto, Brassey, Jackson and Betts. For the Quebec and Richmond their contract price was £6,500 stg. a mile, for the Trois Pistoles section and a loop line from Belleville to Peterborough, £8,000 and for the Montreal-Toronto section, £9,000. The Victoria Bridge was set at £1,400,000. The Gzowski contract was revised on the same terms and specifications, being put at £8,000 a mile. By a most unusual provision both contracting firms were obliged to pay interest at 6 per cent upon the cost of construction until completion.

The total capital was fixed at £9,500,000. Of this, £1,416,400 had already been raised for the St. Lawrence and Atlantic and the Quebec and Richmond. £837,600 was reserved for the Canadian shareholders in these roads and for the bondholders of the Ontario, Simcoe and Huron (later the Northern), who might wish to share in the opportunity. The remaining capital was to be provided, half in shares, one quarter in company debentures and one quarter in debentures convertible into provincial 6 per cent bonds. The guarantee, or more strictly speaking, the loan, thus made by the province amounted all told to £1,811,500.

Eight or ten days before the prospectus was issued − April 12, 1853 − the banking firms involved insisted upon a provision which, while meant for the best, proved a source of serious trouble for the company in the future. They began to doubt whether it would be possible to float the whole seven millions sterling called for, and urged that only half should be issued at once, the remainder to be issued a year later, with a further provision that if called upon, the English contractors were to take it up. To this requirement Sir Morton Peto strongly objected, but finally agreed.

The prospectus was then drawn up by the chief negotiators. It was a compelling document. The British directors were the best names in London − Thomas Baring, George Carr Glyn, Henry Blake, Robert McCalmont, Kirkman Hodgson and Alderman Thompson. The Canadian directors were Hon. John Ross, Hon. Francis Hincks, Hon. E. P. Taché, Hon. James Morris, Hon. Malcolm Cameron, and Hon. R. E. Caron, all members of the provincial cabinet; Hon. Peter McGill, President of the Bank of Montreal, Benjamin Holmes, Vice-President of the St. Lawrence and Atlantic, George Crawford, of Brockville, W. N. Ponton, of Belleville, W. Rhodes of Quebec, and E. F. Whittemore of Toronto. The new road, it was pointed out, would be 1,112 miles in length, thus constituting the most comprehensive system of railway in the world. "The Grand Trunk Railway of Canada, it will be therefore seen, commencing at the debouchure of the three largest lakes in the world, pours the accumulating traffic in one unbroken line throughout the entire length of Canada into the St. Lawrence at Montreal and Quebec, on which it rests at the north, while on the south it reaches the magnificent harbours of Portland and St. John on the open ocean." Special stress was laid on the completeness of the railway and its freedom from competition; the definite limitation of the cost by having the contracts signed in advance, removing all fear of the capital being insufficient; the high standing of the English contractors, and the large government guarantee. In the light of later events, the most interesting and most controverted section was the estimate of net revenue.* It need only be said here that in 1860-1861, when the railway

* The estimate of net revenue was wildly optimistic. The gross annual revenue was calculated at £1,479,660. When the working expenses, interest on debentures, and rental of the St. Lawrence and Atlantic were deducted, a net revenue of £549,696 was expected. This would have given a handsome profit of 11½ per cent annually on the share capital (Currie, *The Grand Trunk Railway*, pp. 19, 63-64).

was opened throughout, the gross traffic amounted to only £714,956, and the surplus over working expenses was only £103,469. The low estimate of working expenses, 40 per cent, as against the actual 65 or 70 with which we are now familiar, was based upon the expectation that the standard of construction would be so much higher than that customary in America that all records of low operating costs would be distanced. This optimistic estimate was framed by the Chief Engineer, A. M. Ross, who had spent a year in Canada on behalf of the English contractors, gathering data.

Three days after the issue of the prospectus, Galt wrote to Benjamin Holmes, Vice-President of the St. Lawrence and Atlantic, as follows:

The reception of the scheme by the public has been marked by the most perfect success. The shares are already at a large premium and a perfect rush exists to get them. . . . I am gratified to state that I have been met in the most honourable and open manner by Hon. John Ross, as representing the Government; and also by Messrs. Jackson, Peto, Brassey and Betts, to whose influential position and admirable arrangement it is only due to say, that the successful introduction of this scheme is in my judgment mainly attributable. The delays, difficulties and anxieties attendant on my present mission have, as you may suppose, been a source of infinite solicitude to me, but I trust the great advantages flowing from the completion of the work will now soon enable me to forget them.

Once the negotiations were completed and the new company so successfully launched, Galt hastened to return to Canada, where the details of the arrangement made were awaited with keen interest. The provisional agreements entered into were laid before the directors of the various companies he had represented, and were speedily approved. His efforts on their behalf were recognized by glowing resolutions and by cheques written in a more restrained mood. With these transactions Galt's official connection with the Grand Trunk and all its works, except as a member of the contracting firm of Gzowski and Company, came to an end for some years, though he was constantly called upon by President Ross for counsel in the many difficulties which soon beset the company.

These difficulties were at the outset due to the sudden clouding of the international horizon. Western Europe had seemed about to enter a period of prolonged peace; only the year before, the navy of the German Bund had been sold by public auction, and the International Exhibition of 1851 at London had been the occasion for many prophecies of a new era in foreign relations. But Eastern Europe was not yet ready for peace. The Turk still held the Balkans in uneasy grip; from Montenegro to the Black Sea a reviving sense of nationalism was stirring revolt, and Russia and Austria were openly or secretly plotting to share in the spoils. Napoleon III, the newly crowned Emperor of France, was eager for foreign conquest to consolidate his power at home, and English fears of Russian domination at Constantinople led them to join that pseudo-warlord in the unavailing attempt to prolong Turkish barbarism and misrule.

Before the year was out the Crimean War was begun, and early in the summer the market had felt the coming storm. Money rose from 2 or 3 to 6 or 8 per cent, and was not easy to get even on these terms. The Grand Trunk found it extremely difficult to secure the balance of the capital required for the vast undertaking. The shares set aside for Canadian investors were not taken up, as they fell below par at once. The Portland roads were found to require heavy expenditure to bring them up to the standard set for the rest of the line, and these expenditures still further straitened the company's resources. The English contractors were released in 1855 from their agreement to take up the remainder of the stock and bonds authorized, undertaking only to accept half their future payments in the company's securities now selling at a discount.

In these circumstances the company turned again and again to the provinces as the readiest source of aid. From 1854 to 1862 scarcely a year passed without some Grand Trunk legislation. The demand for a provincial guarantee of the company's stock, made again and again by directors, shareholders' committees and contractors, was not assented to, but an additional bond guarantee of £900,000 was given in 1855, and by subsequent acts the province first took a position as second mortgagee, in order to permit the issue of preference bonds, and later postponed its lien still further. Its guarantee of bonds became practically a gift, amounting in principal and interest to over $26 million by Confederation. The amount is still carried on the books of the Dominion as a liability of the Grand Trunk, but it has long since ceased to be considered as more than a nominal debt.

The financial straits of the company greatly hampered the

contracting activities of Gzowski and Company, and compelled them in 1855 to acquiesce in the suspension of the section of their contract between Stratford and Sarnia. Fortunately the partners possessed in Galt and Holton two financiers of unusual capacity – both later Finance Ministers of Canada – and they succeeded in turning every difficult corner.

Even with the financing secure, the difficulties were not ended. All calculations of cost were disturbed by the boom which developed in the province before work was fairly begun. The Crimean war shut out Russia from the western market and sent wheat up to two dollars a bushel. Reciprocity with the United States opened a vast and growing market. Farm lands doubled in value and town lots shot up still faster. Every phase of the speculative orgy with which Canada again became familiar for a brief period in the eighties and still more markedly in the first dozen years of the twentieth century, now developed. The demand of the contractors themselves, employing as many as fifteen thousand men at one time, sent prices soaring. Wages and supplies and right of way all rose to heights undreamed of in the sleepy provinces of the pre-railway years. Sub-contractor after sub-contractor was threatened with bankruptcy, and a readjustment of the contract price was time and again made necessary.

These unlooked-for evils of too much prosperity lessened the profit Gzowski and Company had counted upon, but good management saved the day and brought all the partners a more than modest competency. They were more fortunate than their English fellow-contractors, who lost heavily in money and prestige in their Canadian work and found it necessary to abandon the Maritime contracts altogether. Their loss was partly due to being required to take part of their compensation in depreciated securities, but it was due in greater degree to their inability to cope with the peculiar conditions which construction work in America demanded. All their work had been done in countries where wages were low, and labour-saving methods had not been a necessity, as they were to Gzowski and Company and other contractors accustomed to our conditions.

The financial straits of the Grand Trunk, it had been noted, led late in 1853 to a request that Gzowski and Company should abandon or slacken all construction west of Stratford. It was felt advisable and, in the chastened mood which adversity had brought to both roads, possible, to make terms between the

Grand Trunk and the Great Western which would save unnecessary duplication in construction. In the spring of 1854 Galt visited London and with Hincks and the London directors of the two boards tried to bring about an amalgamation. This was found impossible, but as a temporary measure, the Grand Trunk agreed to halt construction beyond Stratford, and the Great Western to abandon its London to Sarnia branch. The contractors were compensated for the loss caused by this postponement. Meanwhile they rushed ahead the eastern section of their contract. The road from Toronto to Stratford was formally opened in November, 1856. It was two years later before the ten miles further to St. Mary's were completed, and a branch opened from that point to London, to connect with the Great Western.

The section of the Toronto and Sarnia road between Toronto and Stratford, where work was halted, was, in the words of Walter Shanly, then the company engineer of this division, and later general manager of the whole company, "of a more expensive character than any other equal portion of the Canadian lines." The bridge and culvert work was extremely heavy, both because of the number of streams crossed and because of the depth and width of their valleys. The masonry of the viaduct over the Credit river was over one hundred and twenty feet in height, while the Humber, Eramosa and Grand River structures were of almost equally great size. No difficulty or unexpected expense deterred the contractors from doing thoroughly what they had undertaken to do. Complaints were made later of excessive grades, of poor rails, and of inadequate equipment on the Grand Trunk as handed over to the company, but none of these criticisms were directed against the western section. The contract was carried out with an efficiency and a thoroughness which testified strongly to the executive capacity of Mr. Gzowski and the honourable business standards of all the partners.

The real prosperity and the speculative ferment of the early fifties gave rise to countless further projects of railway building. There were few among the more important proposals in which one or more members of the Gzowski firm did not have an interest. The Great Western in its early days received such large traffic and earned such good dividends as to attract attention largely to the Western Ontario peninsula. Plans for double tracking the Great Western, plans for building a branch from London to Sarnia or Amherstburgh, plans for a new road paralleling it but running further south, near Lake Erie, plans for extensions through Michigan, were all actively pressed. The rivalry to secure the contracts was keen, and many and rapid were the shifts of alliance made between the various contracting groups. Samuel Zimmermann, the railway king of Canada, Wythes and Company, the English contractors who had built the Great Western, and Gzowski and Company at one time joined forces and parcelled out among themselves the bulk of the work to be done, but the alliance was not a stable one, and each firm soon went its own straight or devious way, seeking what contracts it could secure by fair means, or by what in the language of the day was termed a "chisel."

When the line to Stratford was nearing completion, the contractors operated it for a few months before it was formally accepted by the company. The experience thus acquired led them to make a proposal which testified to their faith in the road which they had built and had in part promoted. They offered to lease the whole road from Toronto to Sarnia for 6 per cent on the cost, intending to build extensions to London and Detroit and secure through as well as local traffic. It would have been an interesting and probably a successful experiment, but the English directors had not yet lost hope of success under their own management, and declined the offer.

In 1858 Galt and Holton determined to retire from the contracting field. The financial crisis of 1857 had brought a sudden stop to all new projects, and for other reasons they desired to sever their connection with the Grand Trunk, which still had a good deal of work to carry through. They had been growing more and more absorbed in politics. It was understood on all sides that either or both at the next turn of the wheel would probably be called to high office. In any case it would have been impossible or inadvisable for men who wished to do work in the House or Ministry that would count, to remain closely connected with a busy contracting firm. Under the special circumstances which had developed in Canada it was impossible.

For the Grand Trunk itself was in politics. Its repeated requests for provincial aid, the log-rolling by members for the various sections most directly concerned in its further extension, the measure of responsibility assumed by the Hincks ministry and its successors, made its affairs a staple of parliamentary controversy. Charges that Hincks was bribed by English contractors added fuel to the flame kindled by the realization of the burden thrown upon the province by the failure of those contractors to do the impossible in the London money market. George Brown and the *Globe* diligently fanned the flame. In the early days of the Grand Trunk controversy, he had sided with Galt and Holton, but when they joined forces with the Brassey firm he turned all his batteries against them as well. As Chairman of a special legislative committee appointed in 1857 to inquire into "the condition, management and prospects of the Grand Trunk," Brown probed the details of the organization and later operations of the company, and made a special effort to discover some shady transactions involving Galt as well as Hincks. Galt was the chief witness throughout the long inquiry. His straightforward testimony and his able cross-examination of Brown's star witness, Benjamin Holmes, at that time Vice-President of the Grand Trunk, made the real situation clear beyond dispute, and he emerged from the ordeal with his honour henceforth unquestioned and his ability more widely recognized than ever.

Yet in such bad odour was the railway in many quarters, and so certain was it to come to parliament again for aid, that both Galt and Holton determined to sever all connection, even as contractors. The firm of Gzowski and Company was accordingly dissolved in 1858, and a division of assets made. The other partners decided to carry on the work under the same firm name, and before railway construction came to a halt in 1860, they built the extension to Sarnia, a branch from St. Mary's to London, and a loop line in Michigan which gave the Grand Trunk access to Detroit. Perhaps the most notable of these later enterprises was the building of the famous International Bridge across the Niagara River. Both Sir Casimir Gzowski and Sir David Macpherson were destined to attain high place in Canadian public life, and with both Galt maintained close personal relations long after the business tie was severed.

Shortly after retiring from all contracting connection with the Grand Trunk, Galt was urged to become a member of the railway's board of directors. He was reluctant to do so, but at the earnest solicitation of Mr. Glyn and of the new Managing Director, Mr. T. E. Blackwell, he agreed, and was elected a director early in 1858. His term of office was short, however, as he resigned a few months later upon taking office as Inspector-General in the Cartier-Macdonald cabinet.

With this step, Galt's active connection with Canadian

railways came to a close.* It had been a connection of momentous importance for the country. Mistakes had been made, in
which he had his share, but the net result was unquestionably
such as to justify the high reputation which this decade's activity
gave him both in Canada and in Great Britain. The straggling
colony had been bound together from end to end by nearly two
thousand miles of rail, and a good beginning had been made in
linking up the provinces by the sea. The new facilities of transport made it possible to take advantage of the wide markets
opened up both in America and Europe. In this period Canada's
commercial isolation came to an end, and this change involved
the extension and elaboration of the primitive financial structure
of the forties. The fertilizing stream of London capital was
turned into Canadian channels. For good or for ill, Canada was
henceforth more than a pioneer settlement. It had definitely
become a part of the great world of commerce and finance.

For ill as well as good. There was ground for much heart-
searching as to some of the incidents and effects of this transition period. The moral tone of public life had been seriously
lowered. The country had been saddled with a heavy debt
through the failure of the Grand Trunk and other guaranteed
roads to fulfil expectations. London shareholders suffered heavy
losses. For these ill results Alexander T. Galt had little responsibility. The province could not for all time remain in the
untempted garden of an agricultural Eden, and when temptation
came to its public men, nothing but good would have followed
had all possessed the high and unyielding standard of personal
integrity which Galt maintained in all his countless negotiations.
The material loss to the province through its guarantee was
small in comparison with the widespread commercial benefits
received from the building of the road. And if English money
was lost in the building and operation, that only served to prove
the foresight of the man who early in 1852 pointed out the need
of encouraging local ability and local responsibility, and the
difficulty of managing any railway effectively from three

* This statement is technically correct but, as it stands, misleading.
Galt's formal connection with the railways may have come to a
close, but his services in their interest as a member of government
were extremely helpful. It will be seen, for example, that his tariff
policy of 1859 was inextricably linked with the survival of the railways. He was probably more valuable to railway companies as a
minister than as a financier.

thousand miles' distance.* That Canadians could build roads well, and could finance them skilfully, he and his associates amply proved, and possibly if they had been permitted they could have proved, thirty years before the Canadian Pacific demonstrated it, that they could operate them successfully as well.

---

* Not all historians have been as charitable as Skelton in passing judgment on this period in Canadian history. A. R. M. Lower has written: "The money dumped into Canada by the orgy of railroad building in the 1850's has been estimated as high as one hundred million dollars. Nothing remotely approaching it had ever occurred before in the country's history. . . . Much went to promoters and contractors; a little, but no impressive amount, to the English financial interests, who in general found themselves outdone in their own area by the smart colonials; and a great deal in actual costs of construction. . . . Between all these groups, the money was shoveled out. . . . This expenditure . . . gave Canada a positively hectic three years of prosperity from 1854 to 1857, and incidentally some railroads" (A. R. M. Lower, Colony to Nation [Toronto, 1946], pp. 285-286).

4: Canada Under the Union: The Coming of Responsible Government

Galt and the union era; the union of the Canadas; the coming of responsible government; Galt's introduction to politics.

The period of legislative union between Upper and Lower Canada, 1841-1867, was of deep and lasting importance in the making of modern Canada. It was in this crowded quarter-century that the foundations of the Dominion were laid. Institutions were established, policies tested, traditions formed, men trained, all essential for the transformation of the struggling backwoods settlements of yesterday into the nation of today.

As has been seen, it was an era of marked industrial and commercial development. Canals and railways were built which bound the province together and united it with the outside world, and at the same time brought about a growth of commercial enterprise and machinery, and an outburst of speculative activity fraught alike with great good and great ill. But this period was equally important in its political phases. It witnessed the winning and the working out of responsible government, with all that this implied of change in colonial status, in constitutional machinery, and in party organization. It was the era of experiment in legislative union, of the half-hearted and less than half-hearted attempt to make the two provinces one in interest and feeling, an era of sectional rivalries and political deadlock, which found at last their only solution in the federation of British North America.

Some account has been given of the part which A. T. Galt played in the railway and commercial development of this period, especially in its middle years. His career is of equal significance as a reflex of the political activity of the union era, a guiding thread through the maze of experiment and fleeting change. His first incursion into politics was connected with the last determined stand of the old regime against the demand for self-government. He entered Parliament in the session after responsible government was definitely achieved, and save for a brief gap he was in Parliament during all the trying years when legislative union was being given its trial and Canadian politicians were learning to work the system of responsible government they had won. For a large part of this time he was in office, and throughout he was intimately concerned with the political developments of the period, its success and its failures, and still more notably, with the remedy finally adopted for the failures.

The very fact that Galt was not a rigid party man makes his career the more significant. He was a man of independent thinking, and yet so open-minded, so keenly alert to the changing needs and movements of the time, that he reflects better than any other statesman of his day the changes in public opinion upon great issues. Where other men were held back by considerations of party fortunes or by lack of interest in broader principles, Galt never hesitated to take up a new issue or change his opinion upon an old one. These were qualities which sometimes militated against immediate success in political life, but they helped to make him the most representative figure of his time and to enable him to foresee and to speed the coming of the new solutions which each decade's problems demanded.

Galt's first entrance into practical politics, it has been seen, came about through his endeavour, in Metcalfe's regime, to enlist the aid of the provincial government in averting the threatened ruin of the British American Land Company by crushing taxation. He had not been without interest in politics previously; no young man of active mind could be without interest, in the days of the Reform Bill in England and of the struggle in Canada which led to rebellion. Writing to his friend, D. M. Moir, the year before the passing of the Reform Bill, John Galt had declared: "You will be surprised to learn that I take no interest in the Reform question, but the boys are fierce Tories."

Alexander came to Canada just on the eve of the rebellion. His associations and interests in Canada combined with this early bias to throw his sympathies strongly with the "British party," the section which resisted the demands of the popular Assembly because majority rule meant French rule. The Land Company, in fact, had been one of the *bêtes noirs* of Papineau and his followers. It was condemned both because sale of Crown lands helped to enable the executive to get along without the vote of the taxes which the Assembly was trying to barter for power, and because it was believed that the Company aimed at swamping the French Canadians by bringing great numbers of English immigrants to Lower Canada. It was, then, with intense interest that the young clerk followed the double outbreak, the spectacular six months' progress of the great proconsul, Lord Durham, the business administration of Lord Sydenham, and the period of calm that came with the diplomatic Bagot. But it was not until Sir Charles Metcalfe, fresh from ruling India and Jamaica, came to make a last stand against the rising tide of responsible government that Galt saw behind the scenes at all. . . .

~ The Rebellion of 1837 in Upper and Lower Canada failed to realize the aims of the radical reformers who hoped to throw off the oligarchic rule of the colonial Tories. However, it did succeed in breaking down British indifference to the unsatisfactory state of affairs in British North America. It was clear that drastic new measures to remove the sources of discontent were needed and consequently Lord Durham was dispatched to the restive colonies to investigate and to recommend such remedies as he deemed necessary. The results of this inquiry were submitted to the British government in his famous Report.[1] Durham's analysis covered in depth a wide range of topics including land tenure, education, municipal government and taxation, but two recommendations stood out above all others. These were the union of the Canadas and responsible government.

Although the union of Upper and Lower Canada was justified on sound economic grounds, Durham's strong advocacy of union sprang chiefly from his conviction that it was the French who were mainly responsible for political unrest and slow economic progress. The most practical answer to the problem in his view was to submerge the French in the narrow English majority which would result if the two colonies were joined. He advised the merging of the provinces into a single community with a common legislature in which the French would lose their sense of a separate national identity.

Durham's recommendation in favour of colonial self-government was even more radical and certainly more significant for the future of the British Empire. The British government had granted representative institutions in the colonies but continued to govern through local cliques which were not responsible to popular legislative control. It is not clear to what extent Durham accepted the colonial reformers' idea of responsible government, but he urged the imperial authorities to concede the basic principles of self-government without delay. The exact form of self-government was not clearly defined, but certainly the implication of Durham's scheme was that the colonial executive council would become a cabinet on the British model, representing a majority in the popular assembly, and carrying out such measures as the majority supported. The flaw in the proposal was the failure to recognize that such a system, if it were to work effectively, required a coherent party system which still did not exist in the colonies.

In 1839 Charles Poulett Thomson, later Lord Sydenham, was appointed Governor-General and began to implement Durham's recommendations. The union of the two Canada's was accomplished smoothly and in a short time. The experience in establishing responsible government was less happy. Sydenham's interpretation of responsible government led him to look upon the executive as a mere advisory board and he attempted to retain executive power in his own hands. He succeeded in defending the governor's prerogative, maintaining a precarious control over the legislature by exploiting the absence of a party system and by the liberal use of patronage. His successor, Sir Charles Bagot, arrived in Canada in 1842 when Sydenham's policy was on the brink of collapse. Bagot was forced to admit several reformers to his cabinet. He managed barely to hold on to his independent authority but, by the time he died in 1843, the council was well on the way to becoming a true cabinet. Sir Charles Metcalfe, Bagot's successor, was determined that there should be no further erosion of the governor's powers and he quickly became the centre of a political storm. A controversy over the governor's right to approve appointments developed shortly after his arrival in Canada and when he refused to give up his prerogative in appointments, his ministry resigned. A year of political chaos followed as Metcalfe attempted in vain to find suitable men to take their place. ~

It was at this stage in the struggle that young Galt had his first experience of practical politics. The British American Land Company had found itself in straits which compelled it to seek the aid of the provincial government. Settlers and sales were few, development expenses heavy, and now the Company was threatened with heavy local taxation. The district councils established during the suspension of the constitution of Lower Canada had been authorized to levy taxes for local purposes. None had taken advantage of this power except the District Council of Sherbrooke, which had imposed, but had not yet exacted, a tax of a penny an acre on all wild lands, which would amount to £2,500 for the Land Company. It was understood that a new municipal act was about to be introduced. With a view to seeking relief from the existing tax and endeavouring to avert similar ills under the new legislation, the Directors had authorized Galt to proceed to Kingston, the capital of the united province, and see what could be done. His instructions were to induce the government, if possible, to buy back the Company's lands at the bare cost of purchase and subsequent development, to oppose the establishment of municipal authorities at all, or, if this was inevitable, to seek to have their powers of taxation limited or the Company's lands exempted.

Arrived at Kingston, Galt was not long in finding out that the requests of the Company were likely to be given short shrift. Messrs. Moffat and Holmes, local directors of the Company and both Members of Parliament for Montreal, the former a member of the old Tory party and the latter a supporter of the Lafontaine-Baldwin administration, made it clear that the Company was not in favour with the legislature. The old hostility of the French Canadians against the Company was reinforced by the rising hostility of both sections of the province to speculative holding of large undeveloped areas. It was in vain that Galt emphasized the differences between the ordinary large holder of wild lands, who had paid little or nothing for them, and done less to develop them, and the Company, which had paid large sums for purchase and development. Morin, the Commissioner of Crown Lands for Lower Canada, told him that no special favour would be shown the Company. Hincks, the Inspector-General, was still more uncompromising in his hostility. A gleam of hope came from Wakefield, formerly Durham's trusted assistant and now a member of the local legislature. He was endeavouring to enlist interest in a scheme projected by Charles Buller, another of Durham's lieutenants, for the purchase by the province of all granted wild land and its settlement by a systematic emigration policy. Even this gleam soon faded; Wakefield reported that the members of a special committee he had had appointed showed no interest in Buller's suggestion. In one quarter only did the young secretary find encouragement. In two interviews in November, the Governor expressed sympathy but added that "under the present order of things my power is greatly limited."

It was clear that the Company had little influence and less sympathy at the capital. On the advice of Moffat, Galt did not present the petitions for resale of lands to the province and decided to seek exemption from the existing District tax by further negotiations with the local authority rather than by seeking to induce the provincial government to override it. He concentrated his efforts upon securing modification of the taxing powers to be assigned the local authorities by the new Municipal Act, then being drafted by Morin. As a result of repeated interviews, Morin agreed to stipulate that only land benefited by local improvements should be taxed, that value as well as area should be considered in the assessment, and that a limit should be set to the proportion of school taxes assessable on wild lands. With these concessions Galt had perforce to be content.

It was while the young secretary was thus seeking, and in vain, for a glimmer of official favour toward the Company, that an incident occurred which has been recorded by Fennings Taylor, assistant clerk of the Legislative Council. "It was at such a time," the chronicler records, "that the subject of our sketch found himself a visitor at Kingston, probably, and in spite of himself, an idler at the British American Hotel, in the care of a genial landlord, whose heart was as large as his lodgings were small. In such straits different men would act differently. The listless man would probably lounge and dream; the energetic man would move and act; one would sit and think, the other would walk and observe. The writer, who then resided about five miles from Kingston, was informed on his return home one afternoon, that some gentlemen, and one in particular, had that day been walking on the road in front of his house for hours, as if impelled by a vow or constrained by a wager. On inquiring the name of the chief pedestrian, the writer was almost reviled for his ignorance. 'That is Aleck Galt,' said the enthusiast, 'his wager is to walk thirty miles in six hours.' He did it too, and in a plucky way, for he had, if we remember rightly, several minutes to spare. Thus the bet, which was five pounds, was honestly earned. The fatigue of the walk was, we have little doubt, subsequently forgotten in the glow of the wine, and the chaff and chatter, like nuts and biscuit, gave a relishing flavour to the dessert." . . .

~ Galt secured an interview with Francis Hincks, whom he found to be most unco-operative. Hincks told him that wild lands would be taxed heavily and that the government "would have no mercy on the proprietors." Galt was "exceedingly sorry to hear such wild and unjust expressions," but took comfort in the fact that Hincks' influence was confined to Canada West. ~

It was perhaps not surprising that Hincks, who was later to become a close associate of his young interviewer, was not in the best of temper. The very day of this discussion word had reached the members of the Executive Council that the Governor had filled the cup by appointing to the post of Clerk of the Peace in Dalhousie District, the very man whom a leading member of the Opposition had boasted a few days before, in Baldwin's presence, the Governor would be induced to name. Four days later, after futile conferences, the councillors resigned. How quickly Galt turned the crisis to account may be seen from his next letter to Robinson, written from Montreal, on December 7:

I had the honour of addressing you last on the 23rd ult., at which time I stated the probable purport of the government measure and also mentioned the particulars of my interviews with the Governor-General. Circumstances have since occurred materially affecting the whole position of affairs.

On the 27th ult. it was suddenly announced that in consequence of disagreement between His Excellency and the Executive Council the latter had resigned. The particulars attending this resignation I need not advert to, as the Court will no doubt see them fully set forth in the public prints. The point at issue appears to be the exercise of the right of patronage which, it is conceded, under "Responsible Government" belongs to the Executive Council.

I very soon ascertained that whatever the real cause of disagreement might be, it was almost certain the business of the session was at an end, and that the Education and Municipal Bills would be postponed to a future Parliament. It also appeared highly probable, as the late Executive commanded a large majority, that the Governor would soon be required to dissolve the House of Assembly. I anxiously considered whether the Company might not turn to advantage the present state of political affairs. I much regretted now that I had not the advantage of the presence of the Commissioner, and equally so that Mr. McGill and Mr. Moffat were both absent in Montreal, but after giving the subject the best consideration in my power I can only trust that the conclusion I came to and have acted upon may receive the approval of the Court.

When I first met the Directors on my arrival from Canada, I took the earliest opportunity of urging on them as a measure of self-defence, that the Company should endeavour to make use of that local influence which their large property afforded, and at the same time I stated my impression that the best security the Company could possess against injurious treatment either at the hands of the Provincial Legislature or of the Municipal Council was to obtain such an influence in these representative bodies as might render their opposition or support of importance. In these views I understood that the Court coincided. On my arrival in Kingston, I found to my deep regret that the Company were completely disregarded, and though listened to, I had no means of effectually pressing their case on the Government. This treatment, I believed, could be easily traced to the circumstances that of the members returned from the Eastern Townships there was not one who would stand forward as the advocate of the Company, and the natural deduction was that their system of management was unpopular, and that harsh measures toward them would be rather acceptable than otherwise to the inhabitants. At the same time, I could not conceal from myself that if the measures affecting the Company were once passed, it would then become impossible by any means to affect their repeal, while from the strength of the Ministry it seemed vain to hope that anything should occur to interfere with their carrying out their views.

The unexpected resignation of the Ministry appeared to me at once to afford a last chance to the Company to improve their position by decidedly assuming an interest in the election, should a dissolution occur, and endeavour to secure the return of several Eastern Townships representatives favorable to the Company and to a certain extent subject to their influence. Meantime it might be advantageous, while matters were in such an unsettled state, to endeavour to place the Company in a more favourable situation with one or other party, by tendering its support. It appeared, by an analysis of the House, that in the event of any election the members from the Eastern Townships would most probably decide the majority. . . .

It then became necessary to decide in what manner and to whom I should address myself for the purpose of asserting the Company's influence and pledging its exercise. The Executive Council were to all practical purposes the governors of the country, and moreover had the support of a large majority, which, it was very possible, a new election might not materially affect, but then, they were to a considerable extent personally hostile to the Company, and were further pledged to the country in certain measures against the Company's interests. Besides, I felt it very difficult to deal with men who were already receiving from the representatives of the Eastern Townships that support which it was my business to tender. On the other hand, the Governor-General found himself placed in a position of great difficulty, his ministry leaving him at a most important part of the session, and certain that the House of Assembly would support them in any course they chose to adopt. Still, it could not be doubted that the Home Government would support their representative, and if an appeal were made to the people, it might not at all improbably result in the Governor triumphing over his opponents. It therefore seemed to me that as His Excellency was more in want of support, and further, that, as the accession of the Townships members would at once strengthen him and weaken his adversaries, it was with the Governor-General that I could most advantageously treat. . . .

Having come to this conclusion, two days after the resignation of the Executive, I addressed a note to His Excellency of which a copy is enclosed, requesting an audience on the subject. I personally waited on the private secretary with the note, and was happy to find that he entered into the subject with eagerness, and assured me that His Excellency was much gratified with the proffer made; he appointed the next day for my interview. On the 2nd inst., therefore, I waited on the Governor-General, who stated that he was much pleased to receive so early an assurance of the support of the Company, that although it was not at present his intention to dissolve the House, he might ultimately be obliged to take that course, and that in such a case it would be of the last importance that the Government should receive the support of the members from the English section of Lower Canada. After a lengthy conversation concerning the position of the Company and the means they had of acting efficiently, His Excellency concluded by distinctly asking what I supposed the Company would expect at his hands in return for their aid. I had previously thought that this question might be put, and I therefore advisedly replied, that I could not venture to make anything like terms with His Excellency, that the fact was, his late advisers were pursuing a course highly prejudicial to the Company and that could that corporation assist in strengthening his government, I felt assured that they would receive at least justice, and that until they had shown their ability as well as their disposition to serve, I could not say more. His Excellency then replied emphatically in these words: "You may rest assured . . . those who support me, I will support."

Subsequently to my visit to the Governor-General, I had several interviews with Mr. Draper, the probable future Attorney-General (West), and with Mr. De Blaquiere, who is one of His Excellency's advisers in the present crisis. The latter gentleman candidly admitted the great importance of carrying out what I had undertaken, and added, that he need scarce say that with three or four votes in the Company's interests, they need be under no uneasiness as to the measures of the government towards them.

I trust that what I have now stated will induce the Court to approve of the steps which, unadvised, I have assumed the heavy responsibility of taking. I believed that to let matters take their course, as has been hitherto done, would result in the speedy ruin of the Company under the burden of taxation, and I therefore considered that were I to let the present opportunity slip, I should have but ill fulfilled the confidence with which the Court have treated me. . . . If our efforts fail, I do not see that the Company's circumstances would be altered for the worse, for it would evidently be impossible for any party, however strong, to pass a measure through both houses affecting the Company directly, and my last letter showed that the party lately in power were disposed to pass as severe general measures relative to Wild Lands as they could carry.

Another reason why I was anxious at once to offer the Company's support to the Governor, arose from my belief that the people would be themselves disposed to reject their representatives, and, believing this, I conceived that I should be able to take advantage of this feeling and claim credit to the Company.

It is, however, now for the Court to decide whether they will sanction what has already been done, and thus render other steps necessary. For although I have assured the Governor of the best exertions of the Company on his behalf, still I do not propose, until I receive instructions from the Court, openly to show any anxiety on the part of the Company in the approaching elections. I shall, however, personally use every exertion in my power, and I shall hope in this to receive the assistance of Mr. Fraser.

I arrived here today, and immediately waited on Mr. McGill, and fully acquainted him with the steps I have taken, which he authorized me to say, are fully approved by him. My only anxiety is that the Court will coincide in his opinion.

Evidently the young Secretary took to politics like a duck

to water. When a politician of two or three months' training could act and write like this, there did not seem much ground for the fears of those sceptical persons who doubted the competency of colonials, adopted or native-born, to manage the parliamentary machine.

There were few in England, in politics or out, in that day, who did not approve of any course tending to uphold British authority over the colonies. The Governor at once replied, commending Galt's course, though through a miscarriage of the mails he did not receive the letter before he had sailed for England in February to present the report of his work as Secretary.

G. R. ROBINSON TO A. T. G., LONDON, 3RD JANUARY, 1844

Dear Sir:

We have duly received your despatches of 7th and 8th ulto., but the short period elapsing before the sailing of the present packet does not allow of our calling a Court together to consider its contents.

We, however, do not hesitate to express our entire approbation of the course you have taken.

It has always been our conviction that the interests of the British American Land Company were identified with British influence in the colony, and that the prosperity of the Company would greatly strengthen that influence, and tend to the preservation of the connexion of Canada with the Mother Country, and the course so properly taken by His Excellency the Governor deserves the gratitude and support of all persons friendly to British interests.

Should an appeal to the constituencies be made by His Excellency, we are anxious that every proper influence should be used by the Company, and every exertion made by those connected with it, to secure the return of candidates who will maintain the measures of Sir Charles Metcalfe.

We send a copy of this letter to Mr. Fraser, who, we doubt not, will do everything in his power to give effect to our wishes, and should you consider that this important object will be promoted by your prolonging your stay in Canada for another month, you have our authority for so doing.

We are, Dear Sir,
Respectfully yours,
G. R. ROBINSON, *Governor.*
JAS. J. CUMMINS, *Dep. Governor.*

In the course of his stay in England, Galt had ample opportunity to discuss the political situation with the Directors. On his return to Canada, he found that the ministers whom the Governor had secured, the Draper-Viger administration, were anxious to obtain the Company's influence without committing themselves to the repurchase or other schemes. Meanwhile, Galt had succeeded in inducing the Municipal Council of the District to refrain from attempting to collect the Wild Lands tax. Other measures of vital importance to the Company and to the whole Eastern Townships had latterly come to the front, notably the proposal to build a railway from Montreal to Boston, through the Townships. He was, therefore, in no mood to pledge an unqualified thick and thin support to the new administration. Late in September, 1844, he wrote a letter to the Ministerial candidates for Sherbrooke Town and Sherbrooke County, Messrs. Brooks and Hale, in which he declared: "The grounds upon which I have invariably based my expectations of succeeding with the railway project have been, that the peculiar position of political affairs in the Colony was such as to render it absolutely necessary that the Eastern Townships should decide at the next election on such a representation as would, while prepared to support the views of the Governor-General, yet regard themselves as unpledged to the support of any particular class of men whom His Excellency might select to carry out those principles, and who would be prepared to regard the conduct of those ministers favorably or otherwise according to the consideration they might evince for the notorious wants of this section of Canada. . . . I had every confidence in the personal sympathy of the Governor-General, but I did not and do not expect that without strong political reasons he would be able to make good to us those friendly intentions if in so doing he placed his councillors in a difficult position. . . . My fear is that the position in which Mr. Hale stands, as connected with what has been termed the 'Family Compact,' is such as will induce the French-Canadian members to view his election as a determination on the part of this section to revert to a system of exclusion and of irresponsible administration. He will be considered a thick and thin supporter of the Governor."

This formal request brought an immediate joint pledge from both candidates that "so intimately connected did they consider the railway to be with the prosperity of the Eastern Townships that they should look upon the refusal of efficient assistance by the Executive as a denial of that just share of the notice of government to which the Townships were entitled, and that they should, except upon important constitutional questions, hesitate to afford their support to any administration which would not enter into their desires on that head."

The elections were held in November, and resulted in the return of a majority pledged to support the Governor. The Eastern Townships sent a solid delegation of six to his aid. The personal exertions of the Governor, the stirring of racial bitterness, the uncertainty as to the fine points of constitutional lore involved in the controversy, and the feeling among many that British connection was at stake, all contributed to this result. Whether or not the Land Company could claim the credit in its district, at all events it had little to complain of in the legislation of the next few years.

Metcalfe had triumphed, but his victory only served to demonstrate the impossibility of permanent conduct of the government of Canada except on the lines his opponents had urged. By his very assaults upon the opposing party he gave it coherence and definiteness. The parliamentary majority behind his ministers began to break up. It became clear that no ministry could long hold office which was not chosen from below, rather than imposed from above. In the country a strong reaction had set in; every election could not be made a flag-waving election, and in any event the flag was ceasing to have its old force in some quarters. Soon Sir Charles, the third Governor to whom Canada had proved fatal in five years, went home to England to be crowned with honours by an approving ministry, and to carry them to a speedy grave, regretted by friend and foe. The brief governorship of General Cathcart merely marked time. In 1847 Lord Elgin, son-in-law of Durham, and heir to his policy, came to take up the task. From the outset he showed his determination to accept the will of the majority, and to trust to influence rather than to compulsion to recommend his opinions to his ministers. At the election of 1848, the Reformers swept both Upper and Lower Canada, and the second Baldwin-Lafontaine ministry, the Ministry of All-the-Talents, came to power. Draper, himself, Metcalfe's chief supporter, on laying down the reins of office, expressed his conviction that henceforth Responsible Government was inevitable. The long contest was over.

"The day when Lord Elgin, after long hesitation," declared a Canadian public man of wide familiarity with Canadian history [Hon. F. D. Monk], "summoned Louis Hippolyte Lafontaine to ask him if he could form a cabinet which would have the confidence of Parliament; the day when Lafontaine accepted the charge as Premier and took his oath, stipulating that Robert Baldwin, his lifelong friend, should be his colleague; the 11th of March, 1848, was without doubt . . . the blessed day of the birth of free government for our country, the true birth of our nation." It is not possible to maintain that any one day brought the complete fulfilment of the aspirations for which "Responsible Government" had long been the watchword. Even yet, two generations later, the process is not complete. Yet if far from being the final goal, that day was a notable milestone on the way toward it, the beginning of a new political era. Responsible Government had been in large measure irretrievably won. It remained to see what would be its fruits, how it would work in the hands of the public men of Canada.

5: The Aftermath of Responsible Government

Galt's first election to Parliament; the passing of racial ascendancy; the passing of the old colonial system; the annexation movement of 1849.

Galt's brief glimpse behind the political scenes at Kingston in 1843 fired him with an ambition to play a part himself when the time came. Then and there he made up his mind that he would some day become the Inspector-General, or Finance Minister, of Canada. The determination showed a discriminating knowledge of his own powers; fifteen years later it was fulfilled to the letter. His frequent journeys to Montreal, which had become the capital in 1844, on land and railway business, brought him into close and frequent contact with members of the legislature and of the administration, and confirmed his belief that he could hold his own in their company. His successful management of the Land Company and his active interest in the Portland railway had brought him wide reputation. He had already become recognized as the outstanding representative man of the Eastern Townships. When, therefore, Samuel Brooks, the member for Sherbrooke County, died, it was to Galt that all looked as his successor.

His position on this occasion can best be stated in the words of a letter to the Governor of the Land Company, Alexander Gillespie, in April, 1849:

In my last communication I had the honor to advise the Court of the sudden and lamented death of Samuel Brooks, the late representative of Sherbrooke County in our provincial parliament, and I now beg to state the events which have placed my name before the public as his probable successor.

Immediately after Mr. Brooks' funeral, the subject of his successor was discussed amongst the leading men of the County, and I was informed that the desire was becoming general that I should accept the nomination. This was intimated to me on the 29th ult., and, on the 30th, I received Mr. Exham's letter of March 9 wherein he states that "the Court thought it better that the Company and its officers should avoid being mixed up with any political agitations." The receipt of this letter reminded me of the doubts previously expressed by the

Court as to its being desirable that their Commissioner should have a seat in the lower House. After full consideration I came to the conclusion that as the Directors might deem it incompatible with my other duties I ought to decline the proffered nomination.

On the afternoon of the same day a large meeting was held, to whom I briefly explained the reasons why I could not serve them, and handed in to the Chairman for publication my written refusal, of which I enclose a copy. I then retired from the meeting and considered the matter closed, but the gentlemen present appeared to have so much difficulty in selecting any other person, that after a protracted discussion I was sent for and was informed that in the present circumstances of the Townships and especially of the Railroad, they were unanimously of the opinion that I was likely to be more useful than any other person available. They desired that I should withdraw my refusal and consent to allow them to return me (if the county acquiesced), subject to the sanction of the Directors of the Company. I at length withdrew my refusal, and agreed to leave the matter in their hands, expressly stating, however, that if elected, I held myself at liberty to resign if required to do so by the Directors. I left Sherbrooke next morning so that no one might hereafter say that I had sought for, or exercised any improper influence to obtain, my election.

Being distrustful of my own judgment in a matter where my personal feelings were more or less interested, immediately on my arrival in town, I waited upon Mr. McGill and Mr. Moffatt, and begged their candid advice of what the Company's interests dictated. Both these gentlemen concurred in the opinion that my presence in the House would promote the Company's interest, and authorized me to state this opinion to you.

I need not remind the Court that the principle upon which the government of this province is now conducted has placed all power in the hands of the leaders of the House of Assembly, and that in fact no appeal exists to any other adequate tribunal. The British government would, I am sure, decline interfering to protect the Company in the event of any local measure pressing with undue severity upon them. To the Executive government of the day, therefore, the Company must be prepared to address their remonstrances and petitions.

The influence of public bodies as well as of men in this province is now very much regulated by their political power.

This truth has been experienced by me in every representation I have had occasion to make to the government. I could point to the long protracted applications relative to the Railroad, when the answer made to my most urgent entreaties was, Why do not your representatives take the matter up if it is so important? I could point to the Acton Road and to many other proposals with which the Court is familiar, where our efforts have been paralyzed by the mere suspicion that the Company would be benefited. I am far from desiring to arrogate to myself any peculiar claims, but I have felt for the last four years that the representatives of the Eastern Townships were jealous of my exertions on behalf of the country and offered a cold support that chilled all my efforts and effectually barred success with the government. . . .

I will frankly admit to the Court that if instructed to confine myself to the sale of lands and collection of debts, I cannot adequately give value for my salary, and that it is only by striving to remove the weighty evils that press on the country that the Company itself can prosper. No one can question that so long as the Townships languish and their best inhabitants seek elsewhere for prosperity, no system of management and no exertions confined to the Company's own business can restore success to their operations. On the other hand, diffused as their lands are, if the Townships do but thrive, no interest will so soon reap benefit as that of the Company. I consider the interests of the Company and of the country to be identical. . . .

I ought perhaps to add that I am not the least likely to become a political partisan; my views are all for objects of material advantage.

The Court gave a reluctant consent to their Commissioner's request, declining, however, to commit themselves for more than the term of the existing Parliament. Before this word arrived, the election day had passed and A. T. Galt had been returned as member for Sherbrooke County without opposition. Not entirely without question, however. It is significant of the shifting and uncertainty of party lines at this time that a week after he had consented to stand, the Chairman of the election committee found it necessary to write him at Montreal to find out on which side of the House he would sit if elected. The Chairman, Mr. J. G. Robinson, wrote:

After the frequent interviews which some of us have had with you on the subject of the coming election, and after the expression of your opinions at the meeting at Cheyney's on the 30th ult., it may appear like a want of confidence in you for us to make any further inquiries as to your political views. But since you left for Montreal, circumstances have arisen which seem to render it proper that we should be placed in a position to say beyond the possibility of contradiction what your course will be if returned to parliament for this county.

As individuals, we have the utmost confidence that you will not disappoint the expectations of your Conservative friends, founded on your previous political conduct and the free and candid expressions given on the occasions alluded to. We are, however, constrained to say that your political opponents understand your political position very differently from what we do. Some of them do not hesitate to say that you pledged yourself to go with the ministry.

The political course which we have hitherto taken, the character which this county has maintained and the position which it holds in the Townships and in the Province, as well as our private feelings, forbid that we should be a party to the election of any candidate who would take his seat on the minis- terial side of the House. We have no wish to bind our represen- tative to oppose the ministry for the sake of opposition, on the contrary, we would have every measure calculated to promote the general welfare supported come from what quarter it might.

In a private letter Mr. Robinson threw some further light on the situation:

The difficulty lies mainly as to the place, let me say bench, you are to occupy. Some may say it makes little difference whether you sit on the ministerial or on the opposition benches, if you vote right, yet, as a county is counted by the side its member occupies, it is a matter of considerable importance after all.

Some individuals, who go so far as even to uphold the pay- ment of all rebellion losses, have claimed that you were a thoroughgoing ministry man. I may also mention that I have heard many who signed your requisition say: If the support of the ministry to our railroad is to be purchased by Mr. Galt's joining their ranks so far as to sit on their side, and be counted a ministry man, let the railroad go to blazes.

The reply was soon forthcoming:

Your esteemed favour of today with resolution of the Committee asking whether I have pledged myself to support the ministerial party, has, I confess, occasioned me much surprise, after my frank and public declaration that I was not disposed to pledge myself to support the extreme views of either political party in the House. I have not the least hesitation in replying that I have given no such pledge, nor have I ever, to the best of my belief, given any ground for such supposition. At the same time I am bound to say that I will support a good measure let it come from either side of the House.

I trust that this explanation will prove satisfactory to the Committee.

Whether entirely satisfactory or not, the explanation had to suffice. The new member took his seat on the Opposition benches, and voted against the government on the Rebellion Losses Bill. Two days later a Tory mob stoned the Governor-General and burned the Parliament buildings to demonstrate its superior loyalty, and six months later the same ultra-loyalist element, reinforced by Radical stragglers, issued a Manifesto calling for the annexation of Canada to the United States. . . .

~ The Montreal riots and the annexation movement had their origins in the changed political and economic conditions in Lower Canada (Canada East). Under the union and after the grant of responsible government, the English-speaking minority of Lower Canada was chagrined to find itself at the mercy of the French majority, represented in the legislature by Lafontaine, in alliance with Baldwin's Upper Canadian reformers. Hitherto the English in Lower Canada had enjoyed a privileged position and had been protected by the imperial authority exercised through the governor. When the British government accepted responsible government, they also accepted majority rule which meant, in the eastern half of the union, French rule. The first manifestation of the new situation became apparent in the Rebellion Losses Bill introduced by Lafontaine and designed to compensate those who had suffered damages in the Rebellion of 1837. The inclusion of rebels among those to receive compensation caused the pent-up frustration of the Lower Canada English to explode in rioting and personal abuse of the Governor-General, Lord Elgin, who went ahead and signed the measure despite the objections. In refusing to veto the bill, Elgin was merely accepting the principle of responsible government in practice, but his action was viewed by the Lower

Canada English as an indication that they had been abandoned by the Mother Country.

The sudden supremacy of the French was not the only source of English dissatisfaction. An equally strong motivating factor was the commercial depression of 1847-49 which the English merchants of Lower Canada attributed to the collapse of the old colonial system. For years the old colonial system had provided favoured treatment for colonial produce in the British market by means of shipping regulations and preferential duties. These subsidies were gradually reduced in the early 1840's and disappeared entirely with the repeal of the Corn Laws in 1846. At the very moment when the British government swept away this basis of prosperity in Lower Canada, the American government removed duties on imports from Canada if the goods were destined for sale outside the United States. This meant that produce from the Canadian interior could be shipped cheaply through the New York route rather than by way of the St. Lawrence.

In 1849 the English, and most particularly the merchant class, understandably felt that they had been betrayed, economically as well as politically, by Great Britain.[1] ~

In October, 1849, a manifesto was issued, strongly worded, forcefully argued, impressively signed, urging peaceful separation from the Mother Country and annexation to the United States. All the other political possibilities were reviewed and one by one declared of no avail. The only remedy lay in securing an entrance to the markets of the United States, and an infusion of the energy and the capital of that more favoured land. The signatures read like a blue-book of the men of wealth and weight in English-speaking Montreal. A future prime minister of Canada, J. J. C. Abbott, three future cabinet ministers, John Rose, D. L. Macpherson, and Luther H. Holton, leaders in commerce like the Redpaths, Molsons, Torrances, Workmans, were only the more notable of the signers. A few French-Canadian Rouges, with A. A. Dorion at their head, joined in because of their republican sympathies. The newspapers reflected the force of opinion. The *Herald* and *Courier* came out strong for annexation, the *Pilot* and *Transcript*, the Reform organs, as strongly opposed; the *Gazette* compromised on independence, while the *Witness* characteristically saw in the movement "the hand of divine Providence." In Canada West a few Reformers of republican sympathies echoed the movement, but Baldwin set his face strongly against it, and the *Globe*, now, under Brown, the leading newspaper of the province, backed him so effectively that little headway was made.

Galt had been opposed to the Rebellion Losses Bill, but he felt no bitterness on the racial or political issue. The economic advantages of union with the United States appealed to him strongly, familiar as he was with the much greater prosperity of the states adjoining the province.[2] Like most of his strongly protectionist contemporaries, he could not at the time see any permanent basis for imperial unity now that the tariff tie was gone or going.[3] Further, he had come to have the closest personal and business relations with the Montreal men prominent in the agitation. When, therefore, he was requested by a petition from over a thousand of the inhabitants of the County of Sherbrooke to give his views on the pressing question, he came out strongly for annexation.

After reviewing the political discontent and economic misery of the province, he declared that the colonial status was admitted by English statesmen to be one of tutelage only, from which they would gladly release the people of Canada, when the latter so desired. "It will be a far nobler cause for pride in Great Britain," he declared, "to have educated such a vast nation in the proper enjoyment of freedom, than to possess forever the nominal control of the whole continent as discontented and suffering colonies. . . . To make Canada great, there must be opened to her inhabitants those elements of emulation and pride which will call forth all their energies; the dissensions of her citizens must be terminated by abolishing distinctions of race; they must be made to feel that they are part of one great country, and that its destinies are entrusted to their guidance. Knowing as we do the Constitution of Great Britain, it is not a question of choice whether we shall be incorporated with Great Britain or with the United States, but, shall we remain a dependency of the former or become an integral part of the latter country? . . . Although no longer dependent upon Great Britain, we shall feel that we have served her well in ensuring that harmony between the two countries which is now constantly in peril from conflicting interests."

The reply of Galt made it clear that so far as the political aspects of the movement were concerned, it had its root in the inability of men on both sides to see any means of reconciling the claims of self-respecting nationhood with imperial connection. Imperial leaders had taught that British connection was impossible without colonial subordination, and that the connection was chiefly valuable for the pounds, shillings and pence results. Now they reaped where they had sowed; no subordination, no empire; no profit, no empire.

Shortly after issuing this statement, Galt decided to retire from politics for the present. The Directors had criticized, in a friendly way, his attitude upon the question, and the decision of the government to punish Montreal by moving the seat of the capital to Quebec and Toronto alternately had made it impossible for him to spare the time parliamentary duties would require. Upon his resignation, a contest upon annexation lines took place in the County, resulting in the return of the Annexationist candidate, Sanborn, by a narrow majority.

But already the movement was dying out. Lord Elgin set his face strongly against it, and was backed up by the Colonial Secretary, Lord Grey, though the Premier, Lord John Russell, expressed his opinion that separation was only a matter of time. Canada West was almost a unit against it; French Canada, save for a few anti-clerical Rouges, was equally hostile, and the government took a strong lead. Montreal found itself in a small minority, and then healing time and reviving trade gradually weaned it from the agitation. Finally, Elgin secured reciprocity and reciprocity killed all desire in Canada for annexation. Galt and all the other men prominent in the movement became within a very few years strong opponents of the policy they once had advocated. Another stage in Canada's tortuous political development was passed.

Other interests more important than politics had now entered Galt's life. In the intercourse with Montreal merchants, he had become particularly intimate with the family of John Torrance of St. Antoine Hall, then and for many years later prominent in business and shipping circles. In 1848 he was so fortunate as to win the hand of his daughter, Elliott, but their happiness was cut short by her death shortly after the birth of a son, Elliott Torrance, in May, 1850. Late in the following year, Galt married his wife's younger sister, Amy Gordon, with whom he was to pass a lifetime of true and close companionship. Through all the vicissitudes of politics and business, and however outer affairs pressed him, his thoughts were never far from his family, and in a home life which was as nearly perfect as falls to human lot, he found and gave abiding strength and comfort.

6: Parties and the Union

Sectional strife and party instability; Clear Grits and Rouges; the Hincks-Morin ministry; the achievements and the fall of the Great Ministry; Galt, the Rouges, and the Ministry; John A. Macdonald and the Liberal-Conservatives.

~ The grant of responsible government brought the struggle for colonial self-government to a close, but the union of the two Canadas which accompanied it introduced an equally bitter sectional conflict. Durham's assumption that union would destroy the French sense of national identity was proven wrong. The French continued to form a bloc within the new political framework. The terms of union were in many respects generous toward Lower Canada which, as Canada East, retained the official use of the French language, the former legal system, a privileged status for the Church, traditional forms of land tenure, and a distinctive educational system. In the common legislature, Canada East was assigned a representation equal to that of Canada West. The equal balance of representation facilitated the emergence of a "quasi-federal" system. It became a feature of government that every ministry must have two premiers, one from Canada West and one from Canada East. It likewise became common for legislation to apply exclusively to one section or the other, and it was customary in the case of common legislation to insist upon separate majorities from both sections. Since a clearly defined party system was slow in developing, it became increasingly difficult to obtain the requisite overall majority in favour of important measures. A stable party system was in turn rendered almost impossible by virtue of racial antagonism between sections and by the internal differences within each section.

The great reform ministry of Baldwin and Lafontaine, which triumphed in the struggle for responsible government, continued in office until 1851 and enacted several constructive measures. When the two reform leaders retired from politics, their places were taken by men of lesser stature, Francis Hincks and A. N. Morin. The Tories, meanwhile, defeated in their efforts to obstruct the coming of responsible government, went into eclipse as they sought new political bearings. In Canada West, increasingly effective opposition to the Hincks-Morin government came from the Clear Grits led by the rising politician and editor, George Brown. The Grits demanded further concessions in the form of universal suffrage, secret ballots, elective officials, biennial parliaments and the abolition of Clergy Reserves. The opposition in Canada West was equally radical. The Rouges under the leadership of first Papineau, and then A. A. Dorion, were dedicated to the principles of popular sovereignty, non-clerical education, and the abolition of seigneurial tenure.

The Hincks-Morin administration ran into trouble over the questions of Clergy Reserves and seigneurial tenure. Hincks made little headway on the secularization of Clergy Reserves as he was almost totally absorbed in railway projects. He did request, and was eventually granted by the British government, the power to carry out the reform but he postponed action on the plea that a general election should be held first. The ministry's policy on seigneurial tenure was similarly a source of dissatisfaction. While it was generally agreed that the feudal system of land tenure still prevalent in Canada was a barrier to industrial development and a burden upon the habitant, there was difference of opinion on whether it should be abolished with or without compensation to the seigneurs. Morin encountered strong opposition when he proposed partial compensation.

In 1854 Hincks suddenly dissolved the legislature hoping to secure a stable majority in a general election. The results were disappointing. The combined ministerial party was successful in returning the single largest group but it was doubtful that they would command a working majority in the legislature. In Canada West the Conservatives (formerly called Tories) and the Grits made gains with 32 and 11 members respectively. The Hincks group was reduced to 22 members. In Canada East the situation was more confused. The Morin Liberals claimed 46 seats, but it was a group that could not be depended upon, especially in view of the personal following of Joseph Cauchon which numbered 18. The Rouges managed to elect 19 members. On the fringe of the Rouges group and in general sympathy with them, but still calling himself a Liberal and prepared to support the ministry, was Alexander Galt. Since none of these groups could be described as parties in the strict sense, the alignment in the legislature would only be known on the first day of the opening session when the members would vote on the election of a Speaker. ~

The great majority of the English-speaking people of

Montreal district and the Eastern Townships, or at least their leaders, had called themselves Conservatives in earlier days, when they adopted any party label. In reality they deserved better the title of "British party" or "official party." They included men of both conservative and radical leanings. The Union, and the coming of responsible government, eased for a time the racial tension, so far as Lower Canada was concerned, and so permitted these latent divergencies to appear. At the same time the world-wide swing to Liberalism was not without its effect. The influences which transformed Peel and Gladstone from "stern and unbending Tories" into founders of latter-day Liberalism were at work in Canada. On a man like A. T. Galt, closely akin to Peel in open-mindedness, in financial interests, and in disregard of party traditions, these influences operated with full force. Together with his personal friendship with Holton and Dorion, they carried him for a time far toward the Rouge camp.

Galt, it has been seen, resigned from Parliament early in 1850 when the removal of the seat of government from Montreal made it impossible for him to combine legislative duties with his work as Commissioner of the Land Company. The wide expansion of his business interests in the next few years gave the Land Company a subordinate place in his activities. Its work in any case was being reduced to a routine which did not require his continuous supervision, and the directors were glad to retain him on his own terms. When, therefore, late in 1852, the member for Sherbrooke town, Edward Short, was appointed to the bench, Galt agreed to stand and was returned at the by-election in March, 1853, without opposition. J. S. Sanborn, it may be noted, still sat for Galt's first constituency, Sherbrooke County. The boundaries of both constituencies were materially altered in the redistribution of this session, but Galt continued to sit for Sherbrooke town for the remaining years of Union, from 1853 to 1867.

In the adjourned session of 1853 Galt gave an independent support to the ministry, because, in his own words, he "desired a speedy settlement of the seigneurial tenure and Clergy Reserves questions, and believed that ministry more likely to settle both questions than any other that could be formed." When the new Parliament opened, he was prepared to continue this qualified support, and voted for the ministerial candidate for Speaker. When, however, the Address from the Throne was delivered, making it clear that the ministry was not going to take an aggressive stand in either issue, he determined to vote against them.

The first test of party strength came on the opening day of the session, September 5th, with the election of a Speaker. The ministry put forward George Etienne Cartier, the Clear Grits, John Sandfield Macdonald, and the Rouges, Louis V. Sicotte. The various sections of the motley Opposition planned that the Rouge candidate should first be put forward, and doubtless be beaten, and that then the whole Clear Grit, Rouge and Conservative vote should be swung to Macdonald. The alliance worked to the extent of defeating Cartier, by a vote of 62 to 59. But when Sicotte's name came up, and it was apparent he was also to be beaten, Hincks, who hated the foes of his own household more than those of Lower Canada, suddenly called out, "Put me among the yeas," and threw the whole ministerial vote to Sicotte, who was thus easily elected.

Next day the speech from the Throne was delivered. It contained no definite indication of aggression on either the Clergy Reserves or seigneurial tenure question. The revolt among the western ministerialists continued, and Hincks gave way. On September 8th the Hincks-Morin ministry resigned.

The trend of events at this critical juncture is clearly shown in letters exchanged between Hincks and Galt. . . .

~ In a letter to Galt, dated August 13, 1854, Hincks sounded him out on how the Rouges would vote on the Speakership. He also referred to the "immoral combination" of the Rouges and Cauchon factions in the last session and predicted that the Cauchonites and ministerialists would draw still farther apart. He expressed the hope that there would be no "crisis" which would affect the development of "a more Liberal party in Lower Canada."

A week later Hincks wrote again expressing his disappointment that the Rouges were evidently acting in concert with "the Tories, Cauchons and Browns." The hostility of the Rouges he attributed to the personal hostility of Holton. The course they were following could only result in forcing the Liberals of Lower Canada into the Conservative camp. "A coalition of the Tories, Cauchonites and ministerial party," he wrote, "would be a most formidable combination." He went on to answer Galt's questions as to his proposed policy if he managed to get a majority when the legislature met. Galt's suggestions on a suitable programme he dismissed as unacceptable and designed merely to provide an excuse for the Rouges to vote against him. On the question of the secret ballot, he personally had no strong feeling but argued that there was no point in raising such an issue, since there was such a wide difference of opinion on the question among his followers. "The same remark," he said, "applies to your other measures."

Galt's position was made clear in a letter written to Hincks on the day of the Throne Speech, September 6, 1854. He explained that he had not committed himself previously because he wished to see if the policies outlined were ones he could conscientiously support. The Speech had been so ambiguous on the subject of the Clergy Reserves and so unacceptable regarding seigneurial tenure, that he was not prepared to support the ministry.

Hincks replied with a bitter letter on September 7. He wrote that he wanted no vote from a man who would doubt his word that he was prepared to secularize the Clergy Reserves. On seigneurial tenure he acknowledged that he and Galt were in complete disagreement. ⌁

The result which Hincks had prophesied now came about. The extreme Liberals were disappointed in their hope of a junction between the radical forces from both sections and an accession of sufficient men of middle views to afford a majority. It was about the other pole of political thought that the scattered units grouped. A working agreement was effected between the Conservatives and the Moderate Reformers of Upper Canada, which later strengthened into a merging of these two groups into the great Liberal-Conservative party. At the same time a close alliance was formed between this combination and the Ministerial party of Lower Canada, who had long been recognized as at least as much "conservative" as "liberal." Attempts had been made under the Draper and Sherwood administrations to form a Conservative–French-Canadian alliance, but had failed. They could not well succeed until the principle of self-government had been firmly established, until the fundamental reforms upon which the "Liberals" of both sections were agreed were realized, or at least well on the way to realization, and until the alliance, the personal ties, which bound Baldwin and Lafontaine had ceased to have effect. Now the hour had come – and with it the man, John A. Macdonald.

Under the guiding hand of the young Kingston lawyer whose ten years' experience in the Assembly had taught him

much of tactics and more of men, the MacNab-Morin administration took office on Hincks' fall. Its titular head was the old
Tory warrior, Sir Allan MacNab. A third Conservative, William
Cayley, was taken into the Upper Canada section of the cabinet,
while Robert Spence and John Ross represented the Hincks
wing of the coalition. The Lower Canada section remained for
a time the same as in the Hincks-Morin ministry.

The new ministry undertook to carry out the full Liberal
programme, to secularize the Reserves, to commute seigneurial
tenure, and to make the Legislative Council elective. The Tory
position on the most controverted issues of the day was thus
definitely abandoned, and a Conservatism more consistent with
the changed conditions took its place. It might be said, indeed,
that Liberalism provided the platform and the votes, and Conservatism the leaders. Gradually the Liberal-Conservative party
became more united. The Hincksites, or Baldwin Reformers as
they preferred to call themselves, maintained a separate existence for a time, but eventually disappeared as a party, joining
either the Liberal-Conservative or the Clear Grit party, as
temperament or issue urged.

The reconstruction of 1854 had given the country parties
more logically divided and more firmly based. A long step had
been taken toward party stability. But for years to come this
advance was nullified by the effects of the ever growing sectional conflict. The Opposition in Upper Canada and the coalition in Lower Canada grew in strength until the two sections
stood arrayed against each other in almost unanimous strength
– deadlocked.

7: Sectional Conflict and the Way Out: 1854-1856

The rise of Macdonald and Cartier; the achievements of the coalition; the growth of sectional conflict; the remedies: repeal of the Union; American models; Rep. by Pop.; the Double Majority; federal union of the Canadas; the federation of British North America; the services of Galt.

~ The Liberal-Conservative ministry of 1854, in its first session, took up the two questions which had led to Hincks' downfall and settled them to the general satisfaction. The Clergy Reserves were secularized and seigneurial tenure was abolished with generous compensation to the seigneurs. In 1856 the Legislative Council was reformed. Once these measures had been enacted, the pace of legislation slackened. The sessions of 1856, 1857 and 1858 brought forth little that was constructive. At the same time there was a bewildering series of ministries. In the four years from 1854 to 1858, six different administrations held office. The only significant development among the rapid shifts of government was the steady emergence of John A. Macdonald in Upper Canada and George Etienne Cartier in Lower Canada as the dominant figures in the Liberal-Conservative alliance.

As constructive achievement lessened, sectional controversy increased. The issue of representation in the legislature became the subject of bitter agitation in Upper Canada. By the terms of Union, both sections of the province had been allotted an equal number of seats. However, the population of Upper Canada grew rapidly after Union until it exceeded that of Lower Canada by several hundred thousand and Upper Canadians began to insist upon a greater representation in the legislature on the basis of population. This demand for a greater voice in government took on added weight in view of the fact that Upper Canada contributed twice as much to the provincial revenue but received only half as much in the form of government expenditure.

Ministerial instability accentuated the difficulties. Clearly defined parties, so essential for a parliamentary system to work well, had not developed and, in the meantime, personal loyalties

and sectional groupings made for constantly shifting alliances.*
Bribery and corrupt electoral practices were rampant, and
debates in the legislature frequently became exercises in personal abuse. Eventually the political forces came into such a
nice balance that there was complete deadlock. The futility of
the stalemate appeared to be amply demonstrated when the
legislature failed to reach agreement on the location of a permanent capital and finally had to request the British government to decide on a site. The situation was clearly serious and
required a drastic remedy. But it was one thing to feel the need
for change and quite another to see the proper solution.

In the decade before Confederation, several plans for a way
out of the intolerable situation were proposed. At various times
such widely divergent schemes as representation by population,
repeal of the Union, separation of executive and legislature, the
double majority, and the federation of the two Canadas were
put forward. All, for one reason or another, were found to be
unacceptable to a majority. Representation by population appealed to Upper Canada, but could not be supported by any
politician from Lower Canada. Repeal of the Union was super-
ficially the simplest solution, but economically unfeasible. The
separation of executive and legislature on the American model
ran counter to a deep-rooted belief in the British parliamentary
system. The principle of the double majority, that is, the rule
that legislation affecting one section alone should not be passed
unless there was a majority from that section in its favour,
proved impossible in practice. The federal union of the two
Canadas was supported in some quarters but was considered
too restrictive until it was merged in the ultimate solution, the
broader concept of a federation of all the colonies in British
North America. The prospect of a union of all the provinces
had been discussed intermittently for years, but it had remained

---

* Skelton in this and the preceding chapter assumed that the absence
of a clear party structure was the fundamental cause of political
instability in Canada. A recent study of political alignments in this
period would suggest a revision of the traditional view is in order
(Paul G. Cornell, *The Alignment of Political Groups in Canada,
1841-1867* [Toronto, 1962], pp. 82-86). This careful examination of
individual voting records indicates that most members consistently
voted with one group or another, suggesting that groups were
reasonably stable in their membership. The members with no strong
affiliation (aptly described as "loose fish") who supported the
ministry which offered them the greatest rewards were actually very
few.

the dream of a few visionaries. In Skelton's words, "neither the time nor the man had come." ~

. . . It is A. T. Galt's chief title to the grateful memory of future generations of Canadians that at the critical juncture he was ready to bring forward the only abiding solution. It is not implied that Galt did more to bring about Confederation than the other men who share with him the honour of being numbered among the Fathers. There is no need to make invidious comparisons, for there is glory enough to go round. What is beyond question is the fact that Galt took a peculiar and essential share in the movement. By his advocacy in 1858 he brought the question once for all into practical politics, and went far towards committing at least one great party to its support. By winning over Cartier, he removed what might otherwise have proved an insuperable barrier – the opposition of Lower Canada to a proposal which would greatly reduce the relative importance of French Canada in the union. By linking the federation scheme with the growing demand for incorporating the vast west in Canadian territory, he gave added strength to both movements. And when the time came for hammering the vague dream of federation into a workable scheme, he once more contributed important factors.

Galt's training and temperament were such as to make him peculiarly fitted to perform this service. He had an interest in general ideas, a readiness to take far views, an impatience with the personal controversies that engrossed other men, which prepared him to take up a proposal for sweeping change at the initial stage. The very characteristics which militated against his success as a leader of a political party made him more inclined than men absorbed in the opportunist work of the moment to commit himself to broad programmes of action. Again, his position as a representative of the English-speaking minority in Lower Canada made him able to understand the point of view of both Upper Canada and his French-Canadian compatriots, and at the same time kept him from adopting either the "Rep. by Pop." cry of the one or the "J'y suis, j'y reste," tactics of the other. And not least, his railway experience had led him to see both how possible it would be to connect the Canadas and the Lower Provinces by rail, and how effectual such a connection would prove in bringing about the frequent intercourse and the mutual understanding necessary for the making of a nation.

The session of 1858 was notable for the full discussion of

the various solutions offered of the constitutional angle. In May, Joseph Thibaudeau moved a resolution for the adoption of the Double Majority. In July, Malcolm Cameron's motion to establish "Rep. by Pop." led to a long debate. During the discussion of these motions, which were both substantially defeated, the advocates of repeal and of written constitutions also found occasion to voice their views. Finally, on July 5 and 7, Galt secured an opportunity to present the resolutions in favour of Federal Union of which he had given notice early in the session.[1]

Galt's case for federation was presented in part during the debate on "Rep. by Pop." and in part in moving his own resolutions. Naturally he gave first place to the contention that a federal union would provide a solution of the constitutional difficulties of the province, by removing to local legislatures the most contentious issues. He did not content himself with this negative recommendation, but proceeded to show how desirable federation would be in itself. It would greatly widen the area within which trade might be carried on without restriction – give a free trade area as great as that which had so materially contributed to the prosperity of the United States; each section had resources which would admirably supplement the others. It would give more than commercial prosperity; it would bring national strength and national prestige. He believed "that the people desired to be a nation, and they could only be so by adopting some such plan." If 3,500,000 colonists were united there would be no danger that their interests would be disregarded by Great Britain, and no danger of attack from the United States. "It is the old story of the bundle of sticks," he declared, "the provinces now are liable to be every one of them broken in detail by the United States, while united they would withstand any power on the continent."

Turning to the North West, then much in the public eye, thanks chiefly to the persistent campaign of George Brown, who manifested herein that constructive side of his nature which never found adequate expression, Galt showed how great was the opportunity and how necessary was the federal solution as the means of grasping it. "The Province of Canada," he declared, "was the foremost colony of the foremost empire of the world, and able to exercise a prodigious influence on the future of the continent, but instead of thinking of the future the House had spent three or four months in disposing of matters which, without meaning any disrespect, he thought might have been disposed of in as many weeks. . . . The House ought to assume the responsibility of occupying that great empire . . . that region ten times as large as the settled heart of Canada, a thousand miles long by seven hundred broad and capable of sustaining thirty millions of souls. Such a thing had never yet occurred to any people as to have the offer of half a continent. . . . The door should be opened for the young men of Canada to go into that country, otherwise the Americans would certainly go there first. . . ." What political arrangements would the acquisition of that distant territory involve? "If the territory were assumed now it would fall under the management of the Crown Lands Commissioner, who no doubt would do the best he could for its organization, but such an agency was not calculated to govern such a territory. Men who went to settle there must have a chance to make a name and identify themselves with something in the new country. . . . If I refer to these things it is to point out that under the present system it is not possible to assume the government of that territory, while if federal government were set up a local government might be given to the people of the Red River or any other locality, and they might be welcomed into Union with Canada, which would form a bond of material strength between all the parts of the federation. . . . We could offer immigrants a great opportunity. . . . Half a continent is ours if we do not keep on quarrelling about petty matters and lose sight of what interests us most."

It is interesting to note how little support from the leaders of Parliament Galt received at the moment. Neither Macdonald, Cartier nor Brown spoke on the resolution. Only one member, Playfair, gave it full support; he declared that he had long favoured such a step and had so spoken at the British American League meeting in Toronto nearly ten years before. Turcotte agreed that the idea merited discussion. Drummond, who had recently left the cabinet, believed federation would come eventually, and looked on it as desirable because a step towards independence. But it was not possible until England had built a railway to the eastward, and the colonization of the Hudson's Bay territory was a dream which could not be realized for a great length of time. Sicotte opposed federation on the same ground – that it would lead to independence. Dorion admitted it might be needed in a century. There was no menace requiring defence. We knew nothing of the other colonies and had no trade with them. He was ready to consider federal union of the two Canadas or even Representation by Population if

Lower Canada were given proper safeguards for its religion, language and laws. Cauchon opposed it strongly; as for defence, Canada was protected by England; the Maritime Provinces would only use Canada's money to build local public works. Merritt was also decidedly opposed; the colonies were too isolated to be brought under a single government.

Clearly the proposal would not have plain sailing. There was no great competition then for the honour of being one of the Fathers of Confederation. The resolution would undoubtedly have been overwhelmingly defeated had they come to a vote. But before that opportunity offered, a sudden crisis in the ministerial fortunes had both blocked the path of all unfinished business, and opened up to Galt a way of advancing his cause from within instead of from without the cabinet councils.

8: Party Changes and the Federation Proposals

Personal changes; the seat of government crisis; Galt offered the premiership; the Cartier-Macdonald ministry; Galt's federation policy adopted; negotiations in England; the issue postponed.

The chief constitutional reforms proposed in this stirring time have been reviewed. It is, however, essential to bear in mind that until the very eve of the triumph of the federation movement there was a powerful group, both in Parliament and in the country, which denied the need of any organic change whatever. John A. Macdonald, the greatest figure in this group, was inclined to minimize the evils of the existing regime, and to believe that such difficulties as did exist could be met by personal rather than by constitutional changes. His attitude was in part due to the fact that he was in power for the greater part of this period, and therefore more prone than hungry opposition leaders to believe that all was well with the world. It was based also on deep-seated traits of character and on consciousness of his power over men. Macdonald was never the man to take up a policy in its pioneer stage, or to agree to changes until the impossibility of making the old system work had been overwhelmingly demonstrated. He showed always what his friends called a wise practical opportunism, and his critics, who later dubbed him "old To-morrow," called hand-to-mouth procrastination. True, the existing machinery was creaking badly, but it had not entirely broken down, and a master mechanic could manage to get a few kicks out of the old engine yet. It was characteristic of Macdonald that he was the last of the big men of his province to be brought to see the need of the federation policy, and characteristic also that he was the most indispensable in getting it through when at last converted.

Throughout this period, therefore, Macdonald persisted that all was well with the province, save for the perversity of pestilent agitators and the dangerous rivalry of opposition leaders. To remove the objections to the existing system he sought to win over the objectors. "Sir John Macdonald could truly say at the end of his days," declares his biographer, "that he had the proud satisfaction of knowing that almost every leading man who had begun political life as his opponent ended by being his colleague and friend." Until Confederation brought a certain fixity, the parties in opposition to him were continually finding that their leaders had joined forces with the tempter, and that they were compelled to face anew the task of building up their organization. All through the period under review the skilled hand which had detached the Baldwin Reformers and the French-Canadian leaders from their old allies, and was in future to captivate a notable share of the Reformers who unwarily entered into the coalition government that carried Confederation, was busy making new combinations to stave off the inevitable day.

In Upper Canada a notable instance of this policy was the sudden accession, in 1858, to the ministerial ranks, and to the cabinet, of Sidney Smith, who had hitherto been one of the Opposition stalwarts. Even Malcolm Cameron, one of the founders of the Clear Grits, gave the ministry an independent support during this session. Early in the same year John A. Macdonald proposed to his brother clansman, John Sandfield Macdonald, to give three seats in the cabinet to him and two other Reformers — "not Grits" — and though John Sandfield declined the offer in the famous laconic telegram, "No go," it was apparent that the negotiations had not been without hope.

In Lower Canada the administration was overwhelming in numbers, but its opponents were stronger in individual ability. In the session of 1857, a decided coolness had grown up between Holton, Dorion and Galt on the one hand, and Brown on the other. It was based on their dislike of the lengths to which Brown was carrying his campaign against "Lower Canada domination," and on their resentment of his criticism, especially of Galt and Holton, in connection with Grand Trunk matters.

Brown had been closely associated with Galt, Holton and J. A. Macdonald in 1852 when they were opposing the attempt of the English contractor-promoters to secure the charter and government guarantee for the Grand Trunk Railway. When their opposition had proved unavailing, Galt and Holton, who were not then in Parliament, made the best terms they could, but Brown continued to fight. The financial difficulties of company and contractors, and the consequent necessity of applying again and again to Parliament for aid brought the company into bad odour in Canada, and Brown endeavoured to make his political enemies bear their due share of this disfavour. Hincks, as the recipient of what was alleged to be a bribe of £50,000 from one of the contractors, Sir Morton Peto, and Cartier, as the salaried solicitor, first of the contractors and later of the company, were the chief objects of his criticism.

But Brown's muckraking zeal did not stop here. In May, 1857, as Chairman of a special Committee appointed to investigate "the condition, management and prospects of the Grand Trunk Railway Company," he made a strong attack upon Galt. He made the accusation or insinuation that Galt was chiefly responsible for the exaggeration and failure of the Grand Trunk project, that he had misused his position as Grand Trunk director to secure for his firm unfairly high terms for the Sarnia contract and for himself huge profits on large blocks of stock in the Montreal and Portland roads on which he held an option, and which were unloaded upon the Grand Trunk at preposterously high prices. Galt at once met the attack, and by a thorough cross-examination of the chief officials of the old St. Lawrence and Atlantic, and the production of all the official correspondence demonstrated the absolute groundlessness of the charges. It was shown that the calculations as to earnings and profits contained in the prospectus were based on investigations carried on in Canada by the Chief Engineer, A. M. Ross, during the previous year, that Galt's tenure of office as a director of the original Grand Trunk had been only nominal, as he never took his seat at the directors' table, that the contract for the Sarnia road was made with independent representatives of that company and was varied in consequence of changes in the specifications, that this part of the Grand Trunk was pronounced to be beyond criticism by every engineer who inspected it, that the optioned St. Lawrence stock held by Galt was taken for the purpose of facilitating the negotiations and was sold for the Company's benefit at the option prices, that the recompense made for his services by the St. Lawrence and Atlantic and Atlantic and St. Lawrence stockholders whose agent he was, instead of being prodigious, was unduly small, and that during the negotiations he never dealt in a share of the old company. This answer did not silence Brown, but it convinced the public that Galt's honour was still as stainless as before.

Later in the session Brown crossed swords with both Galt and Holton because of their support of the government bill for the relief of the Grand Trunk. Both men, on deciding to adopt a political career, had severed fully and fairly, as their private papers show, all connection with the railway, either as contractors or as stockholders, with the explicit purpose of leaving their hands free to deal with any railway issues that might arise in

Parliament. Brown refused to believe that their support of the relief act was disinterested. Dorion, who had also supported the government's policy, came in for less violent attack.

At once Macdonald saw the opening. During the recess of 1859, he negotiated with the Lower Canadian Opposition leaders, and especially with Dorion, to whom he offered a cabinet portfolio. Dorion hesitated, but at last declined. Holton approved the decision, but Galt thought it unwise.

Galt was in fact drifting steadily away from his former political allies. Party ties at no time held him strongly. Now he was no longer bound to the Rouges by strong common principles. The democratic programme he had endorsed had already been adopted in the two instances he had most at heart, the secularization of the reserves and the abolition of the seigneurial tenure. He had long since given up the belief in annexation which in earlier days had been a Rouge plank. Only in his hostility to ecclesiastical domination was he still Rouge in opinion, and at the time this question was not to the fore. And now, with the strong attacks of Brown fresh in memory, personal ties were going the way of ties of common principles.[1]

Macdonald, with his usual acuteness, notes the transition in a half jocular letter:

Toronto, 2nd November, 1857

My dear Galt:

. . . You call yourself a Rouge. There may have been at one time a reddish tinge about you, but I could observe it becoming by degrees fainter. In fact you are like Byron's Dying Dolphin, exhibiting a series of colours – "the last still loveliest" – and that last is "true blue," being the colour I affect.

Seriously, you would make a decent Conservative, if you gave your own judgment a fair chance and cut loose from Holton and Dorion and those other beggars. So pray do become true blue at once: it is a good standing colour and bears washing.

Yours always,
JOHN A. MACDONALD.

It was not surprising, therefore, that in the elections of 1857 Galt announced that he would stand as an independent, and denounced the Upper Canada Opposition. He was again returned for Sherbrooke by acclamation. When the House met, it was found that in Lower Canada the Rouges had been reduced to a mere handful, even Dorion himself as well as Holton being beaten, though in Upper Canada the Opposition had scored. Galt did not at once pass to the government side. He took his seat on the cross-benches and opposed the government forces when they refused an adequate inquiry into some colossal election frauds in Quebec city. Yet in the debate on the Address he showed a decided leaning towards the ministry: "If the government were defeated," he declared, "Mr. Brown would be called on, but it would be impossible to govern the country with his views. Neither J. S. Macdonald nor Mr. Dorion could hold a seat with Mr. Brown. . . . He would not for one moment attempt to become the defender of the government; he was not a supporter of theirs. Yet his view was distinctly at the moment that it was not desirable that any change in the government of the country should take place, and he would not vote against them on what he considered a want of confidence amendment."

Two comments on this speech may be cited. Speaking later the same evening Brown shrewdly retorted: "It edified me to hear the honourable gentleman talk of extreme views. What a charming picture of candour and moderation he drew of himself sitting on that cross bench! . . . Is it possible that the honourable gentleman in the midst of these dire hatreds that he painted was seeking to build up a position for himself as the *juste milieu* in the next crisis? Does the honourable gentleman already fancy himself sent for, and with a soft word for this side and a soft word for that he might manage to patch up a new coalition!"

Holton took the evident separation more to heart:

Montreal, March 10th, 1858.

My dear Galt:

As your speech of Monday night is an event not only in your own career but in the politics of the country in regard to which I cannot if I would maintain silence in my intercourse with others, it is due to the frankness of friendship that I should at the earliest possible moment reveal to you the feelings it has awakened and the opinions I have formed both as to the soundness of the position you assumed and the probable effect on your interests as a public man of the step you have taken.

I read the speech as reported in the Globe *when I first came down this morning, and for hours it had the effect of some great calamity, some sudden bereavement in depressing my spirits. I felt and I still feel like throwing politics to the dogs.*

. . . You refuse to confirm the commercial policy we have

all of us advocated because it might turn out the men we had all up to Monday night opposed, and opposed mainly because they would not adopt that very policy, . . . When we were together in Toronto last week I understood that you proposed taking perfectly independent no-party ground, voting on each question as it arose, regardless of whom it might put in or keep in, but it strikes me you have gone quite beyond that and become a pronounced ministerialist. That is an easier position than the other. Indeed, I question whether it could be maintained for a fortnight. . . .

I regret your separation from a party with which I must from sincere conviction continue to act, for the sake of the party that can ill afford to spare your talents; for my own sake, not only because of our past associations but because I have looked to your speedily attaining the high position in the country to which your talents are fitted, through that party thus possibly benefitting myself as a humble member thereof, and for your own sake, because I believe you will be exposed to a great deal of unmerited obloquy.

Always faithfully yours,

L. H. HOLTON.

The shock which crystallized Galt's decision to join the Conservative party came with the defeat of the government on the question of the capital. In 1857, after the defeat of the proposal to make Quebec the permanent capital, the Taché-Macdonald government was afraid to make the question a ministerial one: they could only please one city and would displease four or five. Accordingly they adopted the ingenious device of passing a resolution requesting the Queen to choose among the rival cities. At worst, the proposal would postpone the decision for a session. At best it might quell altogether the objections of the disappointed claimants, since criticism would then become "disloyalty." And meanwhile there was nothing to prevent the government or its leading members making privately what recommendation they pleased. No one in administrative circles really imagined that Queen Victoria or the Colonial Secretary, Labouchère, would attempt to make an independent choice in a matter which required so much local knowledge, and a matter in which such knowledge was sadly lacking in England, to judge by a ponderous pronouncement from the London *Times* in favour of Montreal, based on the assumption that Montreal was in Upper Canada! The decision was really made on the advice of Sir Edmund Head, acting with what degree of independence it is not possible now to say. By whomsoever made, the choice has been ratified by the judgment of succeeding years as a wise one. Ottawa was still "a backwoods village," but its position on the border line between Upper and Lower Canada made it to some extent a compromise and its distance from the United States border increased its military security.

If posterity has expressed content, not so the men of 1858. The Opposition at once saw an opportunity to rally against the government all the disappointed sections. An amendment moved by M. Piche, "that in the opinion of this House the city of Ottawa should not be made the seat of government of the province," was carried by 64 votes to 50. Brown followed up this opening by moving the adjournment, as a distinct expression of want of confidence in the ministry. This motion was rejected by a vote of 61 to 50, but the Upper Canada majority against the government was unusually large and two days later, on July 29th, the ministry resigned.

Then followed an episode which gave rise to controversies and recriminations that echoed for years – the rise and fall of the Short Administration, the two-day cabinet of Brown and Dorion. Upon receiving the resignation of Macdonald and Cartier, Sir Edmund Head sent for Brown, as the leader of the Opposition, to invite him to form a new government. Brown consented, and after a few days' negotiations, succeeded in organizing a strong administration. The new ministers, upon accepting office, at once resigned their seats, according to established custom, in order to present themselves to their constituencies for election. During their absence, in defiance of constitutional precedent as well as ordinary courtesy, a vote of want of confidence was moved by Hector Langevin and J. B. Robinson and carried by a large majority. Brown at once requested the Governor-General to grant a dissolution, but the Governor, as he had intimated after Brown had accepted his invitation, though before the negotiations were completed, refused to grant it. There was nothing for the new ministry to do but resign.

At once the flood gates of denunciation were opened. The Governor was accused of secretly conspiring with Macdonald, who had been surprised at Brown's success in forming a ministry, and of aiming to make himself a second Metcalfe. Brown, on the other hand, was attacked as greedy of power, rash and reckless in ever attempting to form a ministry knowing that he faced an almost solidly hostile Lower Canada. The charges of conspiracy brought against the Governor-General were partisan exaggerations; Head, whatever his failings, was a man of honour. Nor did he exceed his constitutional privileges in refusing to accept the advice of his new ministers to grant a dissolution; a Governor-General may always disregard the advice of his ministers, provided he can find, as Head soon found, new ministers willing and able to support the contrary policy. Yet it is clear that Head was actuated by a strong partiality for Macdonald, with whom he was on terms of intimate personal friendship, and by a strong prejudice against Brown. His assertion that there was no ground for holding a new election, since there was no indication that the Opposition would obtain a larger vote than they had won the year before, was hardly borne out by the hesitation of the Cartier-Macdonald ministry later to face the country, which led to the famous Double Shuffle. Brown, it cannot be denied, was ambitious to hold power, but no more so than Macdonald or Cartier, and no more than his capacities and his influence in Upper Canada warranted. It was unfortunate that he was not given an oppor-tunity to exercise the great constructive powers which he un-doubtedly possessed, instead of relapsing into more violent opposition than ever. Whether he could have found a working basis of agreement with his Lower Canada colleagues which would have permitted them to secure support in both sections was doubtful. The fact that in the few days of cabinet negoti-ations Brown and the Lower Canadian leaders came so close to working out a compromise on the chief sectional issues was at once a condemnation of the failure in the past of the two wings of the Opposition to find common positive ground, and an augury of good promise for their future.

Upon Brown's resignation, the Governor-General tried a new tack. The strong partisan chiefs had failed: why not seek an independent who could draw strength from the moderate men of all groups? There was no question as to who that inde-pendent leader would be. In his five sessions of parliamentary experience Galt had made his mark. He had distinctly impressed the public by his breadth and sincerity of view, his judicial fairness and his financial acumen. His championing of federa-tion, while it had as yet won few out-and-out adherents, had increased his prestige. In the House his unfailing kindliness, tact and bonhomie had won him many personal friends. It was accordingly to Galt that Sir Edmund Head next turned, inviting him to endeavour to form a ministry.

No man could receive such an invitation without a feeling of pride. At forty-one, and with barely five years' political life behind him, the offer of the premiership of Canada was a great honour. Yet without hesitation Galt declined the Governor's commission. He had his share of ambition and of confidence in his own capacity. Yet he understood clearly also the limitations of his position. Party lines were far from fixed, yet they were at any moment too firmly drawn to make it possible for a man who had flaunted his independence and had criticized both parties to improvise a following. As a representative, too, of the English-speaking minority in Lower Canada he was in a weak strategic position for attaining party leadership. While he was on very friendly terms with Cartier and while he had not yet taken the attitude of strong opposition to ultramontanism which later was to bring him into open conflict with the Roman Catholic church, yet he could not look to the French-Canadian members for support, and the English-speaking members were few and growing fewer. As a Lower Canadian, again, he was debarred from leadership of the Upper Canada members. Time and again in later days, John A. Macdonald, recognizing this fact, urged him to stand for an Upper Canada constituency, but Galt always preferred to stay by his life-long friends and associations in the east. In view of all these facts, Galt informed the Governor-General that he could not act, and advised him to send for Cartier.

Sir Edmund acted on the advice and invited Cartier to form an administration. Cartier at once accepted, asking Macdonald to head the Upper Canada section. The new cabinet was in essentials simply a revival of the old one, save that Cartier now took precedence as premier, or as "first premier," and that Galt agreed to enter it as Inspector-General.[2] Cayley, the former inspector-general, resigned to make way for him, and to keep the balance even between Lower and Upper Canada, Loranger also resigned, making way for Sherwood. As eventually constituted the Cartier-Macdonald cabinet stood as follows:

LOWER CANADA	UPPER CANADA
G. E. Cartier, Premier and Attorney-General East.	J. A. Macdonald, Attorney-General West.
A. T. Galt, Inspector-General.	P. M. Vankoughnet, Commissioner of Crown Lands.

N. F. Belleau, Speaker of the Legislative Council.

Sidney Smith, Postmaster-General.

L. V. Sicotte, Minister of Public Works.

John Ross, President of the Council.

C. Alleyn, Provincial Secretary.

J. Sherwood, Receiver-General.

Before this adjustment had been made the old ministers had carried through their famous or infamous "Double Shuffle." Constitutional precedent required that ministers upon accepting office should seek re-election. This they were not prepared to do, as the temper of Upper Canada made it very doubtful if they could be returned. Accordingly, they took advantage of a provision, designed to avoid unnecessary appeals to the electors, to the effect that minor changes of office within the ministry should not operate to vacate the minister's seat. Each of the members of the old Macdonald-Cartier administration included in the new ministry was appointed to a post different from that formerly held, and then next day most of them were re-transferred to their former post. None but the two new ministers, whose seats were safe, therefore, had to face the electors. Coming on the top of what had appeared to many the conspiracy of Head and the discourtesy shown to the Brown-Dorion ministers, the transaction aroused the most violent criticism. It was not the constitutional crime it was pictured, but it was at best a smart trick, which helped to embitter and lower the tone of political life.

As a consideration of accepting office, Galt insisted that the government should adopt his federation policy. It is doubtful if Cartier and Macdonald would have agreed had not the proposal seemed to open up a way to rid the minority of the embarrassing question of the choice of the capital. The new government would undoubtedly have a good majority in the House on other issues, but there was still good ground for fearing that if they adhered to Ottawa or indeed to any other city, a majority would again be found against them. Confederation, if it came, would involve considering anew where the seat of government for the wider land should be, and so long as negotiations looking towards Confederation were pending, the troublesome question would be shelved. Accordingly the government took up Galt's policy. In announcing the ministerial programme on August 7th, Cartier bound the two questions together, though strangely the significance of his action escaped the notice even of the lynx-eyed Opposition critics:

The government felt themselves bound to carry out the law of the land respecting the seat of government, but, in the face of the recent vote on that subject, the Administration do not consider themselves warranted in incurring any expenditure for the public buildings until Parliament has had an opportunity of considering the whole question in all its bearings; and the expediency of a Federal Union of the British North American Provinces will be anxiously considered, and communication with the Home government and the Lower Provinces entered into forthwith on the subject; and the result of this communication will be submitted to Parliament at its next session.

The new ministry lost no time in carrying out their promise. Cartier, Ross and Galt were appointed a Committee of the Executive Council to visit England and interview the authorities in Downing Street, not only on the federation question but on the Hudson's Bay territory and Intercolonial Railway issues. They sailed early in October, and as soon after their arrival as could be arranged, obtained an interview with Sir Edward Bulwer-Lytton, Secretary for the Colonies in the Conservative administration of Earl Derby. The formal Federation memorial presented to Lytton has often been printed, but for completeness' sake it must be included here; the draft in Galt's handwriting shows that the surmise of the *Globe* [that Galt was the author of the memorial] . . . was correct:

London, 23rd October, 1858.

Sir, –

We have the honor to submit for the consideration of Her Majesty's Government that the Governor-General of Canada, acting under the advice of his responsible advisers, has been pleased to recommend that the subject of a Federative Union of the Provinces of British North America should form the subject of discussion by Delegates from each Province, to be appointed under the orders of Her Majesty's Government, and we have been instructed to urge the importance of this step as well upon grounds peculiar to Canada as from considerations affecting the interests of the other Colonies and of the whole Empire.

It is our duty to state that very grave difficulties now present themselves in conducting the Government of Canada in such a manner as to show due regard to the wishes of its numerous population. The Union of Lower with Upper Canada was based upon perfect equality being preserved between these provinces, a condition the more necessary from the differences in their respective language, law and religion, and although there is now a large English population in Lower Canada, still these differences exist to an extent which prevents any perfect and complete assimilation of the views of the two sections.

At the time of the Union Act Lower Canada possessed a much larger population than Upper Canada, but this produced no difficulty in the Government of the United Provinces under that Act. Since that period, however, the progress of population has been more rapid in the western section, and claims are now made on behalf of its inhabitants for giving them representation in the Legislature in proportion to their numbers, which claims, involving, it is believed, a most serious interference with the principles upon which the Union was based, have been and are strenuously resisted by Lower Canada. The result is shown by an agitation fraught with great danger to the peaceful and har-monious working of our constitutional system, and consequently detrimental to the progress of the province.

The necessity of providing a remedy for a state of things that is yearly becoming worse, and of allaying feelings that are daily being aggravated by the contention of political parties, has impressed the advisers of Her Majesty's representatives in Canada with the importance of seeking for such a mode of dealing with these difficulties as may forever remove them. In this view it has appeared to them advisable to consider how far the Union of Lower with Upper Canada could be rendered essentially federative — in combination with the provinces of New Brunswick, Nova Scotia, Newfoundland and Prince Ed-ward Island, together with such other territories as it may be hereafter desirable to incorporate with such confederation from the possessions of the Crown in British North America.

The undersigned are convinced that Her Majesty's Govern-ment will be fully alive to the grave nature of the circumstances referred to which are stated by them under the full responsibility of their position as advisers of the Crown in Canada. They are satisfied that the time has arrived for a constitutional discussion of all means whereby the evils of internal dissension may be avoided in such an important dependency of the Empire, as Canada. But independent of reasons affecting Canada alone it is respectfully represented that the interests of the several Colonies and of the Empire will be greatly promoted by a more intimate and united Government of the entire British North American Possessions. The population, trade and resources of all these Colonies have so rapidly increased of late years and the removal of Trade restrictions has made them, in so great a degree, self-

sustaining, that it appears to the Government of Canada exceedingly important to bind still more closely the ties of their common allegiance to the British Crown, and to obtain for general purposes such an identity in legislation as may serve to consolidate their growing power, thus raising, under the protection of the Empire, an important confederation on the North American Continent.

At present each Colony is totally distinct in its Government, in its customs and trade, and in its general legislation. To each other, no greater facilities are extended than to any Foreign State and the only common tie is that which binds all to the British Crown. This state of things is considered to be neither promotive of the physical prosperity of all, nor of that moral union which ought to be preserved in the presence of the powerful confederation of the United States.

With a population of three and a half millions, with a foreign commerce exceeding Twenty-five million Sterling, and a Commercial Marine inferior in extent only to those of Great Britain and the United States, it is in the power of the Imperial Government, by sanctioning a Confederation of these Provinces, to constitute a Dependency of the Empire, valuable in time of peace, and powerful in the event of war — forever removing the fear that these Colonies may ultimately serve to swell the power of another Nation.

In the case of the Australian Colonies the Imperial Government have consented to their discussion of the question of Confederation — although the reasons for it, as relates to the Empire, can scarcely be either so urgent or so important as those which affect British North America.

The Government of Canada do not desire to represent the feelings of the other provinces. Their application is confined to the request that the Imperial Government will be pleased to authorise a meeting of Delegates on behalf of each Colony and of Upper and Lower Canada respectively, for the purpose of considering the subject of a Federative Union, and reporting on the principles on which the same could properly be based.

That such delegates should be appointed by the Executive Government of each Colony, and meet with as little delay as possible.

That the Report of such Delegates should be addressed to the Secretary of State for the Colonies, and that a Copy of it as soon as it is prepared, should be placed in the hands of the Governor and Lieutenant-Governor of each Colony, in order that he may lay the same before the Provincial Parliament, with as little delay as possible.

Upon the Report of such Delegates it will be for Her Majesty's Government to decide whether the interests of the Empire will be promoted by Confederation and to direct the action of the Imperial Parliament thereon – with the concurrence of the Legislatures of the respective Colonies.

We have the honour to be,

Your most obedient and humble servants,

G. E. CARTIER.

JNO. ROSS.

A. T. GALT.

Of much greater interest was the confidential letter submitted to Lytton the same day, in the name of the whole Committee, but as Galt's draft again shows, entirely his own composition:

London, 25th October, 1858.

Dear Sir Edward:

In the official communication which we have this day the honour to address to you, on the Confederation of the British North American provinces, we have felt it improper to offer any opinion upon the details which will form the subject of the proposed discussion by Delegates. It is also our duty not to cause embarrassment by advancing views which may yet have to be greatly modified. We venture, however, in compliance with your desire for a confidential communication on these points to suggest: –

That the Federal Government should be composed of a Governor-General, or Viceroy, to be appointed by the Queen, of an Upper House or Senate elected upon a territorial basis of representation, and of a House of Assembly, elected on the basis of population, the Executive to be composed of ministers responsible to the legislature.

That the powers of the Federal legislators and Government should comprehend the Customs, Excise and all trade questions, Postal Service, Militia, Banking, Currency, Weights and Measures and Bankruptcy, Public Works of a National Character, Harbours and Light-houses, Fisheries and their protection, Criminal justice, Public Lands, Public Debt and Government of unincorporated and Indian Territories. It will form a subject for mature deliberation whether the powers of the Federal Government should be confined to the points named, or should be extended to all matters not specially entrusted to the local legislatures.

The Confederation might involve the constitution of a Federal Court of Appeal.

The general revenue, having first been charged with the expense of collection and civil government, to be subject to the payment of interest on the public debts of the Confederation to be constituted from the existing obligations of each, – the surplus to be divided each year according to population. The net revenue from the Public Lands in each province to be its exclusive property, except in the case of the territories.

It may be expedient for a limited time to provide from the general revenue a certain fixed contribution for educational and judicial purposes until provision is made for the same by each member of the Confederation.

It will be observed that the basis of Confederation now proposed differs from that of the United States in several important particulars. It does not profess to be derived from the people but would be the constitution provided by the imperial parliament, thus affording the means of remedying any defect, which is now practically impossible under the American consti-tution. The local legislature would not be in a position to claim the exercise of the same sovereign powers which have frequently been the cause of difference between the American states and their general government. To this may be added that by the proposed distribution of the revenue each province would have a direct pecuniary interest in the preservation of the authority of the Federal Government. In these respects it is conceived that the proposed Confederation would possess greater inherent strength than that of the United States, and would combine the advantage of the unity for general purposes of a legislative union with so much of the Federation principle as would join all the benefits of local government and legislation upon ques-tions of provincial interest.

We have, etc. etc.

G. E. CARTIER.

JNO. ROSS.

A. T. GALT.

This document, written on brief notice, shows cleary how thoroughly Galt had studied the question and how closely he anticipated the chief features of Federation as eventually drawn up by the combined wisdom of the leaders of all the provinces.

The list of the specific powers allotted to the federal government, the appreciation of the possibility of assigning to it all
matters not specifically entrusted to the local legislature, the
provision for a Supreme Court, the payment of federal subsidies
to the provinces, the division of public lands, and the emphasis,
two years before the outbreak of the Civil War had made the
issue clear to all men, upon the points whereby the weakness
of the federal government of the United States was to be
avoided in the case of Canada – these all form a remarkable
evidence of the judgment and foresight of the new minister.

Three days later the Canadian ministers joined delegates
from New Brunswick, Charles Fisher and A. J. Smith, and
from Nova Scotia, Charles Tupper, W. A. Henry, and R. B.
Dickey, in bringing before the Colonial Office the question of
imperial aid to the Intercolonial Railway. They reviewed the
history of the discussions, stressing especially the promises of
Grey in 1851 and Pakington in 1852 to give an imperial guarantee, and noting that the outbreak of the Crimean War had
suspended further consideration. Then in 1857 Messrs. Macdonald and Rose from Canada and Messrs. Johnston and
Archibald from Nova Scotia had revived the question with
Labouchère. Since 1852 Canada had spent on the part of the
Main Trunk line originally under discussion, £3,111,500 stg.,
making an annual charge of £186,000; New Brunswick had to
face an annual burden of £48,000, and Nova Scotia about the
same, on account of their railway enterprises. It was estimated
that it would take £3,500,000 to fill up the gap from Rivière
du Loup in Canada to Truro, Nova Scotia. If the British
government would appropriate to this purpose the £1,500,000
Sydenham loan, guaranteed by the British government, which
Canada was about to repay, the three provinces would each
promise £20,000 a year to meet interest charges, leaving
£60,000 for the United Kingdom to assume. A supplementary
memorial, presented November 12, pointed out that the savings
in ocean subsidy and in carriage of mails, men and munitions
would be nearly twice this amount, and declared the willingness
of the three colonies to accept Britain's share of aid in the form
of steamship subsidies similar to those which were being paid
to the Cunard line from Liverpool to Boston and which were
building up American ports at the expense of Canadian ports.

A few days after the departure of his colleagues, Galt
addressed a confidential note to Lytton on the same subject,
from which the following passages may be given:

London, 17th Nov., 1858.

Dear Sir Edward:

Presuming on the kindness with which you have received both my colleagues and myself, I venture to address to you certain considerations on the subject of the Intercolonial Railway which could not safely be enlarged upon in official documents.

The position of Canada is both peculiar and exceptional. A population now numbering three millions of British-born subjects reside in the interior of America and during the winter season are absolutely proscribed from any intercourse with either Great Britain or the other colonies except through a foreign country jealous of the power of England on the Continent. . . .

The result (of the adoption of the bonding system) is that the whole winter and spring trade of Canada passes through foreign territory. I cannot help remarking that the policy of the Imperial Government in subsidizing the Cunard line has largely tended to this result. . . .

The present state of the case is that Canada is at this moment at the mercy of the American Congress for the continuance of her trade between December and June. The repeal of the American bonding laws would at once arrest the whole commerce of the Province. It would entail ruin on every merchant and trader in Upper Canada. . . . The only security we have against such action by the American Government lies in the value of our trade to their railways, forwarders and merchants – we have none in their policy as a government. . . .

Canada has no other interest in the Intercolonial Railway than to be freed from a painful state of subordination to the United States. She has no local interests to serve, no population to benefit. She desires only to serve her allegiance and connection with the British Empire. . . In this as in the question of Confederation our statesmen desire to strengthen our intercourse with the Mother Country and the Sister colonies, to free our trade from foreign trammels, and to build up a nation worthy of England from her North American possessions.

I do not for a moment pretend to say that Canada would use the Intercolonial Railway for her trade while shorter and cheaper lines exist, but if at any time a different trade policy were adopted by the United States or war were to break out, then she would possess another outlet and would gladly suffer any inconvenience from the greater length and enhanced charges. The provision of such an outlet is the security against its being needed.

A letter to Mrs. Galt, written a few days after the first interviews, throws light on the progress of the negotiations:

London, 29th October, 1858.

. . . Mr. Ross and Mr. Cartier have gone to Paris for a few days and I remain here to attend to our matters with the Government. Sir Edward Lytton, finding I was alone, was kind enough to invite me again to Knebworth, where I spent two days this week and had much conversation with him. He wished me to go down again to-morrow, but I declined. However I am to go again next week. It is a high honor and no small advantage to my business. . . .

I hope we shall make some progress next week. As yet it has only been preliminary work, preparing their minds for what we want, but our papers are now all before the Government, and we have only to wait a decision. I think we shall certainly get some points settled as we desire. . . .

He writes again the next week, a little more dubious of satisfactory results:

London, 4th November, 1858.

Since Monday I have been trotting about the public offices, seeing one man and another, fancying myself busy but as yet seeing no results.

Yesterday when at the Colonial Office, Sir Edward sent for me to say we were to be presented to the Queen on Friday at 2 p.m. at Windsor. I therefore telegraphed to Ross and Cartier to come back from Paris, but they had already started, and arrived last night. We were all at sea to know what we should wear, fearing we should be obliged to exhibit ourselves in all the toggery of a Court dress, but it appears this is unnecessary, and we will be received in 'plain dress'. . . .

I wish I could say that our business went on satisfactorily, but the fact is, that it moves so slowly I do not know whether we are going to succeed, or to spend so much time that we shall be obliged to leave without any answer at all. Everybody is very courteous, but very slow, owing no doubt to the vast number of questions they have before them. . . .

Next day he gives an interesting glimpse of the visit to the Queen, not yet sorrowed by the loss of the Prince Consort:

London, 5th November, 1858.

I have just one moment to write you on our return from Windsor. We were most graciously received by Her Majesty, who permitted us to kiss her Royal Hand, which by the way is a small one, though not as pretty as your own. The Queen then entered into a short conversation with each of us in succession about Canada. Mr. Ross suggested that we hoped to see Her Majesty in Canada. She laughed very heartily, saying she was afraid of the sea, but she thought it very likely some of "the children" would visit Canada. After a few more observations in which Prince Albert joined, we took our leave.

Our audience was quite private, no one being present except Prince Albert and Sir Edward Lytton, who introduced us. The Queen was dressed in a green silk dress, handsome but plain, nothing to distinguish her from any other lady. She is rather short, but has a very good face and fine eyes, and her manner is very agreeable. Prince Albert is a very handsome man, speaking with a slight accent. We were presented after Mr. Gladstone, who went down to Windsor with us. In this we were rather lucky, as we got lunch with the gentlemen and ladies-in-waiting at the Palace, while waiting for the Queen; otherwise we should have had to wait looking at the pictures.

We went in our ordinary dress, frock coat, and black cravat, no state dress at all. . . .

A week later he writes again:

London, 12th November, 1858.

Mr. Cartier sails to-morrow, and I trust to get away with Mr. Ross on Wednesday by the Canadian steamer to Portland. . . . I had an interview with Mr. Disraeli on Wednesday and he in a great measure assented to what I want, but I have not yet received his official answer in writing and until I get it I cannot be certain of the result.

The Canadian Club gave us all a grand dinner yesterday. Sir E. Lytton, Lord Carnarvon and Lord Goderich, with other distinguished men, were present. It went off extremely well.

Our business is not yet completed but I fear we shall not be able to wait. . . .

Hope deferred is the note in a letter of still a week later.

London, 19th November, 1858.

There is also too often nothing but disappointment in this world, and I am doomed to experience it in finding myself again detained here for another week. But it has proved unavoidable as I have not yet succeeded in bringing any single part of my business to a close. The Colonial Office have asked me to remain another week, and promise to get all done by that time, either for or against my wishes. . . . I have commenced an energetic system of attendance upon them and like the widow and the unjust judge I may get from my importunity that which would be denied to any claim of justice. I know that you value perhaps more highly than I do my reputation, and I therefore feel certain that you will reconcile yourself to our prolonged separation. . . .

I am going to dine with Sir Edward Lytton to-morrow. I fancy it is a party he is giving in return for that of the Canada Club. . . .

Yet in spite of importunity and of dinners and country-house weekends neither Galt nor his colleagues had any appreciable degree of success in their undertakings. There was no lack of polite words, but the plain fact was that neither the permanent officials nor the government nor the general public had any interest in the problems of the American colonies. One may read ministers' diaries or the Queen's letters, Grenville's gossipy memoirs or the London press of the day and in all alike there is not the faintest sign of concern over the distant possessions. One would find much talk of the visit of Palmerston and Clarendon to Compiègne, of the Newmarket races, of the aftermath of the Indian Mutiny, of the removal of Jewish disabilities, of the closer relations between Lord John Russell and Lord Stanley, of Gladstone's mission to the Ionian Islands or Disraeli's latest Duchess and diamonds dinner, but in the circles of the governing classes Canada was as much in mind as Kamschatka. As will be seen in a later chapter, it was not until the outbreak of the Civil War threatened further complications that any heed was given to Canadian affairs.

On the railway question, the British government gave a frank and flat refusal to extend any aid whatever, on the quite sufficient and legitimate ground that "the national expenditure must be regulated by the national resources, and however important may be the foregoing advantages, it has been found that objects of interest to Great Britain yet more urgent must yield to the necessity of not unduly increasing at the present moment the public burthens." Disraeli, as Chancellor of the Exchequer, had simply more pressing demands to meet than this far off and politically inconspicuous proposal. . . .

On the question of Federation the lukewarmness evident in Downing Street was more surprising. At best the official outlook was one of indifference, and it appeared that if any feeling existed, it was one of hostility rather than of approval. Realizing this at last, Galt endeavoured to have as good a face as possible put upon the matter. Just before sailing he sent the following confidential note to Sir Edward Lytton:

London, 22nd November, 1858.

Dear Sir Edward:

Taking advantage of your very kind permission to address you on the subject of Confederation, and having in mind the outline of the decision which has been arrived at, I venture to suggest that in communicating it to the Governor-General it might be stated,

"That Her Majesty's Government have given their best consideration to the Order-in-Council of the Government of Canada of the fourth of September last on the subject of a Union of the British North American Colonies, and to the request therein that the Secretary of State for the Colonies should authorize a meeting of delegates, etc. Her Majesty's Government have also had under consideration the letter of the twenty-third of October last from certain of His Excellency's advisers now in London on the same subject.

"Her Majesty's Government are impressed with the grave nature of the difficulties which are stated to attend the administration of public affairs in Canada and will be prepared to do all in their power to remove them, in conjunction with the provincial legislatures, consistently with the maintenance of the Queen's authority and of constitutional Government.

"The question of the Union of the North American Colonies is one, however, which involves not merely the interest of the important Province of Canada and its relations towards the Empire, but also equally the position and government of the other provinces. It appears to Her Majesty's Government that it would be premature to invite the proposed meetings of Delegates without communications from the Governments of the other Colonies, expressive of their desire that such meeting should take place. . . .

"Her Majesty's Government are fully alive to the great importance of promoting the consolidation and strength of the possessions of the Crown in North America and should it appear to be the general wish of the Queen's subjects in these Provinces to attain a more intimate alliance between themselves,

Her Majesty's Government would be prepared to give such desire the most serious attention and to do all in their power to meet it, having in view the preservation of the integrity of the Empire and of the Royal Authority."

In the foregoing suggestions, which you have so kindly permitted me to make, I have endeavoured to embody precisely what my understanding was of your decision. I need scarcely add that I deeply regret that it is not more favourable and that I feel that even if conveyed in terms such as I have myself now outlined, it will cause our Government much embarrassment, and I fear weakness, especially in dealing with the Seat of Government question.

I can only entreat that in conveying Her Majesty's decision, you will, if it is possible, avoid expressing any opinion hostile to the Confederation. Apart from all personal or political considerations, I venture to suggest that inasmuch as the question will certainly and necessarily be discussed in the Colonies, it would be a serious and I may almost say, dangerous complication if such discussion took place in the face of an adverse decision from the Home Government.

My deliberate opinion is that the question is simply one of Confederation with each other or of ultimate absorption in the United States, and every difficulty placed in the way of the former is an argument in favor of those who desire the latter. I trust you will pardon my frankness, but on such a question duty forbids me to conceal my apprehensions, even if you should deem them groundless.

The official reply of the Colonial Office was despatched to Sir Edmund Head four days later. It is interesting to note both how the reply conforms to Galt's outline in basing the refusal of the British government to take action upon the necessity of consulting the other colonies, and how it fails to incorporate even the contingent and tentative expression of sympathy with the object in view which he had sought. It does, however, equally avoid the openly hostile attitude which he had evidently had strong ground to fear:

Downing Street,
26th November, 1858.

Sir,

I have on a former occasion acknowledged your despatch No. 118 of the 9th of September, accompanied by a minute of a committee of the Executive Council of Canada proposing that

Her Majesty's Government should authorize a meeting of Delegates to discuss the expediency and the conditions of a federal Union of the British North American Provinces. By this name I understand to be meant an arrangement for establishing a common legislation in the Provinces upon matters of common concern. I have since received a letter on the same question, dated the 23rd of October, from those members of your Executive Council who have recently visited England, and I have to inform you that the proposal has received from Her Majesty's Government the careful consideration which its importance demands.

The question, however, is one which involves not merely the interest of the important Province of Canada and its relations towards the Empire, but also the position and welfare of the other North American Provinces. The Government of one of them has afforded some indication that it deems the question of a Legislative union of some or all of the Colonies as equally deserving of consideration. With this exception Her Majesty's Government have received no expression whatever of the sentiments which may be entertained by the Governments of the Lower Provinces. We think that we should be wanting in proper consideration for those Governments if we were to authorize, without any previous knowledge of their views, a meeting of Delegates from the Executive Councils, and thus to commit them to a preliminary step towards the settlement of a momentous question, of which they have not yet signified their assent to the principle.

A communication in terms corresponding with the present despatch will be addressed to the Governors of the other Provinces, in order to place them and their responsible Advisers in full possession of the actual state of the question.

I have, etc.,

E. B. LYTTON.

Naturally the communication of this lukewarm epistle to the ministers of the other colonies did not awaken enthusiastic echoes. Nova Scotia sent no reply; Newfoundland agreed to appoint delegates if a conference were authorized; New Brunswick declared the question had not been sufficiently discussed to permit a decision, and Prince Edward Island merely authorized receipt of the circular.

Meanwhile the ardour of Galt's colleagues at home had cooled. Discussion of federation could no longer serve to postpone the thorny task of choosing the seat of government. The ministers were divided. When the ministry was formed, Sicotte had declared he would resign if the attempt was again made to force the choice of Ottawa, and Macdonald and Vankoughnet declared they would resign if this were not done. Upon his return from England Cartier threw in his lot with Macdonald, and Sicotte resigned, to become soon the leader of the Lower Canada Opposition. In spite of his defection, the ministry was able, by the narrow majority of five, to have the choice of Ottawa ratified, and, this ticklish question settled, they breathed easier. There was no longer any need to discuss heroic remedies.

Questioned in the House at the opening of the session of 1859, Galt admitted the difficulty of proceeding further in the face of the apathy of the Imperial Government and the Lower Provinces. He declined to give any particulars of the federation scheme, beyond the official documents submitted to Parliament. His speech (February 8th, 1859) gave the *Globe* occasion for summing up the situation in a paragraph not wanting in shrewdness:

"The secret is out: the ministry has no policy, even on Federation. The garrulity of Galt has spoiled the whole affair. Of the entire Cabinet, Mr. Galt alone has shown the slightest interest in the subject. He was the writer of the letter which Messrs. Cartier and Ross were obliging enough to sign; he pressed it upon Sir Bulwer Lytton; he talked with the Earl of Derby about it and therefore all things considered he may be accepted as a tolerably competent witness. He declares that his colleagues and he have no scheme to propound, have not so much as the outlines of a plan. Half-smoke, half-air . . . . No wonder that the Leader fixed ten years as the shortest period in which the marvellous conception could ripen into reality."

The federation idea had been planted in the public mind. Time was needed to permit it to germinate and develop. The harvest of fact could not be reaped in a day or a year. It was to be five years before 'events stronger than advocacy, stronger than men,' were to force the issue. For the present, the Opposition, by their advocacy of a federal union for the two Canadas and the North West, did much to familiarize the public with the general principles of federal union, and the press of both parties kept up a sporadic discussion. The first steps in an eventful road had been taken.

9: Galt as Minister of Finance: 1858-1862

The fortunes of the Cartier-Macdonald ministry; a financial crisis; locking the stable doors; debt conversion, and Canada's credit; fiscal policy; free ports; the government, the decimal currency, and the note issue.

The Cartier-Macdonald ministry was destined to enjoy a longer tenure of office than any other Union administration. It held power from August 6th, 1858, until May 23rd, 1862, or over three years and nine months, as against the three years and six months of its nearest rival, the Baldwin-Lafontaine ministry, and three times as long as the average of other administrations of this period.

This comparative success was due in part to the strength of the Government and in part to the weakness of the Opposition. Macdonald, Cartier and Galt made a very effective combination. Macdonald's skill and shrewdness in managing men, Cartier's vigour and ascendency over the French-Canadian members, and Galt's financial ability and breadth of view on general questions, made it difficult for any but an aggressive and united Opposition to make headway against them. And the Opposition, though aggressive by fits and starts, was very far from united. The alliance between the Upper Canada and Lower Canada sections of the Opposition, always precarious, was broken completely when in 1859 the Clear Grits resolutely opposed a government measure appropriating still further sums to complete the purchase of seigneurial rights for the benefit of the habitants of Lower Canada.

Even within the ranks of the Upper Canada Opposition itself there was dissension. Brown had never been without enemies and rivals in his own ranks. Sandfield Macdonald particularly was unwilling to admit his claim to leadership, and many others, because of his hostility to Lower Canada, considered Brown, in his own frank words on one occasion, "a governmental impossibility." Brown never displayed so clearly as in these years his strength of brain and his dominating personality. His criticisms of the financial policy of the government were vigorous, lucid and compelling; his speeches in the House in 1859 on constitutional reform were among his broadest and most statesmanlike efforts, and in the great Reform popular convention held in Toronto in 1859, which resulted in the adoption of Federation of the Canadas as a supplementary policy to "Rep. by Pop.", he was easily master of the field. Yet antagonism to him persisted, ill-health hampered his campaign, and his own defeat at the polls in 1861 kept him out of Parliament for two sessions. The general election of 1861 left the parties much as they were. But while with Brown's retirement the vigour of the Opposition attack was somewhat slackened for the moment, the reorganization of the Opposition under the more moderate leadership of Sandfield Macdonald and Sicotte, in time made it more formidable and once again brought about a deadlock, from which on this occasion there was to be no escape by merely personal shifts and ministerial patchings.

Aside from party controversy on the wellworn themes of sectional rivalry and ministerial corruption, the chief political interest of this period centres in three matters – the financial administration, the relations of Canada with the United States, and its relation with the Mother Country. These questions, in all of which Galt played a notable part, will, therefore, be discussed in order, in the three chapters which follow.

Galt took up the task of administering the finances of the province at a most critical and difficult time. The country was sobering up after the orgy of speculation and rapid expansion which marked the first railway-building era. Railway building had now ended, and with it the flood of English capital which had quickened trade, raised prices, and made mushroom millionaires. The reaction was intensified by the influence of the crisis which in 1857 brought the trade of the United States to a standstill. And to prove that misfortunes never come singly, the Canadian harvest of 1857 was far below the average, and that of 1858 a complete failure.*

The financial depression made the task of the Minister of Finance doubly difficult. It lessened the revenue of the province and added large obligations to its expenditures.

For revenue the province had depended mainly on customs

* The lack of British capital was also a contributing factor. While prosperity lasted in Britain, and British capital was freely available, the government was not called upon to redeem its guarantees on railway financing. But the British recession and stock market collapse of 1857 made it impossible to raise new capital. See W. T. Easterbrook and Hugh G. J. Aitken, *Canadian Economic History* (Toronto, 1956), p. 371.

and excise duties, with receipts from the post office, public works, chiefly the canals, and from the sale of Crown lands making up the balance. With the slackening in building and borrowing, importations fell away and customs duties in proportion, while all the minor sources of income showed the working of hard times economies.

At the same time, the province was compelled to shoulder certain indirect obligations, railway and municipal guarantees, the notes it had endorsed in the lavish, optimistic days of the early fifties. With the falling off in traffic, not one of the three larger railways, the Grand Trunk, the Great Western, or the Northern, was able to pay the interest on its capital. The province, therefore, found itself compelled to bear an increasing share of this burden, paying over a million dollars in interest on the guaranteed bonds in 1858.The Great Western eventually repaid the greater part of the advances made to it, and the Northern a smaller part, but the Grand Trunk loans, though for many a long day carried as a credit on the books of the Dominion, were by 1858 well known to be hopeless. Yet the province had not made a bad bargain in its railway deals. By the loan or gift of twenty millions it had aided in bringing to the province sixty millions more of private capital. In ten years two thousand miles of railway had been constructed, and a great stimulus given to the industry and settlement of the province. If, as Brown insisted, taxation had gone up from $1.20 a head in 1841 to $2.63 in 1859, it was equally true, as Galt brought out in his budget speech of the same year, that whereas in 1845 it had cost the shipper, and ultimately the farmer, three shillings to forward a barrel of flour from Lake Ontario to Montreal, in 1858 the cost had fallen to 6d. or 7d.

It was not only the railways that were in default. It had been one of Hincks' most original and most popular strokes to empower the municipalities to borrow freely for the purpose of building or subsidizing public works. By the legislation of 1852, provision had been made to enable the municipalities to pool their credit and to take advantage of provincial prestige and provincial machinery in borrowing in money markets where the separate municipalities were unknown. Two Municipal Loan Funds were created, one for Upper and one for Lower Canada. The province, as trustee, not as guarantor, was to borrow money for the sale of Loan Fund debentures, and reloan it to municipalities making application. The local authorities were to levy taxes to meet interest and sinking fund; if any failed to do so, the provincial government was empowered to send in the sheriff.

The municipalities, especially in Upper Canada – Lower Canada was more prudent or more 'unprogressive' – made full use of their opportunities. Port Hope borrowed $740,000, Cobourg and Brantford each $500,000 – all towns of less than 5,000 – the counties of Lanark and Renfrew $800,000, and other counties, townships, towns and villages as their ambitions prompted. The great bulk of these sums was used to bonus local railroads. In the first flush of enthusiasm over the coming of the railway it was expected that not only would these investments result in building up flourishing trade and great industries, but would yield direct dividends so high as to make taxation henceforth unnecessary. The hard fact was that not a single cent of dividends was ever received on the nine million dollars thus invested by municipalities, most of it through the Loan Fund. Instead, many a town and county found itself saddled with a huge debt and a crushing interest demand. One municipality after another repudiated its obligations. The provincial government had not the courage to send in the sheriff. It declined, indeed, to admit ultimate responsibility for the debts, claiming to be merely a trustee, not a guarantor of the Municipal Loan Funds, but it was to the province that the purchasers of the Loan Fund debentures looked for payment and the obligation had to be met. In 1857 $159,000 was advanced by the province to meet interest payments and in 1858 $365,000.

With fresh and heavy obligations thus thrust upon the province at the very time its revenues were falling, a finance minister who sought to make ends meet faced an almost impossible task. In the year when Galt assumed office, 1858, the deficit was as great as the total ordinary expenditure had been in 1850. He was able, thanks to retrenchments, new taxes, and revival of trade, greatly to lessen this gap, but not until the very eve of Confederation was it closed entirely. Year after year expenditure exceeded income, and the debt kept mounting. Yet within the inescapable limits set by past extravagance and present depression the new minister amply justified his reputation as a skilled and capable financier. The best was made of a bad job. The deficits were reduced within manageable proportions, revenues were increased without unduly burdening or disturbing industry, and the credit of the province in the London markets advanced in marked degree.

Much of the expenditure of the province was practically beyond control. Retrenchments were made here and there in the ordinary expenditure, but Galt, like many another finance minister, found that it is easier to raise standards than to lower them, and that vested interests had been created and undertakings begun which could not be ignored. The increase in expenditure and in debt in these years represented the coming of chickens of an earlier brood home to roost. The only important fresh liability assumed was the agreement made in 1859 to complete the purchase of the seigneurs' claims by a grant of 6 per cent permanent annuities to the amount of $120,000, coupled with a grant of a similar sum to the Municipal Loan Fund of Upper Canada. At the same time, to readjust the balance of favours to the two sections of the province, it was enacted that Lower Canada municipalities should forego the greater part of the privileges conferred upon them by the Municipal Loan Fund Act. Each part of the province had been authorized in 1854 to borrow the same amount, $7,300,000; Upper Canada municipalities had borrowed $7,294,800 but those of Lower Canada only $2,262,540. Accordingly, after allowing for borrowings sanctioned but not made, the balance of the Lower Canada fund authorized was cancelled. At the same time the stable door was locked in Upper Canada. An Act passed in 1859 brought the municipal rake's progress to an end, as far as future borrowings were concerned. Drastic provisions were enacted to enforce the payment of the debt already contracted. The 6 per cent Municipal Loan Fund debentures issued by the province as trustee were taken up and cancelled, being replaced by 5 per cent provincial bonds. The municipalities in default were required to levy a tax of 5 per cent upon the yearly value of taxable property to meet the interest and sinking fund, and this obligation was to be the first charge upon the municipal treasury, to be paid over by the treasurer upon penalty of being held personally liable. To compensate to some extent the prudent municipalities which were now compelled to bear their share of the burdens of their reckless neighbours, it was provided that the funds accruing from the sale of the old Clergy Reserves lands should in future be divided only among the municipalities which had not borrowed or had not defaulted. Neither form of pressure brought the defaulters to time. The lack of adequate administrative machinery to supervise the municipalities' action — a lack persisting to our own day — and the political difficulty of forcing debtors who were also electors, to pay up, defeated the good intentions of the legislature of 1859. It may have been only a coincidence, but if so it is an interesting one, that in 1860 the chief defaulting municipalities in Upper Canada returned government supporters. By 1860 the amount due by the municipalities of Upper Canada for interest alone, was $654,000; the amount paid was $158,000. In the same year Lower Canada paid $66,000 out of $166,000 due.

The burden of debt thus shouldered by the province – its direct borrowings for canals and other public works, the railway guarantees, and the Municipal Loan Fund – had attained very large proportions for that day. The interest on the debt and the sinking fund payments were two and a half times as great as the whole revenue of the province ten years before, and equalled 60 per cent of the revenue in 1858. It was clearly desirable, if possible, to take steps both to reduce the burden of the debt on the taxpayers and to strengthen the credit of the province abroad. Accordingly, Galt devoted much of his efforts in the early years of office to plans for consolidating and converting the debt, and for maintaining Canada's prestige in the London money market.

His first operation had to do with the Sydenham loan of 1841, a loan of $7,300,000 guaranteed by the British government, bearing interest at 4 per cent with another 4 per cent added for sinking fund. This sinking fund was invested by the trustees in British consols yielding 3 per cent. This meant, in brief, that the province continued to pay 4 per cent on the whole loan, while the sinking fund, now half of the loan, brought in only 3, and the province, to meet these payments, was compelled to borrow at 5 per cent. In 1859 and 1860, Galt succeeded in floating a new loan, carrying interest at 5 and sinking fund charges of ½ per cent amounting to $209,000 a year as against the $584,000 formerly required. At the same time he affected an important saving by inducing the imperial authorities to invest the sinking fund in India stock at 5 per cent instead of in consols bearing 3.

Continuing this process of conversion, Galt succeeded in 1860 in floating a twenty-five-year loan at 5 per cent, part of which was used to retire $10,250,000 of the old debt. At the same time a sinking fund of ½ per cent was established. The net result of this transaction was that by adding the trifling additional payment of $17,000 a year to the former interest charges – $615,000 – on the amount converted, Galt succeeded in providing for the entire liquidation of the ten millions in fifty years.

Less tangible but equally effective, was the missionary work done in these years in enhancing the credit of Canada in England. Probably none of our finance ministers had been in such close and intimate touch with financial London as Galt was all through his years of office. His early negotiations in connection with the Land Company and his handling of the Grand Trunk consolidation created a strong impression on the men he met there. Especially in the case of Thomas Baring and George Carr Glyn, for many years the financial agents of the province, and perhaps the leading private bankers of a day before the joint stock companies had swallowed up the private firms, this impression ripened into a close personal friendship which lasted until death. Both were men of large financial experience and mature judgment as well as of high honour. Though their losses and the losses of their clients in the Grand Trunk prejudiced them against Canadian investments, Galt succeeded in securing their hearty co-operation in advancing the interests of the province.

It was with the object of shaping English opinion, and especially investors' opinion, as to the soundness of Canadian affairs, that Galt published in January, 1860, the best known of his writings, *Canada: 1849 to 1859*. In this brief pamphlet of something less than fifty pages, Galt is seen at his best. He marshals facts and figures with compelling force, and treats a subject often dry and obscure in a most interesting and lucid fashion.

He begins his review of Canadian affairs with 1849, as the year when political self-government was completely achieved and when the change in Britain's fiscal system took full effect. The extension of the franchise, the improvement of election methods, the reform of the Upper House on an elective basis, the establishment of an excellent municipal system, the provision of what is somewhat rashly termed "a perfect system of elementary and superior education," the solution of the Clergy Reserves and seigneurial tenure questions, the provision for the settlement of the back districts, legal reforms — such a record of achievements in ten years' time certainly, he contends, justifies self-government.

Passing next to material development, Galt showed forcibly how necessary it was for the province to endeavour by canal and railway building to improve the opportunities which its position in regard to the St. Lawrence, the Great Lakes and the Western States made possible, and the rivalry of New York and other United States cities for the same prize of western traffic made essential to its progress. Practically the whole direct debt of the province had been incurred in furtherance of this policy. Including advances to railways it amounted to £8,884,672 stg., while the expenditure on canals, lighthouses and river improvements, roads and bridges and railway advances totalled £8,862,400. "The public of England can now judge," he continues, "how far the expenditure of Canada has been reckless and unwise, or whether it has not been incurred for objects in which the prosperity of the country was wholly bound up, and which fully justified the sacrifices which have been made to attain them." Finally, he reviews the financial policy, especially the increase of customs duties, adopted to meet these obligations, and defends it against the severe criticisms made by English free traders and manufacturers. In conclusion he declares:

In the foregoing pages I have endeavoured to give to English readers an idea, however imperfect, of the progress of Canada in the comparatively short period of ten years. I am aware that my remarks only furnish, as it were, an index to the volume; but if they produce more inquiry and a stricter investigation into the position and circumstances of the province, they may be the means of removing some misapprehensions and thus prove of service to the many thousands in Great Britain, who anxiously look to the Colonies as their future home.

I have sought to avoid all references to political parties in Canada. We have our differences, and struggles for power, as in every other free country; but these discussions, I think, properly belong to ourselves, as from our own people the Government of the day must receive their verdict. Canada stands at the bar of public opinion in England, to be judged, not by the acts of any party, but as a whole; and no public man, possessing any claim to patriotism, would seek, by parading our sectional difficulties and disputes, to gain position in Canada, through the disparagement of his country and her acts in England. I will venture to add only one remark, and that is called for by an impression which I find to exist as to the political course taken by our French Canadian brethren in Canada. During the entire period from 1849 to the present day, the French-Canadian majority from Lower Canada has been represented fully in the Cabinet;

*and with their active concurrence in the initiation and progress
of every measure, and supported by their votes in parliament,
all the great reforms I have recited have been carried.*

*In conclusion I venture to express my conviction that what-
ever may be the future destinies of Canada, her people will
always value as their most precious right, the free and liberal
institutions they enjoy, and will cherish the warmest sentiments
of regard towards the mother country, from whom they have
received them. The future may change our political relations,
but I feel sure the day will never arrive when Canada will
withhold her support, however feeble it may be, from Great
Britain, in any contest for the maintenance of her own position
as the foremost champion of civil and religious liberty.*

The pamphlet, which found a wide circulation, was a
masterpiece of exposition, and contributed notably to a better
and more sympathetic understanding abroad of Canada's problems and her resources. Incidentally, it did not a little to enhance
Galt's reputation on both sides of the ocean.

No small part of Galt's statement of Canada's policy was
given over to a defence of the measures adopted to increase the
revenues of the province. The central feature of these measures
was a substantial increase of the tariff. For the first time, the
issue of protection now took an important place in Canadian
public discussion. "The tariff of 1859," declared an acknowledged authority in this field twenty years later, "and the tariff of
1858, of which it was an enlargement and expansion, were the
first ever framed in this country for the avowed purpose of
developing home manufactures, and in obedience to a public
demand." But it was not merely the general question of the
expediency of protecting home manufactures that was at stake.
The tariff changes made in 1858 and 1859 set the commercial
interests of Lower and Upper Canada by the ears, contributed
to the breakdown of the reciprocity arrangement with the
United States, and brought a chorus of denunciation from
Great Britain.

From the outset the customs duties had been the mainstay
of Canadian finance. At first the rates were low. The tariff as
revised by the Union legislature in 1841 levied light revenue
duties on the chief articles of import not produced in the country, and 5 per cent on all other articles, with a few specified
exemptions. Slight changes were made in the years immediately

following, particularly in the direction of putting duties on livestock, provisions and agricultural products. In 1847 the duty on practically all imported manufactures, except heavy iron products, was raised to 10 per cent and in 1849 to 12½. In 1856 a further increase to 15 was made. Then in 1858 the Cayley tariff levied 20 per cent on many important manufactured articles, and 15 on all goods not enumerated. Now in 1859 Galt took the remaining step, raising a few items to 25 per cent and goods which provided the great bulk alike of imports and duties to 20. The Galt-Cayley tariff as thus developed remained in force without substantial change until the very eve of Confederation, when the same finance minister was to make another equally striking and significant departure.

As thus reviewed the increase in rates appears gradual and fairly regular. As a matter of fact, however, the increases made in 1858 and 1859 marked a distinct departure. They were made not only because of the increasing need of the province for revenue, but because of a strong popular demand for protection. For the first time in Canada organized pressure was brought to bear upon the government to influence its fiscal policy.*

Protectionist sentiment had been growing steadily in Canada. For a time, the conversion of England to free trade had seemed to put the older doctrine out of court, but gradually American example became more powerful than British. With the growth of the province in population, wealth, and commercial organization, the possibility of supplying its staple needs at home became more conceivable. The persistent advocacy of protection by such able exponents as Mr. Justice Sullivan, Baldwin's cousin and former colleague, and more especially by Isaac Buchanan, of Hamilton, untiring promoter of railways, paper money, and high tariffs, told on the public mind. Horace Greeley's forceful writings on the same side were widely circulated in Canada as well as in the United States. But it was not until the crisis of 1857 brought hard times, unemployment, emigration to the United States, falling off in home demand, and cessation of the stream of British capital, that the seed thus

---

* The peculiarly distinctive feature of Galt's policy was not so much that it was admittedly protective in its effect, but that it was the first serious move toward industrial, as contrasted with agricultural, protection. As such it demonstrated the profound change that was taking place in the Canadian economy. The rates of duty were relatively moderate, but it was significant that duties for the first time were being used in order to encourage manufacturing industries. See Easterbrook and Aitken, *Canadian Economic History*, p. 373.

planted fell into fertile ground. Hard times gave rise to the first protectionist movement in Canada, just as twenty years later they prepared the way for the second and more enduring campaign, the campaign which established "the National Policy."

In April, 1858, an influential organization known as the "Association for the Promotion of Canadian Industry" was founded in Toronto. The moving spirit was Buchanan, but he found ample backing among Toronto, Hamilton, Kingston, Montreal and other manufacturers. The Association demanded the abolition or reduction of the duty on tea, sugar and other articles which Canada could not produce, the imposition of a low rate on imported articles in the dry goods, hardware and crockery trades, not likely for some time to be made in Canada, and the increase to 25 per cent of the duties on "all manufactures in wood, iron, tin, brass, copper, leather, india rubber, etc., competing with our industrial products," and to 20 per cent in the case of cottons and woollens. The Association – or Mr. Buchanan – went further and drew up in great detail a new tariff embodying these principles. A deputation from the Association waited upon the chiefs of the Cartier-Macdonald government and were promised substantial sympathy. The tariff introduced by Cayley in 1858 gave evidence of this pressure. The duty on important articles was increased to 20 per cent on clothing and on manufactures of leather to 25, and 15 per cent was levied from articles not enumerated.

Faced with a huge deficit in the following year, Galt cast about for new sources of revenue. There were three conceivable sources.

The first was direct taxation. Under the circumstances in Canada, this was out of the question. In spite of the beginning that had been made in England toward levying a fair proportion of the taxes upon property and income, and in spite of the fact that many states to the south were raising large sums by a direct property tax, the prejudice in Canada against direct taxation was overwhelming. In 1862 it was the opposition to a trifling direct tax levied in connection with the Militia Bill that contributed largely to wreck that measure and bring down the government. As Galt put it in the pamphlet already cited: "In Great Britain it may be possible to adjust the taxation so as to make realized property contribute more than it now does to the wants of the state; but in a country like Canada no such resource exists, and it would be perfectly hopeless to attempt to raise the required revenue by direct taxation – we neither possess the required machinery to do it, nor are the people satisfied that it is the more correct principle."

Assuming, then, Galt continued, that excise and "customs duties must for a long time to come continue to be the principal source from which our revenue is derived," it remained to decide upon what articles these duties should be levied – mainly on articles not produced in Canada, as the free-trader preferred, or mainly on articles produced or likely to be produced in the province, and thus affording protection to the home grower or manufacturer.

Galt's decided preference would have been to levy substantial excise duties on spirits, beer and tobacco, and customs duties on tea, coffee, sugar and molasses. But one sufficient obstacle forbade – the nearness of the United States and the fact that it levied low or no duties on these important articles of general consumption. Under the border conditions which then prevailed and with the inadequate administrative staff that the province employed, higher duties would simply mean more smuggling. "When peace prevailed in the United States," declared Galt in his budget speech of 1862, "and there was no duty on tea, it was impossible for us to levy a high duty without the danger of smuggling, or the moral certainty that we would be unable to collect it." And those who would not have smuggled, would have loudly complained: "Unfavourable comparisons [with the low prices of tea, etc., in the United States] are even now instituted by our agricultural population."

There appeared, then, no alternative but to impose higher duties on manufactured goods, as the protectionists urged. Galt was not theoretically committed to either free trade or protection. Originally a protectionist, his faith had been sapped by the teachings and practice of the Mother Country in recent years. On the whole, his leanings were now more to free trade. However, like many others of his own and a later day, he found solace in the compromise of "incidental protection" – the position that while duties should be levied primarily to produce revenue, no regret would be felt if "incidentally" they afforded protection to home manufacturers. It was a phrase that soothed free traders by making it appear that the protection given was accidental, unconscious, temporary. To the protected manufacturer it was all one what label was applied, so long as he got what he wanted. For the present, Galt saw clearly, an increase in tariff rates would yield an increase in revenue. Time would tell whether the increase proposed was sufficient to divert production to Canadian factories and thus lessen customs revenues, or even to lessen consumption altogether.*

The chief increases made in the Galt tariff of 1859 fell on cotton goods, raised from 15 to 20 per cent, and on iron and steel, from 5 to 10. At the same time all "not otherwise enumerated" goods were subjected to 20 instead of 15 per cent. The nature of the tariff thus constituted may best be gathered from Galt's own exposition:

The fiscal policy of Canada has invariably been governed by considerations of the amount of revenue required. It is no doubt true that a large and influential party exists, who advocate a protective policy; but this policy has not been adopted by either the Government or Legislature, although the necessity of increased taxation for the purposes of revenue has, to a certain extent, compelled action in partial unison with their views, and has caused more attention to be given to the proper adjustment of the duties, so as neither unduly to stimulate nor depress the few branches of manufacture which exist in Canada. The policy of the present Government in readjusting the tariff has been, in the first place, to obtain sufficient revenue for the public wants; and, secondly, to do so in such a manner as would most fairly distribute the additional burdens upon the different classes of the community; and it will undoubtedly be a subject of gratification to the Government if they find that the duties absolutely required to meet their engagements should incidentally benefit and encourage the production, in the country, of many of those articles which we now import. The Government have no expectation that the moderate duties imposed by Canada can produce any considerable development of manufacturing industry: the utmost that is likely to arise is the establishment of works requiring comparatively unskilled labour, or of those competing

---

* Skelton does not make it sufficiently clear that Galt's primary aim was to rescue the railway companies and those municipalities which had drawn heavily on the Municipal Loan Fund in order to finance railway construction. More recently, economic historians have made this point emphatically clear: the railways were on the brink of bankruptcy and if the Canadian government was not to follow them into insolvency, it was absolutely imperative to find new sources of revenue. In Galt's day the function of the tariff was to raise money to build railroads. (See Easterbrook and Aitken, *Canadian Economic History*, pp. 372-376). Even the protective features of the tariff can be traced directly to railways: "As a source of revenue the tariff helped to finance the railways . . . and as a protective measure it contributed to creating and directing traffic" (Glazebrook, *History of Transportation*, II, 15).

with American makers, for the production of goods which can be equally well made in Canada, and which a duty of 20% will no doubt stimulate. That these results should flow from the necessity of increased taxation, is no subject of regret to the Canadian Government, nor can it be alleged as any departure, on their part, from the recognized sound principles of trade, as it will shortly be shown that the Government were compelled to obtain increased revenue; and it is believed that no other course could be relied on for this result than that adopted.

Analysing the different classes of goods imported, Galt showed that raw materials, to the extent of 29 per cent, were admitted free, and that the duties were graduated roughly according to the degree of manufacture involved, except in the case of liquors, tobacco and other luxuries which were taxed at the highest rates. Any attempt to reduce the duty on manufactured goods would therefore involve prohibitive increases on raw materials or partly manufactured goods.

In Canada this phase of the tariff excited little opposition. A few strong free traders complained, but it was not a party issue, and neither in parliament nor in the press was there any prolonged debate. As will be seen later, the case was otherwise in the two countries with which Canada was most concerned. In the United Kingdom the higher tariff was considered a direct blow at British manufacturers, a demonstration of the uselessness of colonies and empire, and it profoundly affected public opinion on the whole subject of imperial relations. In the United States the increase was denounced as a violation of the spirit, if not the letter, of the Reciprocity Treaty.

In Canada much more attention was paid to another phase of the tariff of 1859 – the application of the *ad valorem* principle. Hitherto in Canada mixed duties, some specific, some *ad valorem*, some combining both methods, had prevailed. Now specific duties were entirely abolished, with the one single exception of the duty on whiskey. There was room for dispute as to the merits of this change, but the chief discussion turned not so much on the general principle as on one feature of its application. Henceforth the duty was to be levied on the value in the market where last bought. This meant that if the merchants in Toronto and elsewhere in Upper Canada continued to buy their tea and coffee, sugar and molasses, in New York, as was the prevailing practice, they would have to pay duty on the price at New York, including heavy freight charges from China or the Indies. Buying at Montreal from importers who brought goods direct from the place of origin they would pay the duty only on the original cost of the goods. Montreal would be able to undersell all competitors in these articles, and would thus attract buyers from all Canada for other goods and displace Toronto and Hamilton as a wholesale centre. Hence, "to the Montreal merchant Mr. Galt's tariff was a veritable balm of Gilead; to the merchant of Toronto, wormwood."

Galt undoubtedly had in mind the effect of this change in diverting trade to Montreal and the St. Lawrence route. His interests and sympathies, so far as they were local, were bound up with that city. Quite aside from this natural prejudice, he considered it a matter of not merely local but of national importance that as far as possible importations from abroad should come by a Canadian port, and help to build up Canadian shipping, railways, canals and importing trade. It was simply the principle of protection applied to commerce as well as to industry. The fact that it was a logical complement of the higher duties charged on home manufactures did not of course prevent those advocates of protection in Upper Canada whose interests were adversely affected from complaining loudly. Newspapers and Boards of Trade fulminated against it, but Galt held firm, and the new arrangement soon became an accepted fact. It did not produce the revolutionary change in trade channels that was both hoped and feared — it was not so easy as it sounded for Montreal merchants to build up direct connections with the East — but it contributed in no small degree to the building up of the St. Lawrence route and to the prosperity of Montreal, or, as the Toronto newspapers preferred to put it, of "a few Montrealers already over-rich."

So far as revenue was concerned, the results justified Galt's expectations. Customs receipts increased from $3,368,000 in 1858 to $4,456,000 in 1859, due in part to a slight revival of trade but more so to the increase in rates. Excise returns and special revenues also increased, while expenditures were cut a million. As a result, the $2,500,000 deficit of 1858 fell to $450,000 in the following year. The deficit increased slightly in 1860, and notably in 1861, when the interruption of trade, through the American Civil War, upset all calculations, causing a falling off in customs duties alone of three quarters of a million in the latter half of the year. For 1862 the deficit, unless still further taxes were imposed, promised to soar to nearly three millions. Looking ahead Galt declared it might be assumed that the normal revenue in the immediate future might be taken as eight million, and the expenditure as ten million. How make up this deficiency? This was the task which he assayed in his budget of 1862, the last framed during this first tenure of office. It is notable as showing the tendency away once more from high tariff duties.

In 1859 the low customs or excise duties imposed by the United States on certain articles of wide consumption, it has been seen, prevented Galt from following his inclination and securing the needed new revenue from these sources. Now the troubles of the Republic were a finance minister's opportunity. Galt at once determined to raise the excise duties on spirits, beer and tobacco to the new level which the needs of war had compelled the United States to adopt, and to increase the customs duties on tea and coffee, sugar and molasses, in substantially the same proportions. These increases, he estimated, would yield a million in what was left of the current fiscal year, and two millions and a quarter in a full year. Stamp duties on promissory notes, receipts and bills of exchange were to bring in $400,000.

As an offset to these increases the Finance Minister proposed to lower the customs duties whose increase had been the feature of the budgets of 1858 and 1859. . . .

~ He suggested that the 20 per cent list might be reduced to 15 per cent, and the 10 per cent list to 7½ per cent. His arguments in favour were that a lower tariff would increase the volume of trade, attract immigrants who might otherwise go to the United States, refute the claims of British free traders who used the protective tariff as a reason for breaking the colonial connection, and improve relations with the United States. ~

The change in policy thus outlined is significant of the change in popular feeling and of the readiness of Galt himself to review his position at any time in the light of new facts. Before the new budget was adopted, the Cartier-Macdonald ministry had fallen. W. P. Howland, Minister of Finance in the Sandfield Macdonald-Sicotte government, accepted the excise increases, and, with some variations, the increased duties on tea, sugar, coffee and molasses, but he omitted the stamp duties, and declined to make the reduction Galt had promised on manufactured goods. It is important to note, as indicating that protection had not yet become a party cry, that though Brown welcomed his promised reduction, Foley and McGee, speaking for the Opposition in the House, attacked Galt for abandoning incidental protection. The changes were not put into operation soon enough to reduce the deficit of 1862 materially, but they added substantially to the revenue in the following year. Meanwhile Galt's plans for lowering the general tariff were postponed until a more auspicious occasion – the first budget of the new Confederation.

In the budget of 1860 Galt introduced an interesting innovation – the establishment of free ports at the two extremities of the province. To encourage the fishing trade in the lower St. Lawrence, and the development of farming and mining in the region north of Lake Superior, he proposed to make two free ports, one comprising the town of Gaspé and the district around it and also the Labrador coast as far as the straits of Belle Isle, the other Sault Ste. Marie and the district west of it. Permission would be given to import free of duty all articles needed for consumption within these limits, or for the use of American fishing vessels which would call at Gaspé. The rapid development of these districts, it was hoped, would much more than compensate the country for the loss in revenue. Owing to the isolation of both districts, the risk of smuggling into the other parts of the province was held to be negligible. The announcement of the experiment was received with approval on all sides. It proved a marked success, though in some ten years' time United States complaints that it facilitated smuggling, and the extension of settlement within the province, made it necessary to bring the experiment to an end.

The final phase of Galt's activities as Minister of Finance in this period which calls for notice is his proposal to alter the basis of the banking and currency system of the country.

The year 1858 witnessed the formal adoption in Canada of the decimal system of currency. As early as 1851 Hincks had introduced resolutions, which passed the House, urging the adoption of the decimal system, with the dollar as the unit, and the provision of a provincial currency to correspond. The confusion between the different standards of account, sterling, Halifax currency and the United States dollar basis, and the multiplicity of coins, gold and silver, which were used as media of exchange, rendered reform essential. The British government urged establishing the sterling standard, and when this proved unacceptable, suggested that the decimal system should be based on the pound currency and not on the dollar as the unit.

The feeling of the business community, however, was over-whelmingly in favour of assimilating the currency to the American system, while retaining the British sovereign as legal tender and as the bullion standard. A measure passed in 1853 legalized the decimal system, with the dollar unit, and from that time the banks and the majority of business houses adopted the new system. A supplementary measure of 1857 required all government accounts to be kept in dollars and cents, and with its coming into force in 1858 the old historic but inconvenient chaos of Halifax and sterling currencies rapidly passed away.

More far-reaching were the proposals for currency reform made in 1860.

The Canadian banking system, modelled in large part on Alexander Hamilton's plan for a national bank, and more indirectly on the Scotch banks, had thus far achieved a high degree of success. The Bank of Montreal, the Bank of Upper Canada, the Commercial Bank, the People's Bank, the Farmers' Bank, the Banque de Peuple, the Gore Bank, the Quebec Bank, and the Bank of British North America, had been in existence and flourishing at the Union. They were all chartered banks; that is, a special act of the legislature was required to permit any bank to start. They were permitted to issue notes against their general credit, and to establish branches. Popular discontent with the restriction of credit practised by the banks in the crisis of 1847-48 led Hincks, in 1850, to introduce a free banking act, which permitted the establishment, on the New York model, of local banks by any group of capitalists who fulfilled the require-ments – purchasing provincial bonds to the amount of notes they desired to circulate. Only three banks came into existence under this law – the Molsons, Zimmerman, and Niagara District Banks – since a bank which had to lock up its capital in the purchase of government securities and received only an equiva-lent amount of notes, was handicapped as against a bank of the older type which could utilize both its capital and its asset-secured currency. Cayley, in succeeding Hincks in 1854, let down the bars further. Charters were granted banks without proper insistence in some cases upon the payment of an ade-quate proportion of the subscribed capital, beyond the one-tenth of the capital now required to be invested in provincial securi-ties. Several banks were chartered at this period, destined to a large and honourable service – the Bank of Toronto, established by the milling interests of Upper Canada, the Eastern Townships Bank, with its head office at Sherbrooke, of which Galt was one of the promoters, the Union Bank, the Ontario Bank, and the Bank of Canada, which later developed into the Canadian Bank of Commerce. But others of a less desirable character were also established – the Colonial Bank, the Bank of Brantford, and the International Bank – all fraudulent devices designed by shady American promoters to float the maximum of worthless bills in the neighbouring states.

The crisis of 1857 was not without effect on the banks and on banking legislation. The essential soundness of the principles in force was shown by the fact that during the years 1857 and 1858 not a single bank failed, though bank after bank was crashing in the neighbouring states. In 1859, however, the Colonial and the International closed their doors under scandalous circumstances; the Bank of Upper Canada, the chief financial institution of the Western section, was really in sore straits, though it managed to conceal its condition for some years longer. There was not a bank which did not have to write off large losses sustained through countenancing the railway and land speculation of the preceding years. Some doubt began to be felt of the safety of the note issues of all the smaller banks. At the same time, resentment was expressed against the banks for suddenly shortening sail at the onset of the crisis. Circulation and discounts were cut one-third, the funds usually provided for moving the crops were not forthcoming, the milling and other industries were hampered, and much distress followed. Undoubtedly it was only prudent to bring the orgy of speculation to an end, and the banks were often blamed for what was the fault of the over-speculative businessman, but still many of the banks themselves had not been without fault and the curtailment of credit facilities was abrupt and in some cases indiscriminate.

It was under these circumstances that Galt endeavoured in 1860 to establish a new policy. In order both to make the note circulation absolutely safe and to obtain a revenue for the province he urged that for the future paper money should be issued only by the state. He proposed to establish a provincial treasury department, with the sole right to issue paper currency, which was to be legal tender, and redeemable in specie on demand. An issue of ten millions was to be authorized; one-fifth of the amount in circulation was to be held in specie and one-fifth in government securities; any issue beyond the ten millions was to be covered entirely by specie or securities. Banks chartered in future were to have no right to issue notes. The existing banks would retain their privileges until the expiration of their charters; meanwhile they were offered inducements, including the repeal of the 1 per cent tax on circulation, to surrender their rights. The banks were to be given notes on delivery of one-fifth the amount in specie, one-fifth in government securities, and three-fifths in the shape of a first lien upon their general assets, and they were to pay a tax of 3 per cent on circulation up to half their paid-up capital and of 4 per cent on the excess.

The proposals were met with a storm of opposition from the banks, especially the smaller ones, which depended more upon their note circulation for their profit. The new scheme would greatly curtail the profit from circulation. This prospect led many businessmen to back the opposition of the banks. The elasticity of the note issue, which was a marked and valuable feature of the Canadian system, would be threatened, smaller branches might be closed, and in some way, it was felt, the banks would endeavour to get out of the borrowing public the profits they had to give up to the government. Some doubt was felt, too, of the wisdom of giving any government the additional power its control of the issue of notes would involve. Accordingly Galt yielded for a time, as Lord Sydenham had been compelled to do in 1841 when he induced Hincks to bring in a somewhat similar measure. Later, Galt and Hincks were to see their schemes meet with at least partial success.

Throughout his tenure of office, Galt enjoyed the confidence of the business public in an unusual degree. Differences of opinion often existed as to the wisdom of specific acts, and the recurrence of deficits throughout his term gave the Opposition regulation openings for criticism, but the public respect for the skill and resource of the Finance Minister was unshaken. The power which he had in unusual degree, a power surpassed only by Gladstone among his contemporaries, of making financial statements lucid and interesting, contributed not a little to the high reputation he attained.

10: Canada and the United States

~ As the first effects of free trade in Great Britain were felt in the colonies, Canadian businessmen and politicians turned to closer economic relationships with the United States in an effort to strengthen the markets which already existed in the south. The idea of reciprocity, that is, the creation in North America of a single market area in which specified types of products could be freely exchanged between the British colonies and the United States, became extremely popular in Canada as a panacea for economic troubles.

The main difficulty was to sell reciprocity to the Americans. The northern states were strongly protectionist, while the southern states, which were traditionally supporters of low tariffs, feared that reciprocity would lead to annexation of the British colonies and add more non-slave states to the American Union. The natural inclination in the North against freer trade, the fear of the South that reciprocity would eventually upset the precarious balance between slave and non-slave territory in the United States, and the general indifference of American politicians toward the British colonies, made the task of putting the reciprocity proposals before the American government a difficult one.

If they were to achieve success, the Canadians had to convince the Southerners that reciprocity would not lead to annexation and to persuade the American administration that there were urgent reasons for taking the proposals seriously. The first of these requirements was met by Lord Elgin's brilliant personal diplomacy in Washington between 1852 and 1854 when he persuaded the Southern politicians that reciprocity was actually the most effective means of forestalling annexation.[1] The second was provided by the announcement that the British government intended to enforce the fisheries convention of 1818 which excluded Americans from fishing within a three-mile limit along the coasts of the British colonies. There was still little enthusiasm for reciprocity in the United States, but the desire for a settlement of the fisheries question was urgent, and the American government realized that they would have to accept some form of reciprocity if they hoped to reach a settlement on the fisheries issue.

The Reciprocity Treaty was signed in 1854. It permitted free access in the coastal fisheries to Americans and abolished duties on a wide range of natural products crossing the British colonial and American borders. The products included grain, flour, fish, livestock, meat, coal, timber and other less important natural produce. At the same time, American vessels were admitted to the use of Canadian canals on the same terms as British and colonial vessels, and the American administration promised to urge the various states to adopt similar arrangements with regard to Canadian vessels on American canals.

This reciprocal arrangement worked reasonably well for several years but, when Galt introduced new tariff regulations on manufactured goods in 1859, there were vigorous protests from the United States. Opposition to reciprocity had developed among certain American business interests in 1858 when merchants in Buffalo, New York and Philadelphia began to realize that they might be injured by the diversion of traffic through the St. Lawrence canals and the Grand Trunk Railway. Galt's imposition of increased duties on manufactures provided them with the opportunity to launch an attack on reciprocity. Their argument was that the United States had accepted reciprocity on the assumption that it would lead to increased export of manufactured goods to Canada. Since this appeared unlikely as a result of Galt's tariff they urged that the United States cancel the Reciprocity Treaty as soon as possible.[2] ~

The task of reply naturally fell to Galt, as Minister of Finance, and advocate of most of the specific proposals in question. It was a task to his liking; few writers on finance had his power of clear and trenchant argument. In a report of the Privy Council, which he drew up in March, 1862, he dealt first with the charge that the increase of duties on manufactures was a violation of the spirit of the treaty, and directed against United States producers. The treaty, he contended, made no mention whatever of manufactured goods. The United States itself had insisted upon a strict interpretation, subjecting flour ground in Canada from United States wheat, and lumber cut in Canada from United States saw-logs, to import duty. Had any obligation existed not to increase duties on manufactured goods, it surely rested on both countries equally, and yet the United

States had also raised its duties much higher. The increase of rates had been absolutely necessary to meet the heavy expenditures of the province, and if, as United States critics charged, a policy of incidental protection had been adopted, and avowed by the Minister of Finance himself, its purpose was to aid Canada, not to injure the United States. At any rate, it was not for the high tariff pot to call the lower tariff kettle black.

As to the discrimination involved in the change from the specific to the *ad valorem* basis of levying duties, Galt could not deny his own statement that the change was made in order to encourage importation by the St. Lawrence rather than by United States ports. He replied, however, with the usual *tu quoque*, pointed out that the change made in 1859 was merely a reversion to the basis which existed when the treaty first went into force, and contended that it merely put Montreal on a level with New York instead of being discriminated against as formerly. The provision for refunding canal tolls, further, gave an advantage to the Canadian route, indeed, but left United States and Canadian vessels on an equality, and it was equality as to vessels that the treaty prescribed. Moreover, the United States had not carried out nor tried to carry out, the treaty provision of urging the separate states to open their canals to Canadian vessels; until they did and until they abolished the tolls, they had no standing in court.

Galt concluded by a strong condemnation of the proposed *Zollverein*. "The project of an American *Zollverein*," he contended, "to which the British provinces should become parties, is one wholly inconsistent with the maintenance of their connection with Great Britain, and also opposed, on its own merits, to the interest of the people of these Provinces. It requires no great foresight to perceive, that a *Zollverein* means the imposition of duties by the confederacy, on articles produced outside the confederation, coupled with free trade among its members. In other words, Canada would be required to tax British goods, while she admitted those of the United States free, a state of things that could only accompany a severance of all the ties of affection, nationality and interest that now unite Canada to the Mother Country. It would also be essentially against the interests of Canada – Great Britain is, to a far greater degree than the United States, the market for Canadian produce – and commercial relations should therefore be extended with her, certainly not interfered with. Besides, in the consideration of the rate of duties to be levied on imports, the United States, as being the more powerful country, would necessarily impose her views upon the confederation, and the result would be a tariff, not as now based upon the simple wants of Canada, but upon those of a country now engaged in a colossal war, which must for many years demand enormous contributions from the people, among the means of obtaining which Customs duties will certainly rank as an important source of revenue."

In the many discussions of the *Zollverein* or Commercial Union project which took place in the next thirty years, the case against such a policy was never more concisely or forcefully stated than in this utterance of Galt's, which was the first official reference to the subject. While opposed to such an alliance, Galt was, however, in favour of every measure of closer trade relationship compatible with the continued separate existence of the colonies. There were, he declared, many respects in which it would be found beneficial to extend the operation of the Reciprocity Treaty with the United States. "The abolition of the coasting laws of both countries on their inland waters, the free purchase and sale of vessels, and the removal of all discrimination on the score of nationality, the extension of the privilege in both countries of buying goods in bond or by return of drawback, the addition to the free list of all wooden wares, agricultural implements, machinery, books and many other articles peculiarly of American manufacture, and the assimilation of the patent laws, all these and many other topics naturally offer themselves for consideration and do not appear calculated to cause any serious opposition."

From this brief summary, it is apparent that there were serious grounds of difference. Both for protectionist and for revenue ends the governments of both countries were being driven to raise new barriers in the path of trade. The Reciprocity Treaty had been negotiated when free trade sentiment was at its height in both countries. In the United States a protectionist reaction had been shortly afterward stimulated, especially in New York State, by the powerful advocacy of Horace Greeley. After the Civil War broke out, the absence of the free trade Southerners from Congress permitted this sentiment to expand without restriction; the Morrill high tariff of 1860 was passed before the actual outbreak, but after the Southern representatives had withdrawn from Congress. In Canada, as has been seen, a similar tendency was well under way. Further, the need of meeting the war bill in the one country and the need of meeting the bill for the orgy of public works construction in the other, called for higher customs rates. Even so, agreement for renewal and extension of the reciprocity arrangement might have been reached, so obvious were its economic benefits, had not the situation been complicated by bitter antagonisms rising out of the conduct of the Civil War and the attitude of Canada, and especially of Great Britain, to North and South. . . .

~ At the outbreak of the Civil War in the United States, Canadian and British public opinion favoured the North. The attitude changed with startling swiftness. Relations between Great Britain and the North rapidly deteriorated when the English recognized the Confederacy and the Northern states established a naval blockade which challenged the cherished British right to freedom of the seas. Before the first year of the war was out, Britain and the North were on the brink of war with Canada as the probable battlefield.

In Canada the shift of opinion was not so dramatic. In general the colonists favoured the North, as their early stand on slavery and the number of Canadians who served in the Northern armies demonstrated. Their position was impaired, however, by the clear preference of the British government for the South and by the activities of Southern agents who used Canada as a refuge and potential base for raids against the United States. The Northern resentment of Britain's support of the Confederacy expressed itself in outspoken hostility toward Britain's North American possessions.

With public opinion in a delicate state, a relatively minor incident threatened to explode into a full-scale war. In 1861 an American warship stopped the British steamer *Trent* on the high seas and removed two Confederate agents who were on the way to Europe in search of military assistance. The British government issued a stiff protest against this violation of freedom of the seas and demanded redress. Preparations for war were undertaken in England and eight thousand troops were dispatched to the colonies. The imminence of war created intense excitement in Canada which was practically defenceless in the face of a possible American attack.[3] ~

It was at this critical juncture that Galt took part in his first diplomatic adventure. During the summer he had had an interview with an unofficial agent of Seward, George Ashman, on the threatened movement in Congress against reciprocity – an interview looked upon with disfavour by Lord Lyons [British minister in Washington, 1859-64], who had all the professional diplomat's jealousy of amateur intervention. Early in December he visited Washington to find how the land lay, and during his visit found an opportunity to visit the President and talk frankly over the situation. A letter to his wife gives a summary of his activities, and his comments on the men and the situation he found in Washington:

Washington, 5th Dec., 1861.

I got here on Saturday night, and was fortunate enough to meet Mr. Ashman, whom you may recollect at Quebec. He has been extremely attentive to me, and as he knows everyone and has access everywhere, I can assure you I have had unusually good opportunities of learning the public opinion of Washington, and I am happy to say it is not of that unfriendly character to us that we might suppose from the papers.

That which has most struck me here is the quiet and order which prevails. No one could suppose we were within 15 or 20 miles of two rival armies of 300,000 men. It is true the streets and hotels are crowded with men in uniform and the roads covered with four-horse or mule waggons carrying stores to the army, but yet there is no disturbance, little or no drunkenness, and very little military music. I have not yet visited the Army in the field, but evidence exists everywhere of the magnitude of the efforts made, and I am bound to add of the success which has attended them.

I dined with Lord Lyons en famille on Sunday. He was very pleasant, and talked freely on public matters here, of which, however, I need say nothing. I also saw Mr. Seward, Secretary of State, on Sunday; he did not impress me much; seemed fidgety, and out of temper. On Monday I went to the opening of the Congress, and was introduced to many of the leading men. There was no ceremony at the opening, merely calling over names. The President's Message was delivered on Tuesday. I did not think much of it, and its tone as regards foreign countries did not please me.

Yesterday I went with Mr. Ashman thro' the Treasury and War offices, calling on Mr. Cameron, Secretary at War. Mr. Chase, Secretary to the Treasury, is shut up preparing his report, and I have not yet seen him.

I went by appointment last night to see the President, and had a long and satisfactory private interview. He is very tall, thin, and with marked features, appears fond of anecdote, of which he has a fund. I liked him for his straight-forward, strong commonsense. I was to have seen Mrs. Lincoln, but she was indisposed.

I dine with Lord Lyons again to-day, and shall to-morrow visit the lines of the Army across the Potomac, and will write you again.
A. T. G.

The interview with the President took place the fourth of December. On the following day Galt prepared a memorandum of it which possesses much interest:*

Washington, Dec. 5th, 1861.

Had interview with the President last evening; Ashman present. In the course of conversation I stated that Seward's circular [ordering the governors of states on the Atlantic sea-board and Great Lakes to prepare for a possible attack by foreign powers] *had caused us uneasiness. The President said that when discussed by the Cabinet, he alone had supposed that result would follow; the rest did not. I said that while we held the most friendly feelings to the United States, we thought from the indications given of the views of the Government and the tone of the press, that it was possibly their intention to molest us, and that the existence of their enormous armed force might be a serious peril hereafter. Mr. Lincoln replied that the press neither here nor in England, as he had the best reason to know, reflected the real views of either government. No doubt they had felt hurt at the early recognition of the South as belligerents, but private explanations of Earl Russell had satisfied him on this point. He had implicit faith in the steady conduct of the American people even under the trying circumstances of the war, and though the existence of large armies had in other countries placed successful generals in positions of arbitrary power, he did not fear this result, but believed the people would quietly resume their peaceful avocations and submit to the rule of the government. For himself and his cabinet, he had never heard from one of his ministers a hostile expression toward us, and he pledged himself as a man of honor, that neither he nor his cabinet entertained the slightest aggressive designs upon Canada, nor had any desire to disturb the rights of Great Britain on this continent. I said such expressions gave me the greatest*

---

* It has been suggested that Galt in this memorandum did not give an accurate report of the mood in Washington (Robin W. Winks, *Canada and the United States: The Civil War Years* [Baltimore, 1960], pp. 75-77).

pleasure, and with his permission I would convey them to my colleagues in the Government, to which he assented.

Mr. Ashman then remarked that there was still a possibility of grave difficulty arising out of the Mason and Slidell affair. To which the President replied to the effect that in any case that matter could be arranged, and intimated that no cause of quarrel would grow out of that.

The conversation then turned upon the slavery question and American politics.

The impression left on my mind has been that the President sincerely deprecates any quarrel with England, and has no hostile designs upon Canada. His statement that his views were those of all his Cabinet is partly corroborated by the statement made to me by Mr. Seward that he should be glad to see Canada placed in a position of defence.

I cannot, however, divest my mind of the impression that the policy of the American government is so subject to popular impulses that no assurance can be, or ought to be, relied on under present circumstances. The temper of the public mind toward England is certainly of doubtful character, and the idea is universal that Canada is most desirable for the North, while its unprepared state would make it an easy prize. The vast military preparations of the North must either be met by corresponding organization in the British provinces, or conflict, if it come, can have but one result.

A. T. G.

. . .

~ As Lincoln had predicted, the *Trent* affair did not produce any serious quarrel, and the danger of war was for a time averted. However, the danger that Canada might become involved in war with the United States did not entirely disappear and several incidents afterward threatened to lead to an outbreak of hostilities. The activities of Confederate agents operating from Canada gave rise to frequent American charges that Canadians were protecting Southerners and, therefore, violating the rules of strict neutrality. The most serious incident was the Confederate raid on St. Alban's, Vermont, in 1864. The conspirators fled into Canada where they were arrested and subsequently freed without punishment. For a short time the situation was tense, but with the cessation of the Confederate activities in Canada, friendly relations were restored. An incidental effect of these events during the Civil War was a growing strain in the relations between Great Britain and Canada. ~

11: Canada and the Mother Country

Changes in imperial relations; internal affairs and the power of the Governor; external affairs; trade relations; tariff autonomy and the Galt Memorandum; negotiations with the United States and France; the responsibility of defence; the Civil War crisis; the storm in England; Galt points the moral: Confederation.

The period between the attainment of substantial self-government under Baldwin and Lafontaine and the coming of Confederation was an important stage in the development of imperial relations. The freedom already won was consolidated and extended. A beginning was made in securing control of external as well as internal affairs. A sharp international crisis brought home the fact that self-government had its duties as well as its privileges. Difference of views as to the responsibility for military defence gave rise to friction which wore the bonds of Empire thin. In the minds of most public men in Britain and of an increasing number in Canada, these pregnant years were proving that colonial self-government would inevitably bring separation in its train.

An interesting interlude was the visit of the Prince of Wales to Canada and the United States in 1860. In spite of friction which developed with Orange societies at Kingston and other points, the tour of the royal party created wide popular interest and intensified the loyal and friendly sentiment of the people. The reception given in the United States was quite as warm and expansive, and prophets pictured an era of undying friendliness, a bare year before the *Trent* was to bring both countries to the verge of war. While in Sherbrooke, the royal party were the guests of Mr. Galt.

Under Lord Elgin, it was commonly understood, responsible government had been won. Responsible government has been shown to involve party government, cabinet government, and self-government. The working of party and cabinet government in this period has been reviewed: it remains to consider the development of self-government. As a matter of fact, self-government was very far from being attained in 1849. The control of Canadian affairs was still divided between the elected representatives of the Canadian people and the authorities of the Mother Country in Downing Street. It was true that a very much larger share of the field was thenceforth resigned to colonial control, but there was still an important if somewhat vaguely defined area within which Downing Street was left supreme. This settlement was by no means accepted as final. In the period under review several issues of the first importance arose, in most of which Galt was deeply concerned, and which led to a readjustment and a much clearer understanding of powers and boundaries.

It had been urged by some early advocates of responsible government, and notably by Baldwin, that the dividing line between colonial and imperial authority should follow the line between internal and external affairs. Lord John Russell had rightly denied the possibility of making such a clear-cut division. The British authorities must, he insisted, as a matter of course, have control of "the questions of foreign war, and international relations, whether of trade or diplomacy." But this was not all; even in the field of internal government, questions might arise involving "the honour of the Crown or the faith of Parliament or the safety of the State" so seriously that the British government must retain its power to intervene. Fortunately, therefore, no such rigid division was made; fortunately, from the standpoint of Canadian autonomy, since the vagueness of the boundaries left it possible for the colonial government, as it grew in experience and authority, to extend its activities into one section after another of the twilight zone, and particularly into the region which Russell had considered imperial beyond question.

While no division between internal and external affairs could be either logically complete or enduring, yet such a rough division was at first accepted. It will serve as a convenient starting point for reviewing the developments of the years that followed. . . .

~ When the British government conceded self-government to the colonies, it was intended that control over colonial trade relations should remain in the hands of the imperial government; there should be one trade policy for the Empire and that policy should be universal free trade. When, in 1850, New Brunswick attempted to place a duty on American imports which was higher than the duty on other goods, the British government insisted that it be withdrawn. In the same year a constitution was drawn up for New South Wales in which the colony was expressly forbidden to impose higher duties on imports from one country or colony than on those from any other source. In 1849 Hincks, when he introduced his budget, stated that to set up a protective tariff in Canada would be equivalent to a declaration of independence. ~

In 1859 Galt had found it necessary to bring in a tariff materially increasing the duties on manufactured goods. Previous step by step increases had been watched with growing suspicion and disfavour in England. Galt's 2½ per cent increase proved the last straw. The manufacturers of Sheffield led the protest. In a memorandum submitted to the Duke of Newcastle, then Colonial Secretary, they declared that in the past eighteen years the Canadian duty on Sheffield goods had advanced from 2½ to 20 per cent. The memorial continued:

The Merchants and Manufacturers of Sheffield have no wish to obtain special exception for themselves, and do not complain that they are called upon to pay the same duty as the American or the German, neither do they claim to have their goods admitted free of duty. All they ask is, that the policy of protection to native manufacturers in Canada should be distinctly discountenanced by Her Majesty's Government as a system condemned by reason and experience, directly contrary to the policy solemnly adopted by the Mother Country, and calculated to breed disunion and distrust between Great Britain and her Colonies. It cannot be regarded as less than indecent and a reproach that, while for fifteen years, the Government, the greatest statesmen, and the Press of this country have been not only advocating but practising the principles of Free Trade, the Government of one of her most important colonies should have been advocating monopoly and protection. . . . We conceive that Her Majesty's Government has a right to demand that what revenue is needed shall be raised in some other way than that which is opposed to the acknowledged commercial policy of the Imperial Government, and destructive of the interests of those manufacturing towns of Great Britain which trade with Canada.

The Duke of Newcastle immediately forwarded the protest to the Governor-General, remarking that he felt there was much force in the argument. He added that while he would probably not recommend the disallowance of the Act, he considered it his duty, no less to the colony than to the Mother Country, to express his regret that the experience of England as to the injurious effect of protection and the advantage of low duties on manufactures, both as regards trade and revenue, should thus be lost sight of.

It fell to Galt to answer this indictment. His report was a strong and convincing document, and constitutes an important landmark in the growth of imperial relations. He had no difficulty in showing that the province needed greater revenue, and that under Canadian conditions the tariff was the only practicable source. Analysing the tariff rates, in detail, he urged that the necessary increase could not have been made to fall on any other schedules than those chosen, and that the tariff taken as a whole showed a lower range of duty than in 1850 – a fact obviously due to the large free list established by the Reciprocity Treaty. So far as Sheffield wares were concerned, he scored a verbal point by showing that the latest tariff had made no change in the duties imposed on the finished product, but had increased the duty on the Canadian manufacturer's raw materials.

Passing, however, to the constitutional question, Galt declared that while the Act had not been disallowed, yet the fact that this course had been entertained made it necessary to state what the provincial government considered to be the position and rights of the Canadian legislature. He continued:

> *Respect to the Imperial Government must always dictate the desire to satisfy them that the policy of this country is neither hastily nor unwisely formed, and that due regard is had to the interests of the Mother Country, as well as of the Province. But the Government of Canada, acting for its legislature and people, cannot, through those feelings of deference which they owe to the Imperial authorities, in any manner waive or diminish the right of the people of Canada to decide for themselves both as to the mode and extent to which taxation shall be imposed. The Provincial Ministry are at all times ready to afford explanations in regard to the Acts of the Legislature to which they are party – but, subject to their duty and allegiance to Her Majesty, their responsibility in all general questions of policy must be to the Provincial Parliament, by whose confidence they administer the affairs of the country. And in the imposition of taxation, it is so plainly necessary that the*

administration and the people should be in accord, that the former cannot admit responsibility or require approval beyond that of the local legislature.

Self-government would be utterly annihilated if the views of the Imperial Government were to be preferred to those of the people of Canada. It is, therefore, the duty of the present government distinctly to affirm the right of the Canadian legislature to adjust the taxation of the people in the way they deem best — even if it should unfortunately happen to meet the disapproval of the Imperial Ministry. Her Majesty cannot be advised to disallow such acts, unless her advisers are prepared to assume the administration of the affairs of the Colony, irrespective of the views of its inhabitants.

The Imperial Government are not responsible for the debts and engagements of Canada, they do not maintain its judicial, educational, or civil service, they contribute nothing to the internal government of the country; and the Provincial Legislature, acting through a ministry directly responsible to it, has to make provision for all these wants; they must necessarily claim and exercise the widest latitude as to the nature and extent of the burthens to be placed upon the industry of the people. The Provincial Government believes that His Grace must share their own convictions on this important subject, but as serious evil would have resulted had His Grace taken a different course, it is wiser to prevent future complication by distinctly stating the position that must be maintained by every Canadian Administration.

In replying to this vigorous defence, the Colonial Office sought the aid of the Lords of the Committee of the Privy Council for Trade. These authorities took the same high ground, contending that even if the protection given were only incidental, it would probably involve the growth of vested interests dependent on these duties, and "that a system of taxation adopted for the legitimate object of revenue, may be continued for the mischievous purpose of protection." The correspondence continued at some length upon matters of detail, but neither in Whitehall nor in Downing Street was any answer attempted to Galt's statement of the constitutional position. Henceforth there was to be no question of the legal right of Canada to control its general trade and tariff policy, whatever might be thought of the expediency of that policy in Canada's own interests, or of its fairness from the Mother Country's point of view.*

Control of the general trade and tariff policy of the country was thus secured. Control of the special trade and tariff relations with various foreign countries obviously involved a still greater assumption of independent authority, and therefore was much slower in coming. In framing its general tariff, Canada did not need to enter into consultation with any foreign state. If, however, special tariff rates were to be given or received from any state, or if fishery or bonding or shipping privileges were to be arranged, it was essential to have the power to carry on negotiations and to ratify the agreements reached.

Naturally, Great Britain considered the control of foreign affairs the very arcana of Empire, and was reluctant to yield any share to the colonies, particularly when she bore alone practically the whole burden of the diplomatic and the defence forces which backed up her policy. Yet, in the case of Canada, relations with the United States were so close and constant that some breach in the rigid rule was here inevitable. The opening was made slowly. In the first important negotiation, resulting in the conclusion of the Reciprocity Treaty of 1854, the leading part was taken by Lord Elgin, as Envoy Extraordinary, though Hincks from Canada and Chandler from New Brunswick took a part in the mission. The treaty was ratified by the votes not only of the British Parliament and the United States Congress but of the legislatures of Canada, New Brunswick, Nova Scotia,

* Discussions of Galt's tariff policies may be found in two articles by D. C. Masters: "Reciprocity and the Genesis of a Canadian Commercial Policy," *Canadian Historical Review,* XIII (December, 1932), pp. 418-28, and "A. T. Galt and Canadian Fiscal Autonomy," *Canadian Historical Review,* XV (September, 1934), pp. 276-82. The reaction of the British authorities is described in David M. L. Farr, *The Colonial Office and Canada, 1867-1887* (Toronto, 1955), pp. 168-71. Despite the arguments presented by Masters and Farr, the myth persists that Galt's statement on tariff policy marked a revolutionary step in British imperial relations. For example, in 1959 on the one hundredth anniversary of Galt's bold assertion, Professor G. S. Graham of the University of London declared: "Henceforth there was no denial of the legal right of a self-governing colony to control its own trade tariff policy." (*The Listener,* November 5, 1959, pp. 769-70). The fact is, however, that the British government was extremely reluctant to make concessions in the field of tariff policy, refusing until 1895, for example, to allow the Australian colonies to levy differential duties in favour of foreign countries. Galt's rejoinder "represented a hope for the future rather than a description of the current position." (Farr, *op. cit.,* p. 170).

Prince Edward Island and Newfoundland. The informal discussion of the working of the treaty which has already been
noted prepared the way for the more formal activities of Galt,
Rose, Macdonald and Brown in the decade which followed.

To open negotiations with any other foreign power was
more difficult, but under Galt's administration an opening was
made. Naturally the first country to be considered was France,
not merely because France was a second mother country to
Canada, but because the negotiation in 1860 of Cobden's
Reciprocity Treaty between England and France had made it
evident that friendlier relations between the two countries were
beginning and that France was disposed to depart to some
extent from her rigid protectionism. . . .

~ In the course of his speech on the budget in 1862, Galt
was asked if any correspondence had been carried on between
the Canadian and French governments concerning trade. He
replied that it was constitutionally impossible for official correspondence to take place between a colonial government and a
foreign country. However, he added, the French consul in
Canada, Baron Boileau, had been active in developing trade
between Canada and France. ~

"No official correspondence can take place," "however,"
illustrates very well the illogical, step-by-step English way of
making constitutional change. Even so, the pace was becoming
too swift for the liking of the Foreign Office, and when Baron
Boileau undertook similar negotiations at Saint John, his recall
was politely requested. It is interesting to note that this method
of negotiation through the consuls on the spot was taken up
and extended by Hon. Mr. Fielding a half century later. . . .

~ The Civil War and the imminent danger of an American
invasion raised the question as to what extent Canadians were
responsible for their own defence. There was no doubt that
Great Britain would continue to assume the major responsibility
for protecting the colonies, and, soon after the outbreak of war
in the United States, several thousand British troops were sent
to North America, bringing the force of regulars serving there
to about eighteen thousand. However, for some time previously
there had been outspoken dissatisfaction expressed in the British
Parliament concerning the heavy burden which the security of
the colonies placed upon the British taxpayer. In the summer
of 1861, a committee urged that the colonies should take on a

greater share of their own defence and Parliament passed a resolution to this effect. During the debate it was pointed out that the North American colonies not only cost the British treasury increasingly large sums annually, but had at the same time reduced whatever commercial benefit Britain might derive from them by adopting a protective trade policy. It seemed to many that the logical conclusion was that the colonies were costing more than they were worth and should be granted complete independence.

In theory the British troops in Canada were supplemented by local militia, but in fact these units existed mainly on paper since they had few weapons, no uniforms and little training. As an effective military force they were absolutely without value.[1] Realizing this, the Canadian government set about to improve the defences of the province. Late in 1861, John A. Macdonald was appointed Minister of Militia, and a few days later a committee, of which Galt was a member, was set up to report on the state of preparedness in case of attack. In March, 1862, the committee recommended that a volunteer force of fifty thousand men be raised immediately, properly equipped and adequately trained. The cost of the programme was estimated at slightly over one million dollars, or one-tenth of the provincial budget. Despite strong criticism of the great expense involved, a bill incorporating the committee's recommendations was submitted to the legislature. It was promptly defeated when French-Canadian supporters of the government defected, forcing the ministry to resign.

When news that the Militia Bill had been rejected reached England, there was a violent reaction. The apathy of the colonials was denounced in the press and Parliament, and there were suggestions that the British troops should be withdrawn and the colonies cut adrift. Canadians generally were astounded at the vehemence of the criticism since they did not share the British opinion of the gravity of the military situation. A more modest Militia Bill was enacted shortly afterward and the crisis passed without serious incident. The clash of views had, however, served to illustrate that the time had arrived for a more exact definition of the relations between the colonies and the Mother Country, with respect to both military and commercial responsibilities. ~

In [a] speech in Manchester in 1862 . . . Galt pointed the moral of the discussion as to the relative rights and duties of the colonies and of the Mother Country both as to trade and as to defence:

> *Before taking or advocating a step which could never be retraced* [separation], *the present colonial policy of self-govern- ment should be thoroughly worked out, further developed and extended. . . . It would be desirable so to harmonize and federate the colonies as to bring them into different groups, so that instead of fifty colonies there would be five or six groups. It was clear that by joining the resources of all, the strength of the whole would be increased for defence, and thus the burden of defending them would be reduced to the Mother Country. The question had been brought under the notice of the Imperial Government three years ago, but no progress had been made. . . In ten or fifteen years the present population of 3,500,000 would probably be doubled, its strength united and developed, and if ultimately it were found necessary to separate, they might then be both ready and able to stand alone and resist further aggression. But if, as I hope, the result were to show that the union of these colonies with Great Britain could be maintained with increasing benefit to both, then how much would the strength of the empire be increased by the possession of such a powerful dependency?*

The two solutions thus pointedly brought forward, separa- tion and Confederation, had gained many advocates in both England and Canada as a result of the events of the past few years. In England, the conviction that separation was inevitable now became became widespread. The angry storm of criticism of Canadian supineness in defence abated as Canadian efforts increased and the danger faded, while use and custom took the sharp edge off the heresy and ingratitude evinced in Canada's tariff policy. The discussion left, however, a legacy in the form of a strong conviction in many men's minds that if the United Kingdom could not defend Canada against the United States, and Canada would not defend herself, and if the trade advan- tages once considered to offset the burdens of defence had disappeared, there was no reason for maintaining an illusory, dangerous and irritating connection. No reason but one – an honourable unwillingness to set the colonies adrift before they were able to defend themselves against any probable foe. Here, then, the policy of Confederation came in to show the means by which colonies could attain the degree of strength necessary to enable them to stand alone. Both by those who looked to

Confederation as the first step toward separation and by those who looked to it as a means of enabling the new state to play a greater part within the Empire, the proposals of Confederation were now given a warm welcome in the United Kingdom instead of the cold indifference exhibited only a few years before.

In Canada, the question of the ultimate future of the relationship, though beginning to be discussed, was less stressed. Here the emphasis was placed on the value of Confederation as a means of meeting the immediate need – increasing the defensive power of the North American colonies. The common danger did much to break down the barriers of provincial isolation. The war which threatened to tear one great federation asunder did much to achieve another.

Yet this factor alone would not have compelled action. It was only the renewed pressure of the difficulty which had first led Galt to urge the solution of Confederation that could bring the question home to politicians who favoured hand-to-mouth policies, and refused to take long views. We may now turn, then, to consider the developments in party and provincial strife which made it clear that only a heroic remedy would meet the situation.

12: The Coming of Confederation

The party see-saw; new converts to federation; the Coalition of 1864; the Maritime provinces come half way; the Conference at Quebec; the Conference draft and Galt's 1858 proposals; Confederation and the people; the Conference with the imperial authorities, 1865; the attempt to prolong reciprocity; a new fiscal policy; ministerial changes: the resignation of Brown and of Galt; the final stage.

The friction with the United States during the Civil War had shown that union of the scattered provinces was desirable. The change of opinion in the United Kingdom on colonial policy and on colonial defence had ensured at last a favourable hearing in Downing Street for any federation proposals. Yet without the development in the provinces themselves of a situation which compelled the practical politicians and party leaders to seek a solution in Confederation, the achievement might have been delayed for years, and that might have meant delay for all time.[1]

In Canada in 1858, when parliamentary and sectional deadlock threatened, it had seemed possible that Galt's proposal to find a way out through federation would be accepted. But the crisis had passed, for the moment. Macdonald and Cartier rallied a strong majority behind them, and the old political coach rattled on once more. For half a dozen years longer the policy of personal rather than of constitutional rearrangement was continued. Then the resources of party manipulations were exhausted, and even the most hand-to-mouth politicians were compelled to seek a more daring settlement.

It is not necessary to follow the see-saw of parties in these troubled years through every move. Only the larger tendencies and the more critical episodes need be reviewed. Broadly speaking, the course of events was that the steady and continued advance of Upper Canada over Lower Canada in population and wealth made the existing system of representation almost intolerable, and that the personal ascendancy of the leaders who had induced the majority to accept it weakened.

The administrations in which Cartier, J. A. Macdonald and Galt were the leading figures held power from 1856 to 1862. In the later years the majority and the prestige of the administration steadily dwindled. Upper Canada was fast becoming a unit in favour of Rep. by Pop. While the elections of 1861 retained the government in office, the break-up began rapidly. It was found necessary to introduce into the cabinet three Upper Canada Conservatives, John Beverley Robinson, John Carling, and James Patton, who were in favour of Rep. by Pop., and to make it an open question in the ministry. Even so, the latter minister was overwhelmingly defeated on seeking re-election in his constituency. Revelations of corruption and inefficiency in the construction of the new Parliament Buildings at Ottawa further weakened the government. Changes in the balance of personality gave the finishing stroke.

The loss of George Brown, by defeat in the elections of 1861, had robbed the Opposition of its most forceful leader, but at the same time had paved the way for closer co-operation between the Upper and Lower Canada sections of the party. Two Lower Canada leaders, Sicotte and Loranger, who had quarrelled with Cartier, rallied a strong group of moderates, together with what was left of the Rouges. In Upper Canada John Sandfield Macdonald, Ishmaelite though he was, succeeded in shepherding a loose group of moderates who were prepared to co-operate with the Lower Canada section. Neither group was ready for Rep. by Pop. or for federation. If they had any constitutional principle, it was the futile plan of the double majority. In fact, however, they were simply on the plane of Cartier and J. A. Macdonald, seeking to preserve the *status quo*, but with themselves in office and the present incumbents out.

The Militia Bill of 1862 was the occasion rather than the cause of the fall of the Cartier-Macdonald government. The bill, as already noted, was unpopular in itself, especially among the Lower Canada members, but had it not been for the weakening of the government on more personal grounds it could have weathered the storm.

On May 24, 1862, the new ministry formed by J. S. Macdonald and L. V. Sicotte was sworn in. It achieved a measure of administrative success by economies in provincial expenditure, but its tenure of office was never secure. The only general principle for which it stood, the double majority, was thrown overboard when its most important measure, an extension of the separate school system in Upper Canada, was forced through only by a Lower Canada majority. Its failure to adopt Rep. by Pop. endangered the adherence of Brown and the *Globe*, in spite of their approval of the personnel of the cabinet, and the separate school policy hardened the attitude of the Clear Grit ring into active opposition. In Lower Canada the ministry was further weakened by the retirement of Dorion, who was not in sympathy with the policy of reopening negotiations for completing the Intercolonial Railway. It was not surprising, then, that toward the close of the first session under the new government, in May, 1863, John A. Macdonald succeeded in rallying enough different shades of opposition to secure a majority of four (63-59) in a vote of want of confidence.

It was only two years since a general election had been held, but there was as yet no alternative to another election. After reconstructing his ministry to include a larger element of the radical group from each section, including Galt's old friend, Luther H. Holton, as Minister of Finance, Sandfield Macdonald went to the country once more. A gain in Upper Canada and a loss in Lower Canada left matters much as they were. The ministers who had been dropped in the reconstruction, Sicotte, Foley and McGee, reinforced the Opposition, and the first two sessions of the new Parliament were given up to interminable personal wrangles. In the vote on the Speakership the government was sustained by a majority of eight, but as the session advanced several members were detached from its support. On October 6 Galt moved a vote of want of confidence, condemning the financial policy of the government, and emphasizing again the fact that Confederation was the only possible solution for the difficulties in which the country found itself. The motion was defeated by only three votes (61-64). Early in the following session, on March 21, 1864, the ministry gave up the attempt to carry on the administration of the country.

The attempts made to construct an alternative ministry reveal the tension and the flux of parties. The Governor-General sent first for Fergusson-Blair, the late Provincial Secretary, as a moderate man who might be able to gather a majority about him. Fergusson-Blair first made overtures to Sir E. P. Taché, who declined to assist; and then asked Dorion to try to form the Lower Canada section, but Dorion, after approaching Chapais, Abbott, and Dunkin, failed, and Fergusson-Blair gave up the task. Next Cartier was summoned, with no greater success. Then Taché himself, who had taken little part in political life since the breakup of the ministry in 1857, agreed to undertake the formation of a new ministry. He invited Alexander Campbell, J. A. Macdonald's Kingston law partner, to form the Upper Canada section; Campbell tried, but again

with no result. Then Taché suggested a coalition, but McDougall, to whom the proposal was made, declined. At last he fell
back on his old colleague, J. A. Macdonald, and on March 30,
by their united efforts, another fleeting administration came to
office, if not to power. The policy of the new government was
announced to include proposals for closer trade relations with
the other colonies, for making efforts to maintain and extend
Reciprocity with the United States, and for more effective
organization of the militia, without any increase in expense.
Rep. by Pop. was left an open question.

The Taché-Macdonald ministry was the last attempt to
make the old machinery work. It was soon clear that its days
were numbered. One of the Upper Canada ministers was defeated in seeking re-election, and others had close calls. The
government's majority at the opening of the session proved to
be only two, and even this margin was precarious.

The end came on June 14, on a motion by Dorion condemning the action of Galt and the Cartier-Macdonald ministry
in general in making an unauthorized advance from the treasury in 1859. At that time certain debentures, to the amount of
$100,000, issued by the City of Montreal in aid of the St.
Lawrence and Atlantic Railroad and for which the Grand
Trunk was now liable, became due. The railway was unable
and the city was unwilling to meet the payment. At the same
time Montreal, like so many other cities, was in arrears in its
Municipal Loan Fund payments. The government was anxious
to have a good example set, and an agreement was made that if
the city would pay up the $100,000 it owed the Loan Fund,
the government would meet the railway debentures of like
amount and look to the Grand Trunk for repayment. Later, the
English bankers of the railway, Messrs. Baring and Glyn, and
the Vice-President, Mr. Blackwell, agreed to assume their just
debt. Unfortunately some misunderstanding arose, which came
to Galt's notice only a short time before he left office in 1862.
He gave instruction to have his successor's attention called to
it, and Mr. Howland attempted in vain to secure the recognition
desired. From that day the former Executive was denounced
unsparingly for this appropriation of funds without Parliament's
consent, and in 1864 Dorion seized it as the readiest stick with
which to beat the ministry then in office. Technically that
ministry could not be held responsible for the deeds or misdeeds
of its fourth predecessor, but the Opposition contended that
since the wicked triumvirate of Cartier, Macdonald and Galt

dominated both, the responsibility came home. The ministers accepted the challenge, and Dorion's motion became a test of the confidence of the House. When it carried by 60-58, Dunkin and Rankin crossing the floor, it was clear that the game was up.

What was to be done? Seek to patch up another ministry out of the existing House? That experiment had been given full trial. Seek a new general election, the third in three years? The Governor-General consented, but the defeated ministers were reluctant to face another inconclusive contest. At last it became clear that the only solution was to do away with the mingling of local and general affairs which led to deadlock, by establishing a federal government.

This conviction had been gaining ground throughout the session. In the previous October Galt had brought the question before the House in the motion of want of confidence in the Macdonald-Sicotte government. In March, the movement gained a notable convert. George Brown had returned to the House in 1863, somewhat chastened by his earlier defeat, and convinced that Rep. by Pop., though a necessary, could not be a final, measure of reform. On March 24, 1864, he moved that a Select Committee of nineteen members be appointed to inquire into the important matters raised in the address of Cartier, Ross and Galt in 1858 – Galt's address to the Colonial Secretary outlining the case for federation. He referred to the gross inequalities of representation which existed, one group of three Upper Canada members representing as many constituents as thirteen Lower Canada members, and declared that the endless crises, the frequent elections, the political turmoil, made a change imperative. "There has been no peace, and there can be no peace, until the question is settled, and settled right," he concluded. The motion carried, though not without many expressions of dissent. Upper Canada members who wanted Rep. by Pop. and nothing else, Lower Canada members who feared their province would be swamped, alike attacked it. Galt opposed a fishing inquiry, insisting on pledging the House definitely to his solution, while J. A. Macdonald, who offered no constructive suggestion, loudly endorsed an Upper Canada member who criticized Galt's scheme on the ground that the Civil War in the United States had proved the folly of federal unions. Yet a committee was appointed, and a strong and representative one. It comprised Messrs. Brown, M. C. Cameron, Cartier, Cauchon, Chapais, Dickson, A. A. Dorion, Dunkin, Foley, Galt, Holton, Joly, McDougall, McKellar, J. A. Macdonald, J. S. Macdonald, Scoble, Street, and Turcotte. The Committee held eight meetings and reported three months after its appointment, on June 14. Brown, as chairman, announced, that "a strong feeling was found to exist among the members of the Committee in favour of changes in the direction of a Federative system, applied either to Canada alone or the whole British North American Provinces, and such progress had been made as to warrant the Committee in recommending that the subject be again referred to a Committee at the next session of Parliament." The Committee had not been unanimous. The yeas and nays had been taken. The last-ditch opponents of any change consisted of John A. Macdonald, Sandfield Macdonald, and Scoble, Dunkin, not being present, but wishing to be recorded "nay."

Immediately after the report of the Committee, Dorion moved his fateful want of confidence vote, as an amendment to Galt's motion that the House should go into Committee of Supply. The crisis and the remedy were dramatically thrown together. While the lobbies were discussing the prospects of an election, Brown seized the occasion to suggest to several supporters of the administration that the crisis should be utilized to settle by co-operation once for all the constitutional difficulties between Upper and Lower Canada. Two of the men thus addressed, Messrs. Morris and Pope, asked and obtained leave to communicate these conversations to Macdonald and Galt. On June 17 the latter two called on Brown at his rooms and discussed ways of settlement. As to the remedy, Brown still held out for representation by population immediately, with federation in the distance, while Galt, as well as Macdonald, who was at last converted, insisted on federation at once. As to the means of securing it, a coalition cabinet was proposed.

The negotiations took a week to conclude. Sir E. P. Taché and Cartier joined the other three leaders at an early stage, and Brown held frequent consultations with his friends from Upper Canada. Finally an agreement was reached as to the end to be sought. "The government are prepared," the memorandum ran, "to pledge themselves to bring in a measure next session for the purpose of removing existing difficulties by introducing the federal principle into Canada, coupled with such provisions as will permit the Maritime Provinces and the North-West Territory to be incorporated into the same system of government, and the government will seek by sending representatives to the Lower Provinces and to England, to secure the assent of those interests which are beyond the control of our own legislation to such a measure as may enable ?ll British North America to be united under a General Legislature based upon the federal principle."

The personal and political arrangements necessary were still more delicate. Brown had at first proposed that the Opposition would support the government in carrying through the policy agreed upon, but Macdonald insisted that as a guarantee of good faith Brown himself should enter the cabinet. Both men knew how surprised, and in many quarters shocked, the country would be to see two arch enemies embrace after years of the most bitter rivalry. Brown hesitated, and the personal question was postponed until after it was found that an agreement as to policy could be obtained. Then, after consulting his friends, Brown agreed to a coalition. As the Opposition formed at least half the House, he suggested that they should be given half the seats in the cabinet, four members from Upper Canada and two from Lower Canada. So far as Upper Canada was concerned, Macdonald was willing to concede three seats, but as for Lower Canada, Cartier and Galt contended, the personnel of the cabinet already afforded ample guarantee for their sincerity and the inclusion of any members of the Lower Canada Opposition would be likely to lead to embarrassment rather than assistance. Brown did not press the Lower Canada matter further, and acquiesced, after some debate, in the proposal to include only three Opposition members from Upper Canada. Accordingly, on June 30, George Brown, Oliver Mowat and William McDougall took their seats in the Executive Council.

The compromise thus affected was probably the only means by which Confederation could have been carried, and was therefore justified. Yet it was not without its unfortunate aspects. Brown was distinctly outmanoeuvred from the party and personal standpoint, and his realization of this later came near to shipwrecking the movement. It was unfortunate, also, that it was not possible to include in the government representatives of the Lower Canada Liberals, who, while opposed to the wider plan of federation, had advocated the federation of the two Canadas long before Brown or Macdonald had been converted. They were, perforce, driven into Opposition, and into taking a more determined position of antagonism than they really felt. Yet there was much force in the contention of Cartier and Galt that a change in the Lower Canada section of the cabinet would have hampered rather than helped. The very fact that Dorion and Holton and their supporters had long been the friends of tolerance and of the closest possible relations between French-speaking and English-speaking Canadians would have made them suspected in the minds of those of their fellow countrymen who feared that in Confederation French-speaking Canadians would be swamped and overwhelmed. It was a paradox, but true, that the mass of Lower Canadians would be much more likely to accept Confederation if sponsored by those who, like Cartier, had hitherto been most unyielding in opposing any constitutional change or any abandonment of Lower Canada's full equality in Parliament.

Both the legislature and the province accepted the new policy with surprisingly little opposition. The union of the most powerful leaders in its support and the general weariness of faction and deadlock compelled consent throughout the Canadas.

It remained to ascertain the attitude of the Lower Provinces. Fortunately they met Canada half way. A vague feeling of dissatisfaction with the isolation and limitations of their existing status had been growing up, particularly among the political leaders. No breakdown of party government, no sectional deadlocks had developed in the provinces by the sea. Yet other factors stirred thoughts of union. Like Canada, they had felt the weakness and the danger of isolation, both in making their influence felt in London and in averting the designs of jingoes in Washington. The desire for an intercolonial railway was still strong, and it was coming to be felt that only political union could achieve it. Many of the leading men, trained in the struggles for responsible government and the party conflicts which followed its achievement, had come to feel that the provincial stage was too narrow for them. They had developed political capacity beyond the needs or opportunities of the three eastern provinces, which all told numbered less than a million souls. It was this desire for larger worlds to conquer which had made Joseph Howe dream visions of an imperial parliament in which a great Nova Scotian might find no mean place, and it was this ambition which led Charles Tupper first to plan a Maritime Union and later to accept with eagerness the proposals for a wider federation.

It was in a Nova Scotia Legislature, 1854, that the first parliamentary proposal of union of all the provinces was made. Nothing came of the proposal, and it was not until ten years later, when Tupper became premier of Nova Scotia, that further steps to union were taken. In that year he invited the governments of the other eastern provinces to send representatives to a conference to discuss Maritime Union. The Conference was called for September, 1864, in Charlottetown. The Canadian ministers decided to take advantage of this happy conjuncture to raise the wider question, and sent a delegation to confer with the Maritime leaders. [The Canadian delegates were John A. Macdonald, George Brown, George Cartier, Alexander T. Galt, William McDougall, Thomas D'Arcy McGee and Hector Langevin.] The local scheme was wrecked by the obstinate insistence of Prince Edward Island that its capital should be made the seat of the new Maritime Government, but this disappointment was soon forgotten in the welcome given the wider plan. Brief discussion made it clear that the plan of federal union would receive careful consideration, if not consent, on every side. Accordingly it was arranged that in the following month a conference of delegates from all the colonies should meet at Quebec to discuss the wider plan. A series of banquets in all three Maritime capitals gave the Canadian delegates an opportunity of bringing the merits of the proposal before representative audiences.*

---

* Skelton is curiously silent on the Charlottetown Conference, especially in view of Galt's significant contribution to the discussions. On the second day of the Conference, Galt was called upon to present the Canadians' proposed financial arrangements for the larger union and he acquitted himself admirably. In the words of Donald Creighton: "This was one of the great moments of [Galt's] career. He was financing the largest of all enterprises, a transcontinental nation; and he could talk, not only in those sweeping generalities and rhetorical flourishes he liked so much, but also with that wealth of convincing illustrative detail of which he was such a master. All the main features of the Canadian plan – the assumption by the new general government of all provincial debt (and possibly the device of the debt allowance by which this transference could be equitably carried out), the payments of subsidies, based on population, to the new local governments, and the division of sources of revenue between the federation and the provinces – all were set out as parts of one great, integrated, and coherent whole. Galt knew the plan to which he himself had contributed so much, down to its smallest detail, and he excelled himself in its presentation." (Donald Creighton, *The Road to Confederation, The Emergence of Canada: 1863-1867* [Toronto, 1964], p. 115). It is perhaps significant that at a luncheon immediately after Galt's speech, the Maritimers expressed approval of the larger federation for the first time (*Ibid.*, p. 116).

On October 10, 1864, the most momentous assembly in the history of the northern half of the continent was opened at Quebec. Each of the five eastern provinces was represented, and the thirty-three delegates included nearly all the foremost leaders of political opinion.

The deliberations of the Conference were held in secret. Such memorials of the proceedings of the Fathers of Confederation as have survived have the same curiously meagre and severely practical aspect as the terms of the Act itself.* There was little, either in the proceedings or in their outcome, of the harking back to first principles, or of the references to the experience of other lands, which marked the forming of the republic to the south. Yet in the sixteen days which were given to the work, the foundations of the future state were laid broad and firm. The measure of the power of the men there assembled to read the need of their own time and to foresee the growth of the future is found in the success and steady progress of the nation they helped create, and in the small necessity yet found for amending their provisions.

The main outlines of the plan were soon determined. In spite of Macdonald's insistence on a legislative union, opinion was practically unanimous in favour of a federal basis. It is now clear that on no other basis could a union have been formed or have been maintained. Lower Canada, insistent on preserving its cherished institutions, and the Lower Provinces, separated from the Canadas by long leagues of territory and years of non-acquaintance, and equally reluctant to hand over their local affairs to a legislature a thousand miles away, would not have entered on any other terms. Even had the attempt been made to frame a legislative union, the hopelessness of harmonizing sectional differences and of extending the union to cross the continent would soon have brought shipwreck. Yet while the federal basis was accepted, the lesson of excessive state autonomy driven home by the Civil War led to giving the central government greater powers than in any other federation yet devised. The right of the federal government to appoint and dismiss the Lieutenant-Governors of the provinces, the right to disallow provincial legislation, the assignment to the federal government of all legislative powers not specifically given the provinces and the power of the federal cabinet to nominate the

* The deliberations of the Quebec Conference are no longer so obscure as when Skelton wrote. See Creighton, *Road to Confederation*, pp. 132-86.

members of the Senate, which was supposed to assure the smaller provinces against aggression, were devices, not all successful, to avoid the ills experienced by the republic.

The composition of the federal legislature was settled without great difficulty.* Following the example of the United States, it was agreed to set up two houses, a Commons in which the cry of representation by population would be given effect, and a Senate in which some approach to federal equality between the various sections would be secured. There was practically no sentiment for universal suffrage even for the election in the Commons, and, at first, the provincial qualifications for franchise were to be accepted in the federal elections. In the first draft, also, it was left to the provincial legislatures to carve out the federal constituencies, and it was only after it was recognized what opportunity this would give a hostile provincial government to gerrymander the federal ridings that the Canadians sought, and successfully, to have this provision changed. As for the Upper House, there were few voices in favour of any other method of selection save nomination. The canvassing required under the elective method, in force ten years in Canada, had proved too arduous and expensive for elderly politicians, and the desirability of winning over the legislative councils of the various provinces by the lure of seats in the Senate strengthened the demand for nomination. Several Lower Province delegates wished to leave the nomination in the hands of the provincial governments, but, with dubious wisdom, the Canadian representatives insisted upon nomination by the federal cabinet, a device which practically destroyed the federal character of the Upper House. An exception was made in the case of Prince Edward Island.

In the division of legislative power between the federal and local governments, the influence of the United States, exerted both by attraction and by repulsion, and of the old controversies in the Canadas, was apparent. The division agreed upon differed from the United States scheme in assigning criminal law, marriage and divorce, with some reservations, and various phases of commercial dealings, to the federal authorities, and as already noted, in making the federal government residuary legatee, a provision which has not proved to be as important as

* The composition of the federal legislature was not settled as smoothly as Skelton suggests. The subject of the composition of the general Parliament was fiercely debated throughout the whole of the session. See Creighton, *Road to Confederation*, pp. 148-167.

was anticipated. The question of courts and laws was settled by giving the provinces the power to establish the courts, save a federal court of appeal, and the federal government the right to appoint and the duty to pay the judges, who were to be drawn from the local bar until such time as the English-law provinces brought uniformity into their civil laws.

The chief stumbling blocks were the question of finance and the question of education, in its religious phase. The Lower Provinces had not developed municipal institutions beyond a very rudimentary stage, and were accustomed to look to their legislatures for many facilities which in the Canadas were provided by the municipalities and met out of local taxation. Their representatives insisted, therefore, not merely upon a federal subsidy to the provinces, but upon a subsidy on a scale which the Canadian representatives deemed extravagant and superfluous. Deadlock threatened, but in a conference in which Galt and Brown represented Canada, Tupper and Archibald Nove Scotia, Tilley New Brunswick, Pope Prince Edward Island, and Shea Newfoundland, an agreement was reached as to assumption of debts and scale of subsidies which met the existing need and which it was fondly hoped would prove permanent.* Crown lands, save in the case of Newfoundland,

---

* Skelton neglects to point out that at this critical juncture, when deadlock threatened and the Conference was on the brink of collapse, Galt saved the situation. He was the only man among the Canadians who was capable of convincing the Maritime delegates that they would not suffer financially by entering into union with Canada (Creighton, *Road to Confederation*, p. 167). The representatives of Nova Scotia, New Brunswick and Prince Edward Island were understandably suspicious that as small units in a federation their own local revenues would dwindle as the federal treasury grew. Galt appreciated that their fears were justified, but he was also convinced that the federal government would require unlimited powers of taxation if his cherished plans of national development were to be carried out. He proposed a compromise scheme, the idea of debt allowance, under which the federal government would assume the provincial debts reckoned on a per capita basis. If the actual debt of a province exceeded its allowance, then that province would pay interest at the rate of 5 per cent on the excess to the federal government. If, on the other hand, a province was fortunate enough to have an actual debt which was less than the allowance, then the federal government would pay interest on the credit balance to the province. In practical terms, Galt's plan of debt allowance meant that Canada, which was heavily in debt, would be penalized, while the Maritime provinces, in a sounder financial position, would benefit by the scheme. Recognizing the statesmanship of Galt's proposals, the Maritime representatives dropped their objections to the financial arrangements of union. (*Ibid.*, pp. 169-71, 179-80).

were to remain in the possession of the provinces, while the chief public works were to be transferred to the federal government.

The question of the control of the schools had long been a vexed one. Under a scheme which gave the control of education to each province, the Roman Catholic majority in Lower Canada had no ground to fear that their views would not be respected. The Protestant minority, however, were in a different position, and Galt, as the special representative of this group, was anxious to have their rights and privileges safeguarded beyond dispute. Accordingly a resolution was included giving the provinces control of "education, saving the rights and privileges which the Protestant or Catholic minority in both Canadas may possess as to their denominational schools at the time when the Constitutional Act goes into operation."

The construction of the Intercolonial by the federal government was an essential condition of the Lower Provinces' acceptance of the union, and was agreed upon without demur. With still more ambitious grasp, the resolutions of the Conference provided not merely for the future admission of the North-West Territories and Pacific provinces, but for improvement of the communications with the West at the earliest possible period that the finances would permit.

The conclusions reached in this momentous three weeks' conference were changed in minor details later, but in substance are the basis of Confederation to this day. It is, therefore, worth while to note at this juncture how closely they correspond to the draft drawn by Galt eight years earlier, at a time when no other public man had entered upon the question of the details of the terms of federation, and at a time before the Civil War had made clear to all men the need of giving a greater measure of power to the federal government. When, further, it is borne in mind that after the second day, on the motion of the Newfoundland representative, Mr. Shea, the resolutions moved were prepared in advance by a committee composed of the delegates from Canada, it will be apparent that Galt's contributions to the all important questions of practical detail were as significant as his share in urging the general policy of a federal union.

GALT'S DRAFT, 1858	THE QUEBEC RESOLUTION OF 1864
1. *A federal rather than a legislative Union.*	1. *Adopted.*
2. *The Confederation does not profess to be derived from the people; the constitution is provided by the imperial parliament, "thus affording the means of remedying any defect, which is now practically impossible under the American constitution."*	2. *So determined.*
3. *The Federal government to be composed of a Governor-General or Viceroy, appointed by the Queen, an Upper House or Senate elected on a territorial basis, and a House of Assembly elected on the basis of population; the Executive to be composed of ministers responsible to the legislature.*	3. *Adopted, except for making the Senate a nominated rather than an elected body.*
4. *The Federal Government to have control over Customs, Excise, and all trade questions, Postal Service, Militia, Banking, Currency, Weights and Measures, Bankruptcy, Public Works of a National Character, Harbours and Lighthouses, Fisheries, Public Lands, Public Debt, and unincorporated territories.*	4. *All specifically assigned to the Federal Government, save Public Lands.*
5. *It will form a subject for mature deliberation whether the powers of the Federal Government should be con-*	5. *The second alternative adopted.*

*fined to the points named,
or should be extended to all
matters not specially en-
trusted to the local legislatures.*

6. *The constitution of a federal
Court of Appeal.*

6. *Adopted.*

7. *Net revenue from the
Crown Lands in each pro-
vince to be the exclusive
property of that province,
except in the case of the
territories.*

7. *The Crown Lands them-
selves so assigned.*

8. *The general revenue, having first been charged with
the expense of collection
and civil government, to be
subject to the payment of
interest on the public debts
of the Confederation, constituted from the existing
obligations of each, and the
surplus to be divided among
the provinces according to
population. For a limited
time a fixed contribution
might be made from the
general revenue for educational and judicial purposes.
"By the proposed distribution of the revenue each
province would have a
direct pecuniary interest in
the preservation of the
authority of the Federal
Government."*

8. *The general principle of
federal subsidies adopted,
on the basis of a fixed contribution rather than "distribution of surplus revenues." The debts of the
provinces assumed by the
Federal Government, with
detailed adjustments.*

In the concluding words of Galt's letter to Sir E. B. Lytton
in 1858, his draft foreshadows with remarkable prescience the
determination of the future Fathers of Confederation to frame
a constitution which "would possess greater inherent strength

than that of the United States, and would combine the advantage of the unity, for general purposes, of a legislative union,
with so much of the Federation principle as would join all the
benefits of local government and legislation upon questions of
provincial interest."

It took less than three weeks to draft the plan of federation,
but it was to take nearly three years to secure its adoption. The
members of the Conference had become thoroughly convinced
of the need and the feasibility of the proposal, but it was still
a question whether it would commend itself to the varied
interests of the five provinces.

In Canada, sentiment soon proved overwhelmingly in
favour. The strongest leaders of both parties were united in its
advocacy, and the constitutional agitation of the past ten years
had prepared men's minds for sweeping change. A series of
banquets and public meetings addressed by the leading delegates gave opportunity immediately after adjournment to put
the case before the people, and the response of press and public
soon showed that the leaders had rightly judged the public
temper. Among the more notable of these addresses was that
given by Galt to a meeting of his constituents in Sherbrooke, on
November 23, 1864. It was a particularly clear and comprehensive summary of the proposed changes, with special reference to the position both of the French-speaking and of the
English-speaking citizens of Lower Canada under the federal
system. The address was widely circulated in pamphlet form,
and contributed materially to a sympathetic understanding of
the union plan.

No time was lost in bringing the issue before the Canadian
legislature. The debate began immediately after the opening
of the 1865 session, in February, and continued into March.
The discussion rose to the level of the high occasion. There was,
inevitably, much turgid rhetoric, much repetition of familiar
points, much evident cramming of historical lore, but particularly in the speeches of eight or ten of the leading men, the
practical grasp, the wide vision, the high courage displayed gave
splendid promise for the future of the new nation.

On the government side, the most notable speeches were
those of Macdonald, Cartier, Brown, McGee and Galt. John
A. Macdonald, in presenting the resolutions, gave a lucid
analysis of the distinctive features of the plan. G. E. Cartier,
who, as usual, was somewhat personal and discursive, devoted

his attention mainly to the effect upon Lower Canada. George Brown made one of his most elaborate speeches, covering the main advantages both negative and positive, of the change, and seeking to prove its consistency with his earlier policy. D'Arcy McGee carried off the palm for eloquence, emphasizing, perhaps overmuch, the danger from the United States as a motive compelling union. A. T. Galt, as befitted the Finance Minister, stressed chiefly the commercial advantages to be gained and expounded the financial provisions of the plan. All declared that the time for union was now or never, and all insisted that the resolutions adopted by the Quebec Conference were of the nature of a treaty, not to be altered by any single province.

The opposition to the proposals came from many quarters and many motives. Sandfield Macdonald, like his fellow-clansman in preferring personal tactics to constitutional change, consistently urged a continuance of the old system, only with better men in charge. Luther Holton attacked the haste and sketchiness of the proposals. A. A. Dorion opposed alike the nominated Senate, the pledge to build the Intercolonial, and the concentration of power in the hands of the federal cabinet, and considered the whole proposal premature. Joly de Lotbinière feared that French-Canadian nationality would be swamped. John Hilliard Cameron, while supporting the proposals, urged, in vain, that they should be submitted to the people through a general election. But it was left for Christopher Dunkin to make the most powerful attack upon the Confederation scheme. That it was a jumbled compromise framed to catch every political and sectional interest, that it was an impossible combination of republican and monarchical principles, that the Senate proposed was ridiculously the worst that could have been devised, that in default of adequate provision in the Senate for guarding federal interests the cabinet would perforce become a body representing all the different sections and creeds, and hence prove unwieldy, that the division of legislative and judicial powers between the federal and the provincial authorities was confused and illogical, that the opening up of railway communication with east and west would entail bankrupting outlays, that the provincial subsidy device would create among the local governments "a calf-like appetite for milking this one most magnificent government cow," and that, as an Englishman, he must deprecate any scheme which was a sure step toward independence and a step away from imperial union – these were only the more notable points in one of the most remarkable speeches ever delivered in any parliamentary gathering. Many of the criticisms of the methods adopted were well taken, many of the prophecies of evil have been borne out by time, but the fact remained that the critics of the plan could give no other solution of the difficulties that faced the province. Fear could not prevail against hope. The resolutions were carried in the Legislative Council by 45 to 15, and in the Assembly by 91 to 33; in both Houses there was a favourable majority among both the Upper and the Lower Canadian members.

So far as the Canadas were concerned, all was well. But not so in the provinces down by the sea. Their representatives at the Conference had returned after their oratorical pilgrimage through the cities of Canada to find a coolness and suspicion which soon hardened into fierce hostility. Fear of Canadian extravagance, of high tariffs and higher debts, of the faction fights whose virulence had been noised abroad, lack of the stimulus which political deadlock had given in Canada, distrust of the unknown, and personal rivalries contributed to rouse wide opposition. In New Brunswick the Tilley government, appealing to the country on a confederation platform, was overwhelmingly defeated in the same month that the Canadian Parliament endorsed the proposals. Newfoundland and Prince Edward Island definitely drew back. In Nova Scotia, opposition developed among businessmen who had hitherto taken little part in politics, and when in addition Joseph Howe, whether from conviction or from personal pique, lent their movement his powerful aid, even Tupper was forced to hesitate. But not for long. A year later the tide turned in New Brunswick; the pressure of the Colonial Office, the reviving fear of Fenian raids, Canadian campaign fund contributions, and the blunders of the anti-Confederate government, combined to put Tilley again in power, pledged to carry out the original agreement. Nearly at the same time, in April, 1866, Tupper carried a motion in the same direction through the Nova Scotia legislature, and thus the ground was cleared for furthur action.

The situation in 1865 was so grave, in the opinion of the Canadian ministers, as to necessitate a conference with the imperial government. Confederation had been jeopardized by the result of the New Brunswick elections, and it was essential to endeavour to have the influence of the British government brought to bear in its favour. The United States had now given formal notice of its intention to abrogate the Reciprocity

Treaty in March, 1866. The military situation was again causing alarm. The border raids had revived United States hostility, and the institution of a passport system and a proposal to end the Rush-Bagot convention were the first fruits of this attitude. Many feared armed attack, now that the triumph of the North had set millions of trained men free, and, with more justification, the designs of Fenian plotters caused alarm. It was advisable, therefore, to concert measures for defence. Finally, the programme of annexing the North-West Territory and of overriding or settling the claims of the Hudson's Bay Company called for consultation. It was, therefore, decided to send a delegation consisting of Macdonald, Cartier, Brown and Galt to discuss all these matters with the British cabinet.

Cartier and Galt sailed a fortnight earlier than Macdonald and Brown, and had the negotiations well under way when the others arrived, the first week in May. Palmerston was still in power, with Cardwell Secretary for the Colonies and Gladstone at the Exchequer. A special committee of the cabinet was named to confer with the Canadian delegates, consisting of the Duke of Somerset, Earl de Grey and Ripon, Mr. Gladstone and Mr. Cardwell, but most of the preliminary discussion was with Mr. Cardwell alone.

As usual, the social phase of the negotiations was very marked, and Galt's letters to his wife gave many evidences of the increased attention Canada was now deemed to warrant, as well as throwing some interesting sidelights on the life of London half a century ago.

London, 2nd April, 1865.

On Tuesday, Cartier and I commenced operations. We saw a great number of people, and generally gathered from them that we had a most difficult task before us. We did not see Mr. Cardwell, the Colonial Secretary, as he was detained at a Cabinet Council. His private secretary, however, called and gave us an appointment at his own house, yesterday morning, and we were with him for upwards of two hours. It was only a preliminary conversation, but we were both pleased with his general tone. One thing he assured us of, that the Imperial Government were prepared to give us their full and hearty support in the Confederation. We are to see him again to-day and he goes with us to Lord de Grey, the Secretary at War, and we shall meet the Duke of Cambridge either then or to-morrow. We are both quite satisfied that it has been most useful our coming in advance of our Colleagues, as we have thus established the basis of negotiations in our own way. It is particularly satisfactory to me on my account. Our division of labor is that Cartier takes up the Confederation question, and I take the Defence. . . .

> London, 4th May, 1865.

Macdonald and Brown have arrived and we are holding daily interviews. I cannot yet say anything as to the result. I have never been sanguine, and am not so now, though public opinion is generally favorable. Still, I doubt whether the people are prepared for the magnitude of the requirements.

We are full of invitations and from distinguished people. Cartier and I having arrived first have rather got the advantage of the others, as our arrival was chronicled in the press, and theirs was not. We went last night to two "At Homes" – the Marchioness of Salisbury's and the Countess of Waldegrave's. They were brilliant affairs and crowded with the nobility. We went at 11 p.m., spent about three-quarters of an hour at Lady Salisbury's and about half an hour at Lady Waldegrave's. There were many beautiful women and of course extremely rich dresses. I met Sir Edward Lytton, who was very glad to see us, also Lord Lyons, Sir John Polkington, Lord Robert Cecil, Marquis of Salisbury, Lord Houghton, and a number of other well-known men. I did not expect to like it, but was agreeably disappointed. Mr. Elliott of the Colonial Office, who has always been very civil to me, went through the rooms with us and introduced us to all whom he thought we would like to meet. At Lady Salisbury's we met the Conservatives, and at Lady Waldegrave's the Liberals, so we saw both sides.

We are going to an "At Home" at the Countess of Stanhope's. We dine with Lord Abinger to-morrow at the Political Economy Club, and on other days with Mr. Cardwell, Lord de Grey, Lady Waldegrave, Lord Elcho, Sir John Polkington and several other great people. We are decidedly in the "haut monde" at present, but I confess I would rather mix with my own class. It shows, however, that politics form the only short cut from the middle to the upper ranks. No amount of wealth would secure the attention we receive, and these attentions are given not to us but to our offices, and in compliment to our people. Out of office these people would not bother their heads about one of us and I should not, therefore, go to their homes if it were not that in going I serve the object of my visit. Still it

is no doubt pleasant to be the recipient of marks of attention.
Dr. Hellmuth called a day or two ago. He was very well and
wanted me to attend and speak at the public meeting of the
Colonial Church Society on Thursday, which I have agreed to
do. There will be a number of the Bishops and Clergy present,
and I shall try to interest them in our progress. I will send you
the report.

We are going to dine with the Goldsmiths Company next
week, it will be a great banquet.

A. T. G.

London, 17th May, 1865.

On Monday I went to the play and was much pleased. But
the great event of Monday was our reception at Court. The
morning was spent partly in arranging our uniforms. I had sent
mine to the tailor's, to put it completely en règle, as you know
the gold lace was not the correct width, and I had also to get
the knee breeches, etc.

We all looked very grand. Our carriages were ordered at
half-past two, and we reached the Palace at a quarter to three.
We were ushered upstairs into a picture gallery, where we found
a crowd of magnificently dressed ladies and men in uniform, all
gorgeous and beyond my powers of description. Mr. Cardwell
had us in charge. We met a good many people we knew, the
Ministers of State and people we have met at dinner.

The Court, as it is termed, is a recent innovation of the
Queen's to relieve her of the fatigue of the Drawing-room, when
a vast number come. At a Court only those attend who are
invited, and it is therefore a great distinction. Before the general
reception began, the Queen ordered that we should be presented
by Mr. Cardwell, as belonging to the Diplomatic circle, and that
we should have the honour of kissing hands. Accordingly when
the door opened, we were ushered in, preceded by Mr. Cardwell, in the order of our seniority, Macdonald, Cartier, Brown
and myself. The ceremony was to bow, to go down on the right
knee (a matter involving, in my own case, a slight mental doubt
as to the tenacity of my breeches), the left arm is then advanced
a little, and the Queen laid her hand upon it, which I touched
slightly with my lips. I then rose, bowed again, and moved off
to the left of the Court circle, which consisted of the Princesses
Helena, Louise, May of Cambridge, the Prince of Wales, and
the ladies and gentlemen in attendance. The Prince of Wales
kindly recognized us by bowing and smiling. The Princess of

Wales was not present. The position assigned to us was that of honour next the Court Circle. The other presentations took place, and the papers I send you will give you the names. The dresses and jewelry of the ladies were most magnificent. They all wore trains, beautiful silk and lace. I was much amused to see how the trains were gathered up. An old gentleman in a grand uniform stood a little to one side next us, and as each lady passed on he picked up her train with great dexterity and placed it over her left arm, and pointed where she was to go. One old lady got slightly embarrassed with her train by turning round the wrong way. I endeavoured, but without much success, to restore her train to her arm, and she went down the room like a ship in distress. The whole affair did not occupy more than half an hour.

The Queen looked very well, but little changed. She was dressed in black, with a long white veil attached to the back of her head. No ornaments, except a heavy pearl necklace. Many of the ladies wore magnificent diamonds and pearls. The Princesses wore white, very plain. They looked amiable, kind girls, especially Helena. The Prince looked very well, and has improved greatly since he was in Canada. The whole scene was a most brilliant one.

. . . We all felt we had been treated with great distinction. Indeed our whole reception in England proves how important our mission is considered. We are treated quite as if we were ambassadors and not as mere Colonists *as we have always been called.*

. . . I dare say you will think that our business is not getting on very well with all this party going, but we are obliged to wait until the Defence Commission has reported, which will be to-day or to-morrow. We open our formal official communication on Friday, and hope a few days will settle things.

A. T. G.

London, 19th May, 1865.

We dined on Sunday with Sir Edward Lytton, and met some literary people, among others Dickens, with whom I had a good deal of conversation. On leaving we went to the Cosmopolitan Club, where I met Mr. Kingslake, the author of Eothen. *On Saturday Mr. Brydges and I went to Windsor and had a very pleasant drive through the Park, enjoying it very much. On Monday Cartier and I dined with Mr. Henry Jackson, and met several of the young literary men of the day. Yesterday, Tues-*

day, we dined with Mr. Cardwell, and met Mr. Gladstone, the Duke of Argyle, Lord de Grey, and Sir R. Palmer, the Attorney-General. It was a purely political dinner, none but members of the Government were present. We therefore had some conversation on our business, but not much.

Thursday, 11th May.

I resume my pen to tell you of our movements last night. We first dined at the Goldsmiths' Hall, the most magnificent display of plate I ever saw. We then drove home, dressed, and went to Lady Waldegrave's At Home, where there was a great crush. We did not stay long, but went on to the Duchess of Wellington's. The ball was, as you may suppose, a very grand affair. After being presented to the Duchess we walked through the rooms, looked at the company and, being rather tired, went home. It is very well to see these places, but it is certainly no great enjoyment for strangers. All was extremely gay and bright. The Duchess has been a very fine woman, but looks faded and sad; she was painted a good deal. We did not see the Duke.

To-day I have been in the city attending the Land Company's annual meeting. I gave them a short account of matters in Canada, and some good advice which I think they will follow. They passed a vote offering me a Dinner, but I do not think it will be in my power to accept. I am to meet the Directors next week.

A. T. G.

London, 25th May, 1865.

Our business here proceeds slowly, and I much fear is going to become very involved. It seems to me as if the Statesmen of England had lost many of the high qualities which used to distinguish them, they seem so timid and hesitating, but at the same time I must admit that the question is surrounded with difficulties. We have had two formal meetings with the Committee of the Cabinet, and we have another to-day which will be very important. The issue is fortunately in the hands of God, who will surely overrule it for good, but I much doubt that serious changes will be necessary in our condition in Canada.

I do not quite like the very marked attention we have received. They have treated us too much as ambassadors and on an equality, and I think it bodes no good, however flattering it may be.

On Monday I dined with Mr. Betts, and went in the evening

to a Concert at the Palace, to which we had the honour of an invitation. It was a very grand affair, the Prince and Princess of Wales and all the foreign Ambassadors and elite of the land. There was a light supper afterwards. I enclose you the carte of the music.

Yesterday we were invited to accompany the Prince to inspect the Great Eastern and Atlantic Cable. We left town at twelve and returned at six, afterwards dining at Mr. Cardwell's (in full dress).

To-day we are invited to the Duke of Cambridge's, but I have sent an apology, not being inclined for festivities, and being very anxious about our business. You must say nothing about it to anyone, but I have the conviction we shall effect nothing satisfactory to our own people. It is very grievous to see half a continent slipping away from the grasp of England with scarcely an effort to hold it. If the worst comes to the worst we shall at any rate be relieved from all danger of war, as the United States will not quarrel with us.

A. T. G.

London, 30th May, 1865.

We had our first official *interview yesterday, and think we have made a good impression. The Cabinet meets to-day to consider the matter, and we may fairly expect that we shall make progress next week.*

Our festivities continue. We dined yesterday with the Prince and Princess of Wales. We were most graciously received, the party was really a Canadian one, the Prince having invited all of his Canadian suite whom he could get. When the party had assembled, the Prince and Princess came in, and we all formed in line and bowed as they went into the dining room. The dinner was of course good, and I have the bill of fare for you. Music (Canadian quadrilles being part) during the whole dinner. After dinner we went into the drawing room, when the Prince presented us each in turn to the Princess, with whom we had a little conversation. She is really extremely pretty, and has the nicest possible foreign accent. She told me she had a horror of the sea, and doubted whether anything could tempt her across the Atlantic, and some little remarks of that kind. After those who had ladies with them had gone, the Prince desired us to go with him to smoke, and we were shown into a handsome Turkish divan, where we had cigars, wine and seltzer water. The Prince put on his dressing gown, to a great extent dropped ceremony,

*and kept us with him upwards of two hours. We left at half-past
one. I had the opportunity of mentioning old Captain Felton
and Mrs. Felton to him and told him how devoted were their
memories of his kindness. He seemed very much pleased, and
desired me to express to them how pleased he was to hear of
their welfare. This of course I shall do on my return, but I
prefer giving you the opportunity of making the old people
happy by calling yourself and telling them, which I hope you
will do. I have got one of his cigars, which he told me had been
sent to him by the King of Portugal; I shall smoke it when I get
home.*

*It seems odd to be visiting on such comparatively easy
terms our future King and Queen, and I know it is a very high
distinction, the highest, I suppose, they can offer us. When we
left the Prince said he must see us again before we went home.*

*We attended the Levee to-day, and were honoured by
having what is called the "Entree," that is, we came in with the
Foreign Ambassadors, and formed part of the Court circle,
going and coming by a separate entrance. And we have now
invitations to the Palace, by command of the Queen, for a
musical party on Monday. We are also to dine with the Duke of
Cambridge. From all we can see we have got the Court party on
our side, and this will be of the greatest use.*

A. T. G.

London, 1st June, 1865.

*Since I wrote last I may mention our doings in the fashion-
able world. We dined on Monday with Col. Jervois, who has
been a warm friend to our mission, indeed, by the way, I may
say we have no stronger ally than the Duke of Cambridge, and
all the Army men. We did not go out in the evening. On Tuesday
we had a magnificent entertainment at Richmond, by Sir Morton
and Lady Peto, 150 ladies and gentlemen, and flowers and music
"à discretion." He had invited all our Railway friends, and we
had a charming evening. Mr. and Mrs. Brassey drove me back
to town.*

*Yesterday was the ever memorable "Derby Day." We had
made up a party of eleven including Bischoff, Grant (whom you
may recollect as G.T.R. secretary), Reynolds (whom you do not
know), Brydges, Russell of the London* Times, *and ourselves
with McGee. We had a basket of lunch and wines from Fortnam
and Mason, and two carriages with postillions. We breakfasted
at eight and started a little after nine. The day was all we could*

wish, but a great deal of dust. We drove down in the midst of a mass of vehicles of all kinds, indulging in good humoured jokes on all sides. We reached the Downs at noon, and got our carriages into a very good place, inside of the course. After settling our arrangements and washing down the dust with sherry and seltzer water we went on a peregrination through the crowd, which thickened every moment.

Macdonald and I went with Russell, who knew every place, and he had got us invited to a very "swell" place close to the winning post. This was a shed and stand erected by a Mr. Todd Heatly, the wine merchant, who supplies most of the Army messes and many of the Clubs and nobility. He opens it on the Derby Day to his friends, who are all the nobility. He provided a magnificent lunch, turtle soup and champagne cup. You would have been horrified to see the champagne go, it was emptied into two large barrels, holding seventy dozen each!! and by a little arrangement of pipes there was a champagne fountain flowing in the middle of the shed. Besides the turtle, there were all the delicacies and substantials of the season. After getting a little preliminary lunch, we walked back to our carriages, and you can scarcely imagine the difficulty we had in finding them, the mass of vehicles was so dense. There we met our own party again, and stayed about an hour, returning to Todd Heatly's to see the race run. Then we had our real lunch, with a little champagne, and then went on the stand, which was not at all crowded, as he evidently in this respect was careful to make his guests comfortable. We had a magnificent view of the course, and could see the horses all the way round. It was really a wonderful sight to see the immense mass of people, and we especially admired the quiet, firm way in which the police controlled them. After nine false starts, the horses got away, and a roar from the multitude announced the fact to those who had not seen it. Immense excitement in every face, hope and fear alternating as the two minutes passed away, which won or lost a million sterling to those who witnessed it. We catch a glimpse of the bright colors of the thirty jockeys flashing along the distant course, and, almost as it were in an instant, we see them sweep round the distant corner and enter the broad, straight course which leads to the winning post. Shouts rise on every side that this or that horse wins. We all watch their approach with eager eyes, not yet sure of the result, till at last one horse singles himself out from the others, and rushes past, while the shouts from two hundred thousand throats proclaim that the French

*horse has won. The excitement becomes tremendous, the vast
crowd rushes into the course, and for full three-quarters of a
mile, nothing but a mass of human faces is seen. I never saw
anything approaching it in actual sublimity. I am satisfied there
were more than a quarter of a million of people rushing together, all eager, excited, gesticulating, shouting, pushing, fighting, and quite uncontrolled and uncontrollable. As soon as it
was known which horse had won, things subsided again, people
cooled, those like ourselves who had no pecuniary interest in the
race, went off to seek more lunch, more champagne, and other
fun, while the fortunates and unfortunates were in all the stages
from perfect bliss to utter despair. Decidedly the race for the
Derby is* an institution.

*The great interest of the day being over, we went to see the
sights of the course, gypsies, music, mountebanks, games of all
kinds, menageries of savage animals, and shows of Irishmen
disguised as savage Indians, and all the rest of the amusements,
till it became time to discuss the great question of getting out of
the crowd home. We were rather lucky in the position we had
chosen, and after spending half an hour in getting ready and
another half hour in hunting up stray members of our party, we
started all merry, but not in the least degree more.*

*The Road, as the return to London is called, is one of the
great celebrities of the Derby, and is in fact the Saturnalia of the
lower classes, who discharge all sorts of wit, humor, and abuse,
with occasionally something broader, at all and sundry. This is
quite understood by everyone, and all go prepared for whatever
may betide. Picture us, then, first providing ourselves with tin
tubes and sundry bags of peas, little wooden dolls, pincushions
filled with bran, then putting on our greatcoats buttoned to the
throats, veils over our hats and faces if need be, cigars lighted,
all as merry as possible and prepared to enjoy the fun of The
Road.*

*I was lucky enough to be in the carriage with Russell and
John A., both masters in the art of "chaffing," and I can assure
you our carriage kept up its reputation all the way to town,
being greeted alternately with cheers and volleys of peas, to
which we made suitable rejoinders. We got blocked for an hour
at a railway bridge, where Russell gained immense applause by
getting on top of the seat, and making an election speech.*

*Every conceivable trap was on the road from the coster
monger's donkey cart to the aristocratic four-in-hand. We were
constantly passing broken down vehicles; no compassion or*

mercy was shown to the unfortunates, who were at once bundled out of the way to shift how they best could. We had good horses and stout carriages and met with no accident, but it took us five hours to get home, sixteen miles, and tired and glad we were to reach our hotel, and pretty looking objects we were, covered with dust and plentifully pelted with flour, making us look like millers.

Altogether it was a wonderful thing from beginning to end, and I would not have missed it for a good deal, though I do not know I should do it again. I send you the account in the Times, *but I hope you will like my own description better.*

A. T. G.

London, 3rd June, 1865.

I wrote you a very long letter by last Canadian mail with account of the Derby. I have therefore only now to chronicle the events of two days. First, as regards our business, it is approaching a termination, which I think will in some respects cause disappointment, but on the whole commends itself to my judgment. I may now say with some degree of confidence that I shall sail on the 17th, for New York.

The great social event since I wrote was our dinner yesterday with the Duke and Duchess d'Aumale. We met the Prince de Joinville, the Count de Paris and the Countess, the Prince de Condé and other distinguished people. Four Princes at once – and two Princesses. Nothing could be kinder or more considerate than the conduct of the whole party, and no one would have imagined that they were other than ordinary ladies and gentlemen.

A. T. G.

The conclusions reached were more satisfactory than some of Galt's forebodings had indicated. As to Confederation, the imperial authorities agreed that without any thought of coercion, they would use every legitimate means to secure the early assent of the Maritime Provinces. The new British Minister at Washington, Sir Frederick Bruce, was to be instructed to urge renewal of the Reciprocity Treaty, acting in concert with the Canadian government. An agreement was reached to make over to Canada all the British territory east of the Rockies and north of the United States, subject to such compensation to the Hudson's Bay Company as should later be found warranted. The settlement of the defence question was the crux of the whole discussion. In the past session it had repeatedly been debated in the British Parliament. The ending of the Civil War, the friction which still existed between Britain and the States, and the publication of a report by Colonel Jervois which made clear the utter defencelessness of Canada in case of war, kept the issue alive. The discussion was less acrimonious than in previous years, but though expressions of willingness to attempt to defend Canada against invasion were more frequent, the feeling that it could not be defended was still dominant. It was recognized that the greater part of the frontier could not be defended, but in order to provide rallying-points for the troops the British government now proposed to spend £50,000 a year on fortifying Quebec, leaving it to the province to fortify Montreal and the communications westward.

In the preliminary interviews with the Colonial Secretary, Galt made clear the attitude of the Canadian ministers. They had been prepared to assent to the proposal of the British government to postpone the settlement of the relative burdens of defence until after Confederation, but the emergency created by the border raids and the possibility, owing to New Brunswick's attitude, of some delay in achieving Confederation, had made them determine to seek an earlier settlement. They were quite prepared to admit that Canada might now assume a larger share of responsibility for her own defence: "the desire and belief of Canada was, in seeking a union, not in any way to weaken the connection with the Mother Country, but rather to remove those causes which now afforded many parties in England arguments for asserting that the connection was mutually disadvantageous." Whether the intentions of the United States were amicable or not, it was felt safer to make adequate preparations which might prove unnecessary rather than run the risk of frightful calamity. In this belief, they doubted whether the defensive works suggested by Colonel Jervois would meet the situation adequately; before they were completed, war would have blown over or have been fought through. Increase of the regular forces, calling out the militia, preparation of supplies of munitions, defence for the inland waters, and a change in the character of the squadrons on the Atlantic coast in view of American ironclad progress, were among the measures suggested. As to the expense, he suggested that the extra cost of maintaining the regular forces in Canada, the expenditure on the militia, fortifications and munitions would be borne equally by Canada and by Great Britain. The battlefield would be local but the cause was imperial. In the opinion of the government, further, the construction of the Intercolonial and the improvement of the canals were essentially works of military defence, but in view of the fact that they also had a commercial purpose, the expense should be borne wholly by the province.

In the formal discussion between the committees of the two cabinets in the following month, a plan for the defence of Canada, prepared by a special Defence Commission, was taken as the basis of arrangement. The attitude of the Canadian delegates, and the agreement reached, may most concisely be quoted from their official report:

We expressed the earnest wish of the people of Canada to perpetuate the happy existing connection with Great Britain, and their entire willingness to contribute to the defence of the Empire their full quota, according to their ability of men and money. But we pointed out that if war should ever unhappily arise between England and the United States, it could only be an Imperial war, on Imperial grounds – that our country alone would be exposed to the horrors of invasion – and that our exposed position, far from entailing on us unusual burdens, should on the contrary secure for us the special and generous consideration of the Imperial Government. We explained, moreover, that though Canada continued to progress steadily and rapidly, it was a vast country, sparsely populated – that the difficulties of first settlement were hardly yet overcome – that the profits of our annual industry were to be found not in floating wealth, but in the increased value of our farms and mines – and that, at this moment especially from the failure of successive crops, the effects of the American civil war on our commercial relations, and the feeling of insecurity as to our position, (greatly aggravated by statements of the defenceless-ness of the country in the British Parliament, and by portions of the British press) – Canada was laboring under a temporary but serious depression. We pointed out that, while fully recognizing the necessity, and prepared to provide for such a system of defence as would restore confidence in our future at home and abroad, the best ultimate defence for British America was to be found in the increase of her population as rapidly as possible, and the husbanding of our resources to that end; and without claiming it as a right, we ventured to suggest that, by enabling us to throw open the north-western territories to free settlement, and by aiding us in enlarging our canals and prosecuting internal

productive works, and by promoting an extensive plan of emi-
gration from Europe into unsettled portions of our domain –
permanent security would be more quickly and surely and
economically secured than by any other means. We did not fail
to point out how this might be done without cost or risk to the
British exchequer, and how greatly it would lighten the new
burden of defence proposed to be assumed at a moment of
depression by the people of Canada.

Much discussion ensued on all these points, and the result
arrived at was, that if the people of Canada undertook the
works of defence at and west of Montreal, and agreed to expend
in training their militia, until the union of all the Provinces was
determined, a sum not less than is now expended annually for
that service, Her Majesty's Government would complete the
fortifications at Quebec, provide the whole armament for all the
works, guarantee a loan for the sum necessary to construct the
works undertaken by Canada, and, in the event of war, under-
take the defence of every portion of Canada with all the
resources of the Empire.

The conclusions reached on the defence question were
alone sufficiently important to warrant the Conference. The
discussions were much more amicable than in 1862; Canadian
authorities were now willing to recognize more freely their
responsibilities, while the British on their part had come to
recognize that if the danger was Canada's the quarrel was theirs.
In addition, as Galt's private letters note, the widespread feeling
in England that Confederation was merely a prelude to separation smoothed the path; why dispute about the terms of a partnership that was soon to end? The discussion is notable, also,
for the first appearance of the argument that the railway and
general development of the country should be counted as a
contribution to military preparedness – an argument which long
did duty in Canadian discussion, which later fell into some
disrepute and which received a new endorsement from the
lessons of the great European war.

When the ministers returned to Canada late in June, the
most pressing question that awaited them was not war with the
United States, but trade with that country. They had hoped
against hope that Washington would take no step to bring the
reciprocity agreement to an end. Now that hope was shattered,
and scarcely nine months remained before the treaty would

expire. As a preliminary step, Galt and Howland made a visit to Washington in July to confer with the new British ambassador, Sir Frederick Bruce.* They came back with the conviction that it would be no easy task to secure the continuance of the agreement. Resentment of war policy, protectionist feeling, revenue needs, all had united Congress in a resolution to put up the bars against the provinces.

Opinion in Canada was unanimous as to the benefits reciprocity had brought, and people and government alike were willing to go great lengths to preserve these benefits. Not all lengths, however, for they believed that the United States had reaped equal advantage, and they would prefer to look elsewhere if Washington's terms proved exorbitant. At this juncture the British authorities, on representations of Canada and of Nova Scotia as to the desirability of consulting them in any negotiations to renew the treaty, suggested a means by which the scattered provinces could co-operate alike in seeking an arrangement with the United States, and, in default of this, in seeking some other outlet for trade. In accordance with this suggestion, a Confederate Council on Commercial Treaties, containing delegates from all the provinces, and presided over by the Governor-General, was organized in August, 1865. Galt and Brown represented Canada, Macdonald and Cartier attending as courtesy members, with Ritchie from Nova Scotia, Wilmot from New Brunswick, Shea from Newfoundland, and Pope from Prince Edward Island. The Council met in September, and drew up certain unanimous resolutions. They advocated seeking a renewal of the treaty with the United States, with any reasonable modifications; failing this, intercolonial trade should be extended, and efforts made to find markets in the West Indies and Latin America. It was also urged that an extension of the treaty should be sought to permit further negotiation, and that a committee of the Council should co-operate with the British ambassador if negotiations were opened.

Shortly after this meeting, Galt carried on a confidential correspondence with David A. Wells, then Commissioner of Inland Revenue at Washington, and a man much after his own heart in breadth of view and lucidity of expression. Wells was

* Galt had intended to go to Washington alone, but when Brown, who deeply distrusted Galt and was probably jealous of him, raised strenuous objections in cabinet, it was decided, "after a long and unpleasant debate," that Howland should accompany the Finance Minister. See J. M. S. Careless, *Brown of the Globe* (Toronto, 1963), II, 211-212.

much more inclined to liberal trade relations than were the interests dominant in Congress. He suggested that Galt should send him in confidence an outline of what Canada would be prepared to do. The cabinet, on considering the suggestion, deemed it more prudent to carry on the negotiations verbally, and authorized Galt to go to New York and if need be to Washington to sound the American authorities. Howland was prevented by other engagements from going, and Brown had just left on a mission to New Brunswick.

In several interviews in New York, Galt and Wells reached a wide measure of agreement. Wells wrote to the Secretary of the Treasury, [Hugh] McCulloch, recommending an extension of the treaty, pending negotiations, and urged Galt to see McCulloch personally. Galt accordingly went on to Washington, and after discussing the question with Sir Frederick Bruce, had several interviews with McCulloch, at the first of which Senator Morrill, the framer of the preposterously high tariff of 1864, was present. McCulloch made it clear that a renewal of the treaty was out of the question, and suggested that all essential ends could be secured by reciprocal legislation. Galt strongly combatted this view, urging the difficulty of inducing six separate legislatures to pass the required measures, and the impossibility of covering the fisheries and navigation matters except by treaty. McCulloch was immovable, however, and Secretary Seward took the same stand. "Mr. Seward," Galt reported to the Canadian cabinet, "in the most emphatic terms declared his belief that no new treaty could be carried, entering into explanations which cannot properly be made public as to why the government could not recommend it. He expressed himself in a very friendly manner toward Canada, and recommended that when the Committees of Congress were organized I should see the Chairmen of those on Finance." Galt reported these interviews to Bruce, who strongly concurred in the policy suggested.

Upon his return to Canada, Galt submitted to the cabinet, on December 18, a memorandum embodying his conclusions. He recommended that in case the United States continued to refuse to consider a treaty, reciprocal legislation should be adopted, and that the arrangement should include reciprocity in natural products, manufactures and shipping, subject to the same terms being given other countries as were given the United States, reciprocal navigation and coasting rights, canal enlargement, and assimilation of excise and customs duties on spirits and tobacco, which were easily smuggled. He suggested that in any case a temporary extension of the treaty should be sought. In the Council, Brown raised strong objections to these proposals. He attacked Galt for entering upon negotiations without his assent and without consulting the Maritime Provinces, declared that the concessions outlined were extravagant, and especially denounced the proposal for reciprocal legislation which would leave Canada dependent from year to year on the whim of Congress. To meet his wishes, Galt agreed to submit a second memorandum, emphasizing the need of extending the treaty until such time as the new federal parliament could act, and assuring the Maritime Provinces that the independent action of Canada did not arise from any intention to take a separate course but merely from the emergencies of the situation. He recommended that the negotiations at Washington should be continued, with Howland and himself as delegates. These proposals were adopted by the cabinet, with the sole but important exception, as will be noted later, of George Brown.

On January 1, 1866, Galt and Howland, accompanied by Henry of Nova Scotia and Smith of New Brunswick, went once more to Washington. They found the leaders of Congress much less open to reason than the administration officials. A farcical free list — millstones, rags, gypsum, firewood — high duties on all the other articles hitherto free, and free admission of the United States to the fishery privileges, were the cool proposals put forward. Under these circumstances there was nothing to do but to accept the plain hint that no agreement was wanted and to reject the offer. The delegates returned to Canada, where their course was everywhere approved, and on March 31 the treaty lapsed. Writing to Lord Monck, February 19, 1866, the British minister at Washington, Sir Frederick Bruce, singles out Galt's services: "Mr. Galt's knowledge, ability and fair spirit made a very favourable impression on the members of the Committee and the Secretary of the Treasury."

Reciprocity had brought prosperity; its rejection clinched Confederation. The provinces were perforce driven back upon themselves, forced to seek east and west a substitute for the trade north and south which high duties checked. "The provinces," declared George Brown some years later, "believed in the practical good sense of the United States people, especially with such a balance-sheet to look back upon as the results of the treaty of 1854 present. They assumed that there were matters existing in 1865-66 to trouble the spirit of American statesmen for the moment, and they waited patiently for the sober second thought which was very long in coming, but in the meantime Canada played a good neighbour's part, and incidentally served her own ends, by continuing to grant the United States most of the privileges which had been given under the treaty – free navigation and free goods, and, subject to a licence fee, access to the fisheries."

The endeavour to find an alternative market to the south came to little. A Commission was duly despatched to the West Indies, Brazil and Mexico, in January, 1866. It brought back much information, but little achievement. Confederation plans and Fenian raids crowded its proceedings off the stage, and it left little net results save to advance a step further the policy of Canadian self-government in fiscal relations. Galt's instructions to the Commissioners, according to Lord Monck, aroused the suspicions of the Foreign Office, "indicating an intention of negotiating with foreign countries independently of England." Writing from England, Monck suggested a modification of the instructions. Apparently, however, Galt stuck to his guns, but the Foreign Office also stuck to its weapons, for when the Commissioners sailed they found reason for believing, according to William McDougall, the chief of the Canadian delegation, that "the despatches which I carried were not the only despatches sent to those governments and to those colonies."

The other question of most importance in the Finance Minister's field was the determination of fiscal policy. It had been intended to postpone any radical revision of existing policy until after Confederation, but the abrogation of the Reciprocity Treaty made it necessary to face the question in the budget of June, 1866. The marked feature of the policy which Galt then announced, in one of his most lucid and forceful financial speeches, was a direct reversal of the former tendency toward protection. Many causes co-operated to this end. Canada, Galt declared, must now choose between two systems, the American and the English or European:

If we take the United States' system of protective duties, of protecting every branch of industry, we shall, to a certain extent, assimilate our system with theirs – a course which I do not think the people of this country would approve. (Hear, hear.) On the other hand, if we adopt what I have called the European system – because the policy of England is now being generally adopted by other European countries – if we adopt that system as

*opposed to the American system, then I think we shall stand in
the position of offering to the people and the capital, which for
various causes are now seeking new homes and employment, a
country possessing more advantages than any other on this
continent. I do not believe that the United States can continue
for any great length of time to absorb the redundant population
of Europe, subject as they are to very high rates of taxation. If
on the other hand we in Canada, or, I would rather say, in
British North America, are able to offer those people land of
equal fertility, and at least equal security for life and property,
and if at the same time we can show them that every article that
enters into ordinary consumption can be bought very much
cheaper here than in the United States, I think we may reasonably hope to be able to attract to our shores much of that
immigration which of recent years has swelled more than anything else the wealth and prosperity of the neighbouring Republic. We are entering on a new state of political existence. If there
is any prominent feature in the future we have designed for
ourselves, it is the establishment of a separate and distinct
nationality; and this can only be accomplished in one way. If
we are in every respect to copy the policy of our neighbours
across the line of 45, the natural course would be to become one
with them. But if, on the other hand, we believe, as we do all
believe, that the continent of North America is sufficiently
extensive for two nations, two empires, then it is time that,
taking lessons from those great authorities on political economy
who have shed light on the commercial transactions of Europe
during the last few years, we should endeavour so to adjust our
system that we may be able to invite immigrants here, telling
them that this is a better country, and governed by wiser
principles, than the country along our borders.*

At the same time, Galt continued, a reduction in duties would
meet the Lower Provinces half way, and would improve relations with the Mother Country. He therefore proposed to reduce
the duty on all manufactured goods in the 20 per cent schedule
to 15, and to make entirely free the semi-manufactured goods
formerly taxed 10 per cent. To meet the consequent loss in
revenue and to provide for the military expenditures occasioned
by the Fenian raids, excise duties, especially on spirits, were
materially raised. He continued:

*The policy of this country has been to make every article of
natural production imported into the Province free, and for*

revenue purposes to impose duties on all those manufactured
articles which it was thought were able to bear the burden,
affording at the same time an incidental amount of protection
to our own manufactures. Now, we propose to decrease the
duties on the largest class of manufactured goods entering the
country. . . .

It is in the belief that that reduction is one that will tend to
develop and enlarge our trade with England, that it will also
cheapen the cost of manufactured goods to every consumer in
the country, that it will benefit the farmer who buys largely of
iron and other goods to carry on farming operations, the manu-
facturer who is interested in obtaining cheaply the materials
that enter into his manufactures, and the mechanic whose
interests lie in obtaining cheaply the clothing and other goods
he consumes; it is in the belief that these advantages will all flow
from it, and that the people of the country will be greatly
relieved by taking some of the burden off the articles they
consume, that the Government venture to propose the reduction
to the Committee.

The policy thus outlined, and adopted without serious dissent from either side of the House, was to remain the basis of
the Canadian fiscal system for a decade, until, in fact, the
commercial depression of the seventies had persuaded the
people to try the "American" rather than the "European"
panacea.

The other important financial measure of this period was
the revival of the provincial note issue plan. Yearly deficits and
the failure of the Bank of Upper Canada, which had been the
government bank, had seriously embarrassed the finances of the
province, and it was found difficult to float debentures in
London even at 8 per cent. Galt, therefore, decided to revive his
1859 proposal, to give the province a monopoly or at least a
share of the note issue. His proposals were strongly fought by
the western banks, but upheld by the Bank of Montreal, then
under charge of the most striking figure in Canadian banking
history, E. H. King, and with which, since 1864, the government had kept its account. In the modified form which resulted
from parliamentary debate and financial pressure, the measure
as passed in 1866 provided for an issue of $5,000,000 provincial
notes, redeemable in specie, and secured partly by specie and
partly by government debentures. The banks were not required
to surrender their privilege of note issue, but inducements were

offered to them to do so, in the form of a remission of the tax on circulation and the payment of interest on the circulation withdrawn until the expiry of the bank charters. Only one bank, the Bank of Montreal, at once took advantage of the offer; it had over two millions locked up in advances to the government and in provincial debentures, and was delighted to be able to convert these credits into provincial notes. In addition, it received a commission of one per cent on all outstanding provincial notes for its services of issue and redemption. The other banks were induced to keep a quantity of the provincial legal tenders on hand, by pressure, in some cases, from the Bank of Montreal, which otherwise insisted on settlement in cash in every town. Gradually, the convenience of the provincial notes as reserves led all the banks to adopt them in large measure instead of specie reserves, and thus the practice which prevailed for nearly fifty years of leaving it mainly to the government to provide the gold reserves needed for the country became established. The process was not without friction; for the moment both Galt and King were highly unpopular in western banking circles, though this feeling soon wore away.

The coalition of 1864 had been formed in a spirit of exaltation above ordinary ambitions and political or personal rivalries. The spirit could not last forever, and soon the partnership between Brown and his former opponents showed signs of strain. When on July 30, 1865, Sir Etienne Taché died, full of years and honoured of all men, Lord Monck asked Macdonald to form a new government. Brown at once demurred, pointing out, with some force, that this meant a complete change of the conditions under which he had entered office. The government hitherto had been a coalition of three parties, each represented by an active leader, Macdonald, Cartier and himself, but acting under a chief who had the confidence of all. He contended that the proper course was to select a nominal head to succeed Sir Etienne Taché. In this course he was backed by his Reform colleagues, Howland and McDougall, and Macdonald perforce gave way. Sir Narcisse Belleau, a somewhat pompous mediocrity, was chosen to fill the post of premier, and the cabinet was patched up once more.

On the next occasion of dispute, Brown stood on much less favourable ground, and failed to carry even his Reform colleagues with him. It has been seen that he protested against Galt's policy with reference to Reciprocity. Doubtless the protest rested in great measure on honest conviction. He distrusted the method of reciprocal legislation as unstable and unsettling. Yet, as the discussion proved, he himself was willing to assent to this procedure if by no other means could agreement be effected. This was precisely Galt's position, but from his knowledge of Washington he appreciated better than Brown the difficulties in the way of effecting agreement on any other lines, or even on these lines. When, nine years later, and with Civil War memories and bitterness fading, Brown himself sought to arrange a reciprocity agreement at Washington, he came to understand more fully the difficulties which the rampant protectionism and provincial isolation of the United States and the lack of co-operation between the executive and the legislature put in the way of negotiations. He had not learned this lesson in 1865, and, accordingly, on December 19, he placed his resignation in the premier's hands. Mr. Howland, after consulting his party friends, decided to remain in office, and the vacant seat was filled by the appointment of Mr. Fergusson-Blair.

It was plain, however, that the Reciprocity policy was only the occasion, not the cause of Brown's retirement from the ministry. The real motive was the galling sense that his accession to it had only strengthened the position of his old rival, Macdonald, and that he had not himself secured the place either in the cabinet councils or in the country's attention which his abilities and his services warranted.[2] The old bitterness which had threatened to turn Upper Canada politics into a bear garden, remained on both sides. Nor was it toward Macdonald alone that Brown was antagonistic. He was intensely jealous of Galt as well, largely because to Galt fell the control of all the financial and commercial measures in which with some justice Brown believed he himself would have found his most fitting field of activity.

It was an unfortunate sequel to a splendid beginning. Yet from that beginning it had been inevitable. Brown by his offer of co-operation in June, 1864, had served his country well but his own ambitions ill. It was not merely that by meeting Upper Canada's demand for fair representations in general and mastery in local issues, Confederation robbed Brown of his most effective campaign cry. He was too true a patriot to let this weigh against his country's gain. His real grievance was that his magnanimous act had given his bitterest rival a new lease of political life. Under the old conditions, Macdonald had nearly reached the end of his tether. His policy of personal adjustment had been played out. Now, by adding new factors to the game, new provinces each presenting opportunities of personal alliance and party combinations, Brown had done his part toward giving his rival precisely the field in which his talents could best be displayed. By separating the Upper from the Lower Canada Liberals on entering the cabinet, he had already weakened his natural allies and strengthened Cartier. Now he had strengthened Macdonald. When Brown was bustling about at Charlottetown, making eloquent addresses on public issues and glowing with anticipations of the prospects the future held for his country and for himself, his rival, no less keenly ambitious but more shrewd, was quietly sizing up the Maritime Province delegate and making an offensive and defensive alliance with Tupper which was to last their lives out. Macdonald played his great and necessary part in the achieving of Confederation, but certainly it was one of the greatest ironies of politics that the very men who had opposed the Confederation scheme to the last were those who profited most, politically, from its success. Barely a day before the coalition which was to carry Confederation was formed, three men had stood out against the proposal to consider a federal solution for Canada's ills. One of these three, John A. Macdonald, became the first premier of the confederated Canada, and a second, John Sandfield Macdonald, became the first premier of Ontario.

Some eight months later, in August, 1866, Galt himself withdrew from the ministry. His resignation was due, not to any thwarted ambition or any serious difference of opinion with his colleagues, but to a point of honour. As the representative of the English-speaking minority in Lower Canada, he had pledged himself to a certain course, and, when this became impossible, he determined to retire from office.

No question had aroused so much concern among the English-speaking citizens of Lower Canada as that of the powers and fate of their schools. Under the law of 1846 any dissentient minority in Lower Canada had the right to establish a separate school to which its taxes should be assigned. This system had worked well, but many feared that with an overwhelming French and Catholic majority in control of the new local legislature, there might be danger that the existing privileges would be lessened. To assure protection for the minority, Galt had insisted upon qualifying the powers as to education which, under the Quebec Resolutions, were to be assigned the provincial governments: "education; saving the rights and privileges which the Protestant or Catholic minority in both Canadas may possess as to their Denominational Schools, at the time when the Union goes into effect." But this was not enough: the minority wished to extend their existing privileges. In his address at Sherbrooke in November, 1864, Galt had declared:

There had been grave difficulties surrounding the separate school question in Upper Canada, but they were all settled now, and with regard to the separate school system of Lower Canada, he was authorized by his colleagues to say that it was the determination of the Government to bring down a measure for the amendment of the school laws before the Confederation was allowed to go into force. [Loud cheers.] He made this statement because, as the clause was worded in the printed resolutions, it would appear that the school law, as it at present existed, was to be continued. Attention had, however, been drawn in Conference to the fact that the school law, as it existed in Lower Canada, required amendment, but no action was taken there as to its alteration, because he hardly felt himself competent to draw up the amendments required; and it was far better that the mind of the British population of Lower Canada should be brought to bear on the subject and that the Government might hear what they had to say, so that all the amendments required in the law might be made in a bill to be submitted to parliament.

In accordance with his promise, the government, in the last session of the old Parliament of Canada, brought down a bill extending and confirming the school privileges of the Lower Canada minority. The changes were chiefly in the direction of setting up independent administrative machinery and providing for separate control in secondary as well as elementary education. All was going well, and a large majority from both sections of the province was assured, when suddenly the situation was complicated by the demand of the Catholic authorities that a similar bill should be passed in behalf of the minority in Upper Canada. A bill to effect this was introduced by a private member, Mr. Bell of Lanark, and received the support of Macdonald, though not of any other of the Upper Canada ministers. This demand was greeted with a storm of denunciation from Upper Canada. The critics of the new measure denied that there was any parallel between the denominational schools of the majority in Lower Canada from which the minority sought exemption, and the public or national schools of Upper Canada, in which, as a matter of fact, three-fourths of the Catholic teachers and pupils of that section were still to be found. Further, the Separate School law had been thoroughly and radically revised only in 1863, and this measure, it was insisted, had been accepted as a full and final settlement.

This situation placed the government in an awkward dilemma. It was found that a large majority of the Upper Canada members would vote against the Bell measure, and that a large majority of the Lower Canada members would vote against the other bill unless the Upper Canada measure was advanced *pari passu*. It would have been possible to pass each measure by a majority drawn chiefly from the other section, but the government rightly felt that to embitter the last session of the Union Parliament by such a struggle, and to impose upon each of the new provinces, by outside votes, a school system which was to be stereotyped by the constitutional safeguards, would be a bad omen for the future. Accordingly it was decided to drop the Lower Canada bill, and thereupon the Upper Canada measure was also withdrawn.

Galt concurred in this action, but in view of his own pledges in the matter felt it necessary to withdraw from the ministry. He writes to Mrs. Galt:

Ottawa, 7th August, 1866.

Before you receive this, you will have learned by telegraph of my resignation, or, if you have not heard, it will have been postponed. The necessity for this step arises from the position in which the Government are placed by the introduction of the U. C. school bill, which has produced so much excitement that we find it impossible to proceed with the L. C. measure. After all that has passed it is impossible for me to remain a member of the Government when this takes place, as I should be exposed to reproaches which, however unjust, would still not the less be addressed to me, of having preferred office to the securing the rights of the Protestant minority.

The difficulty has become so serious, that a total disruption of the Government seemed most probable, but I myself have suggested that my retirement will show the way. My colleagues are very reluctant, and we part on the very best terms, and with the determination to work together. Had we not taken this course, Brown would undoubtedly have carried all U. C. away from us at the next election.

I trust the course I am taking will prove to be right and in the interest of the public. I have sought to do it under the Divine guidance, and the issue is in His hands.

The Government will probably request me to carry through the financial measures in my hands, which will detain me here, but I now think the House will adjourn on Saturday and that I shall be with you that night.

A. T. G.

Speaking in the House on the same day, Galt made clear to the public the reasons for his resignation:

I am bound in all candour to say that I think the course the Government has taken is that course which the interests of the country demand, but at the same time, it is one to which I could not be a party. It is not that I am apprehensive that injurious treatment in regard to this question of education will be directed against the Protestants of Lower Canada, but it is because I have in my position in the Government and as a member of this House, taken certain ground on that question which renders it impossible for me to be responsible for that course. . . . At the same time it is only due to my colleagues from Lower Canada to say that they at least have not shown any disposition to recede in any way from the pledge that was given.

It is of interest to note the comment upon Galt's action made by his predecessor in retirement. Brown, following in the debate, declared that he now had the satisfaction of finding himself completely sustained in the position he had taken at the Quebec Conference, that the resolution attempting to provide guarantees for the minority was unnecessary and inexpedient; whether in Upper or in Lower Canada, the minority would be much safer trusting to the sense of right and justice of the majority than relying upon all the constitutional fetters that could be forged. He continued:

On public grounds I can only rejoice that the honourable gentleman's withdrawal from the Government has taken place. But looking at it from a personal standpoint, I rejoice that my honourable friend has come out on the ground that he could not remain in the Government with honour. When public men act in that manner they add dignity to public life and increase confidence in the public mind. Whoever takes the place of my honourable friend, while he will, I may hope, have sounder views on finance, could not, I am sure, be more happy and

*genial in his manner of addressing the House or one with whom
it would be possible to have more agreeable personal relations.**

It will be seen later than an understanding was reached,
honourably carried out, that the provincial legislature of the
new province of Quebec would give effect to the educational
changes desired, and that in the meantime further guarantees
would be incorporated in the act establishing Confederation.

Though Galt had withdrawn from the ministry, it was felt
imperative to have his counsel in the final drafting of the
Confederation proposals now overdue. The legislatures of Nova
Scotia and New Brunswick had now fallen into line; the one in
April and the other in June, 1866, had authorized the appointment of delegates to take part in arranging with the imperial
government the definite terms of union. These delegates had
arrived in London in July, only to find that their Canadian
confrères had been delayed by the Fenian disturbances, by
personal indisposition, and by Lord Monck's fears that business would be hampered by the change of government in
Great Britain where Russell's ministry, which had followed
Palmerston's, had in turn been defeated on the franchise question and had given way to a Conservative administration in
which Earl Derby was premier, Disraeli Chancellor of the
Exchequer, and Lord Carnarvon Secretary of the Colonies.
They were kept waiting until November, when the tardy Cana-
dians arrived. On December 4, the London Conference was
organized, meeting in the Westminster Palace Hotel, with
Macdonald presiding, and in continuous sesions up to December
24 a revised draft of resolutions was drawn up and sent to the
Colonial Secretary. [The delegates at the London Conference
were as follows: John A. Macdonald, George E. Cartier, W. P.
Howland, W. McDougall, H. Langevin, and A. T. Galt from
Canada; Charles Tupper, W. A. Henry, J. W. Ritchie, A. G.
Archibald, and J. McCully from Nova Scotia; S. L. Tilley, P.
Mitchell, C. Fisher, R. D. Wilmot, J. M. Johnston from New
Brunswick.]

In the December Conference, few material changes were
made in the Quebec plan. The decision of Prince Edward

---

* Privately to his wife, however, Brown confided that Galt's personal
relations were anything but "agreeable," and that he was intensely
indignant at the treatment he had received from his colleagues
(Careless, *Brown of the Globe*, II, 234). There was some suspicion
that Galt would soon be back in the government (P. B. Waite, *Life
and Times of Confederation 1864-1867* [Toronto, 1962], p. 290).

Island to stay out made it necessary to divide the four senators assigned it between the other two Maritime Provinces. Minor amendments were accepted as to the scope of the Lieutenant-Governor's pardoning power, and as to the control of fisheries, penitentiaries and the solemnization of marriages. The provincial subsidies provided were increased so as to give the Maritime Provinces a somewhat larger proportionate share, and the agreement to build the Intercolonial was made definite and binding. The provision safeguarding the rights of religious minorities as to education in the two Canadas was extended to all the provinces, and an additional guarantee was sought in a clause afterwards famous:

And in any province where a system of separate or dissentient schools by law obtains, or where the Legislature may thereafter adopt a system of separate or dissentient schools, an appeal shall lie to the Governor-General from the acts and decisions of the Local Authorities which affect the rights and privileges of the Protestant or Roman Catholic minority in the matter of education, and the Parliament shall have power, in the last resort, to legislate on the subject.

This clause, designed to safeguard the Protestant minority in Quebec, became in later days a guarantee, more or less effective, of the rights of Catholic minorities elsewhere. As the original records show, the draft was Galt's; the wording was slightly changed later.

The progress of the Conference may be gathered from some of the letters which Galt sent his wife; his eldest son, Elliott, it may be noted, was with him in London throughout the negotiations:

London, 13th December, 1866.

We went to Lord Carnarvon's on Tuesday afternoon, spent a pleasant day there, and returned the next morning. There were only a Mr. and Mrs. Holford and a Mr. Herbert there, the former a millionaire with nothing else to distinguish him, the latter, said to be the first fresco painter of the day. We had a long talk with Lord Carnarvon about Confederation, but no points of any material difficulty presented themselves.

A. T. G.

By the way, we had quite a little excitement the night before last. Macdonald, as usual, was reading in bed, fell asleep, set fire to his curtains, and very nearly lost his life. Luckily the fire burnt his shoulder and woke him. He displayed great presence of mind, almost entirely subduing the flames himself. After exhausting his water he awoke Cartier, and afterwards came to my room and awoke me. With the water in our rooms we put it out without causing any alarm in the house, and the burns Macdonald received have proved of no consequence.

A. T. G.

London, 19th December, 1866.

We still continue occupied every day with the meetings of our Conference, in which we are making satisfactory progress, but with a good deal of delay, as our friends from the Maritime Provinces are excessively fond of talking, and very naturally wish to have some changes made in their interest. The Education question came up to-day and, I am thankful to say, our Canadian Delegates all stated that no change could be permitted in what we proposed on behalf of Canada, which however they might extend to the Lower Provinces if they wished. They have taken till to-morrow to decide, and I therefore hope before I close this letter to tell you that so far as the Delegates are concerned, the matter will be settled. . . .

We have hoped to close our preliminary work before Christmas, but I fear to-day that we shall not do so, and I regret also to say that from appearances I much apprehend, that I shall have to be one of those who remain to see the bill through Parliament. Macdonald cannot remain and I feel sure that he will insist on my staying, as our friend Cartier devotes himself so much to society that we do not get much work out of him – this is, however, for your own eye only. Probably Howland, Macdougall and Langevin will go back.

I may tell you as a State secret that it is most improbable Lord Monck will ever return to Canada. I am much grieved to say that such a view is taken of his conduct in the celebrated Lamirando case by the Government here, as will I think induce him to resign. Do not venture to say anything about this, but I thought you would like to know such an interesting piece of news.

Thursday p.m.

I have nothing to add to the foregoing, except that the Education question stands till to-morrow. The difficulty now is as regards the Lower Provinces, not with us in Canada.

With much love, etc. etc.,

A. T. G.

London, Dec. 28th, 1866.

I telegraphed you by the Cable on the 24th, and hope you got the message either that evening or on Xmas. I thought the good news it contained would help to cause a merry Christmas. We closed our preliminary sittings of Conference that day, and agreed unanimously on our report to Lord Carnarvon. I am very much pleased to be able to say that the Education question is all right, and has been extended to and agreed in by all the Provinces, so that there is now, I may say, no fear of its going wrong in the Imperial Parliament. My enemies at home will not have the satisfaction they have hoped for.

The Quebec scheme is adopted, very few alterations, and none that I regard as at all impairing it. . . .

By the way, I hope you did not forget poor little Jeff [Jefferson Davis] at Christmas. I much fear his father will yet be brought to trial.

Praying my blessing you and our dear ones at home, I remain, with much love,

Ever your devoted husband,

A. T. G.

In the conference between the delegates and the Colonial Secretary, the only important change effected was the addition of a clause empowering the Sovereign, on the recommendation of the Governor-General, to appoint one or two senators from each of the three main divisions, in order to avert a deadlock. It is amusing to read of the earnest and prolonged discussions on similar minutiae, while the broad basic fact that the senators, when appointed virtually by the federal premier, would act on party rather than on provincial or dispassionate grounds, was completely ignored.

Of more interest was the difference of opinion as to the rank and title of the new federation. The press had been rich in suggestions for many months as to the name to be adopted: Acadia and Laurentia were among the more popular suggestions, though Cabotia, Ursalia, Septentrionalia and other eccentricities had their sponsors. Finally, however, it was agreed to take the name Canada, finding new names, Ontario and Quebec, for the provinces that once had gone under that name. As to the rank and status of the union, there was also much discussion. During the London Conference it was proposed that the bold title "Kingdom of Canada" should be chosen. This was heartily accepted by the delegates, and the term was embodied in the draft of the bill. It was a splendid stroke, and would have made clear from the beginning, what now after half a century is only dawning on some minds, that the new nation stood upon an equality, "in status if not in stature," with the old Kingdoms of Her Majesty. Objections, however, were raised by the British government through Lord Stanley (afterwards Lord Derby), Foreign Secretary, ostensibly out of fear of wounding the republican susceptibilities of the United States, but probably, it has been suggested, as much out of unwillingness to recognize the equality with Great Britain the terms implied. The ancient term "Dominion" was substituted, and has since been hallowed by time and sacrifice.

Particularly significant is a letter written to Mrs. Galt in January, revealing the deep impression made upon Galt by the evident eagerness of London statesmen to wash their hands of Canada and foreshadowing the conclusions to which that policy was later to lead him:

London, 14th January, 1867.

With regard to matters here, there appears no difficulty as respects our measure, although we have not yet heard from the Cabinet. . . .

I am more than ever disappointed at the tone of feeling here as to the Colonies. I cannot shut my eyes to the fact that they want to get rid of us. They have a servile fear of the United States and would rather give us up than defend us, or incur the risk of war with that country. Day by day I am more oppressed with the sense of responsibility of maintaining a connection undesired here and which exposes us to such peril at home. I pray God to show me the right path. But I much doubt whether Confederation will save us from Annexation. Even Macdonald is rapidly feeling as I do. Cartier alone seems blind to what is passing around us.

They talk of conferring Colonial honours and dignities but I have no faith in this doing any good. It looks like hanging garlands on the victim going to sacrifice. I could wish myself free from all this but I feel that I am useful to my country and duty must be performed. Except Macdonald, I know none of the Delegates who really think enough of the future that is before us, and he considers that our present immediate task is to complete the Union, leaving the rest to be solved by time.

The connection between Canada and England is now one of sentiment, interest in both cases scarcely being in favor of it. Now the sentiment is becoming very weak here, and in Canada will not bear much longer the brunt of the ungenerous remarks

*continually made and the expression which I think will surely
be brought out in the coming Debates, that she is a burden and
weakness, of which they would gladly be rid. When the public
mind in Canada accepts this idea, as that pervading the English
mind, the connection must come to an end. Our danger is, that
meantime a war might arise between England and the U. S. in
which our country would grievously suffer. My doubt is whether
such a risk should be encountered or promoted by me, when in
my own mind I am convinced of the nature of the feeling here.
The issue is, I am thankful to think, in the hands of the Allwise
Governor. . . .*

A. T. G.

A pleasant relief from such forebodings was occasioned by
the marriage of Macdonald to Miss Bernard, sister of his
secretary, Colonel Bernard:

London, 10th February, 1867.

My Dearest Wife:

I write these hasty lines just before I leave for home.

*We have to-day married Macdonald to Miss Bernard; all
went off most agreeably, the day was beautiful, and all were as
happy as possible. The Bishop of Montreal performed the ceremony, and we afterwards lunched at our hotel, since which the
happy pair have started for Oxford to spend two or three days.
There were rather a large party, four bridesmaids – Misses
Macdougall, McGee, Tupper and Archibald – and about
seventy guests. I am going to take a piece of wedding cake to
Elliott.*

*I have just come from the Colonial Office, and understand
that the Queen has desired me to be presented at the private
Court on the 27th. The four premiers, Macdonald, Cartier,
Tupper, and Tilley, are to be then presented, and I am specially
honoured by being included with them. I expect to return from
France on the 24th, and trust I may sail on the 2nd March.*

I enclose you a letter from Elliott.

*You must excuse this short note, as I have to return to the
Colonial Office immediately to see Lord Carnarvon before I
leave, in case he wants anything.*

I hope to see the Emperor when in Paris.

*You will probably not hear from me by next Canadian mail.
With love to all our dear little ones,*

I remain,

Your loving husband,

A. T. GALT.

The bill, as finally agreed upon, was passed by the Imperial Parliament, as Macdonald notes, with little discussion and little interest in England, but with the liveliest hope and widespread rejoicing in Canada. On July 1, 1867, the new Dominion came into being. The plan which less than ten years before had seemed a far off vision had been made a living reality by the foresight, the courage and the unselfishness of some of Canada's greatest sons, and by the pressure of events — "events stronger than advocacy, events stronger than men, which have come in at last like the fire behind the invisible writing to bring out the truth" and wisdom of the policy urged by the few. What the future would mean for the new nation and for the men who had laboured to create it, none could forecast, but nothing that might come could dim the greatness of the achievement already won.

13: The New Nation

Galt's changing interests; last months in office; the "C.B's"; business affairs; new political alignments; Canadian nationality; Canada and the control of foreign affairs; last calls to politics.

During the Union period, the activities of Galt touched on all sides the chief political and business interests of the province. It has, therefore, been necessary to review many phases of this development in some detail. After Confederation, this becomes impossible and also unnecessary. In the wider field no one man's activities could touch all sides of life, and in any event, Galt now came to occupy a different relation to the country's development.

In 1867 Galt was in his fiftieth year. The experience of the previous decade had widened his sympathies, and his know-ledge of men and of affairs. The leading men from the provinces by the sea had been as strongly impressed by his easy mastery of the mysteries of finance, and by his fertility in resource and his executive capacity, as his colleagues and the public in the older sphere. It might have been expected that a long period of service in the administration of the new Dominion was about to open before him. Yet of the twenty-four years of further life which the fates had allotted him, less than one was to be spent in administrative office. Many different factors – the exigencies of his private affairs, the fortunes of his party, his fearless insistence upon taking up causes which lesser politicians termed unpopular and impracticable, and changes in the personal relations of the leading men with whom he had previously acted – combined to turn his energies away from administrative paths. Henceforth it was to be essentially in diplomacy rather than in executive work that his greatest public services were to be displayed.

The task of forming the first Canadian ministry was con-fided by Lord Monck to John A. Macdonald. His position in the existing provincial ministry and the role he had played in the negotiations leading up to Confederation left no room for question that this honour was justly due. His task was made difficult by the necessity, which Dunkin had foreseen, of attempting to give representation in the cabinet to all the sectional, racial, and religious interests which clamoured for a hearing. After a week of deadlock, and after it had at times appeared inevitable that the task would have to be abandoned and George Brown summoned to attempt it, the self-sacrifice of Tupper and D'Arcy McGee at last made it possible to overcome these obstacles, and the ministry was formed.

Galt records the anxiety of the period:

Ottawa, 23rd June, 1867.

My dearest Wife:

I have never before had so much worry and anxiety about political arrangements, as on this occasion at Ottawa. Really it has been so absorbing that I have had no spirit even to write you, as from hour to hour I never knew what aspect things would assume, and I hoped all along to get away on Saturday.

The U. C. Liberals in the Cabinet have insisted on every sort of concession to them. Cartier has resisted and I think with good reason. McGee has been a great difficulty. . . . To help matters I offered to stand aside, but the Lower Canadians would not hear of this, and would not go in without me. The only people who have really been without reproach are the gentlemen from the Lower Provinces, who have done all in their power to reconcile matters.

A final proposition was made on Saturday to the Liberals and rejected by them, but at Mr. Tilley's request they have taken till to-morrow (Monday) to reconsider their decision. It was proposed to meet to-day, but I positively refused to consider such matters on Sunday and all acquiesced.

Macdonald . . . at one moment says he will go on without the Grits, the next, he says he will throw up the cards and recommend the Government to send for George Brown. Things are turning out fast, as I told you I feared would be the case, and I am so thoroughly disgusted that if it were not for the fear of deserting my friends in such a crisis, I would shake off the dust of my feet on political life.

Tom came here on Tuesday and has remained to see how things result. He will however go home to-morrow as he is tired of waiting. . . .

A. T. G.

The elections which followed in August and September of 1867 gave the new government an overwhelming majority from every province save Nova Scotia. The government claimed to be a coalition of both the old parties. In a sense its claim was justified, though the opposition of Brown and the backbone of the Ontario Liberals and of the Rouge remnant in Quebec made it plain that the Liberal cabinet members from the older Canada had not carried their party with them. However this might be, the desire to give the new government a fair trial, the public weariness of personal and factional struggle, and, in Quebec, the influence of the Roman Catholic Church, combined to give the new premier a backing and a majority such as he had never before enjoyed.

Galt had hesitated to accept the post of Minister of Finance which both his colleagues and the public had marked as his. Years of close and unremitting attention to public business had made it impossible for him to give to his private business the attention his many scattered interests required. His brother, Thomas Galt, strongly urged him to stay out of office and devote himself to his own and his family's interests, at least for a time. Pressure was brought to bear upon him by his colleagues, of which the following letter from Hector Langevin may serve as an indication, and his own keen interest in political affairs determined him to forego, for the present at least, the private considerations.

My dear Galt: *Quebec, 5th April, 1867.*

I have received your letter of the 1st instant, and I must add that I have read it with grief.

No one more than myself amongst your friends would regret any difficulty you might have in your private business, and I confess that I expected that it must be so with your affairs to some extent when I knew something of the position of some others of our political friends. True, it is very hard to ask a friend, such as you are, to continue to neglect his own private business and the personal and pecuniary interests of his family, in order that he may continue to attend to the public business of the country and receive the thanks? no, the ungratefulness (so to speak) of his countrymen. But, my dear Galt, you must not forget that you have with us brought about the new order of things which is soon to be inaugurated. . . .

Oh, no, my dear Galt, the country requires you, you cannot leave us now. Your services are specially required. Any one of us might leave, he would be replaced. You know perfectly well, it is not so with you. Finance Ministers are not improvised in one day. Your experience is required; allow me to say it is due to your country.

In the new government, you will not have all the detail of the government of the Province of Canada. Local matters will have fallen to the lot of others, so that the rulers of the Dominion will have more leisure comparatively, and may give to their private and personal matters much more time than we have been able to do during the last three years.

I hope your brother may have considered the matter in a broad sense, and advised you not to leave public life. Be sure that your good work for the good of the country cannot be lost and be detrimental to you. Providence will help you in your public career, and will not allow that, by your attending to your duty as a public man, those that depend on you for their present and future wants should be the losers thereby.

Wishing most sincerely to hear from you soon that you yield to our remonstrances and earnest requests, I remain,

My dear Galt,
Yours very truly,
HECTOR LANGEVIN.

Once more in office, Galt gave himself with energy to the task of organizing the new Dominion's finances. For the most part, the administrative machinery of the old province of Canada was preserved, but the work of adjusting the relations of the Dominion to the old provinces and of the new provinces of Ontario and Quebec to each other, in the matter of debts, property and accounts, was one which called for all his industry and his diplomacy.

The routine of these administrative duties was soon interrupted by dissensions as to what a friend termed the "double plague of C.B.'s" — the grant of the distinction of Companion of the Bath, and the suspension of the Commercial Bank.

On the first of July, when the new Dominion was proclaimed, Lord Monck announced that the Queen had been graciously pleased to confer the honour of Knight Commander of the Bath upon Macdonald, and the honour of Companion of the Bath upon Cartier, Galt, Tilley, Tupper, Howland and McDougall. Up to this period titles and royal distinctions had been rarely bestowed upon colonists, and in those days, as in these, there was a wide difference of opinion as to the advisability of the practice. Assuming that such honours were ever to be conferred, however, there could be no question that the achievement of Confederation was an occasion which called for a generous outpouring. None of the men so honoured was troubled by any democratic scruples. Macdonald, Cartier and Galt had previously declined a proffered distinction, on the

ground simply of its inadequacy. The difficulty lay in the discrimination shown in favour of Macdonald as against Cartier
and Galt. Beyond question, they had taken at least as important
a part in the achievement of Confederation. Without Cartier's
aid it would have been impossible to swing Lower Canada into
line, and in promising that aid he had risked more than any
other Canadian public man. Galt's services, in first bringing
the issue within the field of practical politics, in bringing Cartier
into sympathy, and in helping to frame the terms of the union,
were equally known to all men – except apparently, to Lord
Monck and the Duke of Buckingham, then Colonial Secretary.
The discrimination was especially stupid in the case of Cartier,
since the inferior distinction was taken by his fellow-citizens
from Quebec as a slight upon his province and his race.

At first Galt was prepared to accept the proffered honour,
though without much enthusiasm:

Ottawa, 1st July, 1867.

My dearest Wife:

*You will have learned by my telegram that I have been
made a Companion of the Bath, an honor which I hope you
will appreciate. The Governor, after having been sworn in, said
that he had the pleasure to announce that Her Majesty had been
pleased to make Macdonald a K.C.B., that is a Knight Commander of the Bath, and Cartier, Howland, Macdougall, Tilley,
Tupper and myself Companions of the Bath. Of course this is
intended as a distinction, and no doubt it is, though I confess I
do not attach much importance to it. The honour conferred on
Macdonald is no doubt a worthy one and deserved. . . .*

A. T. GALT.

When, however, he found that Cartier had determined not
to accept, he felt bound to take the same course:

Ottawa, 2nd July, 1867.

My dearest Wife:

*I was sworn in yesterday as Finance Minister, so my public
labours have again commenced.*

*The announcement of the honours yesterday has caused
trouble. Cartier will not accept, and his refusal will necessarily
involve mine, as I cannot accept that which he declines without
either declaring that I think he is wrong, which I do not, or that
his services have been more important than my own, a position
of inferiority that I cannot voluntarily assume.*

It is an ungracious and most unusual thing to refuse an honor publicly conferred, but if Lord Monck is an ass, I cannot help it. We have a good many elements of trouble among us, and this affair will not diminish them.

Of course you will say nothing about this.

Love to all our dear ones.

Your loving husband,

A. T. GALT.

The further procedure of the authorities concerned was of a piece with their original blunder. As there was no precedent for a removal from the Companionship of the Bath except by striking names off its roll, a step taken only in case of disgraceful conduct, it was proposed to accede to the request of Cartier and Galt by cancelling the warrant and issuing a notification omitting both names. Galt immediately, and Cartier a fortnight later, acquiesced in this course, provided that the notification in the Gazette stated expressly that their names were omitted by their own desire. Unfortunately the Duke of Buckingham, without waiting to hear whether the course he proposed would be acceptable, instructed it to be carried out. On Sir Edward Watkin's and Tupper's initiative, the slight was remedied, so far as Cartier was concerned, by conferring a baronetcy on him; this only made matters worse in Galt's case, but slightly over year later the grant of K.C.M.G., under circumstances which will require attention, cleared up the difficulty so far as it could be done. So far only, for in both Cartier's and Galt's minds the incident rankled, and though Macdonald stated that he had had no previous intimation of Monck's intention, the old friendly feelings among the three were never again the same. "Toys! you call these decorations toys!" exclaimed Napoleon, "It is with such toys you govern men!"

More serious in itself was the Commercial Bank episode. This bank, which had its headquarters at Kingston, had long been the chief western competitor of the Bank of Upper Canada, and with the downfall of its rival in 1866 it was left alone. But its triumph was fleeting. Its own management had been reckless, and heavy losses had been incurred. With a capital of $4,000,000, it had to face losses of $1,100,000 on the last ten years' business, nearly one-fourth absorbed by one director who was insolvent when his account was opened. This might have been overcome had it not been for an unwise loan made to the Detroit and Milwaukee Railway, which was supposed, but without ground, to be guaranteed by the Great Western. After long litigation, the bank took $1,770,000 of the railway's bonds in settlement of its claim, but even then its directors, instead of realizing on the bonds, determined to hold them for a rise above their current value of fifty cents on the dollar. At the annual meeting in June, 1867, new directors took hold, and it was proposed to reduce the capital stock by a million. This suggestion, and the shaking of faith by the failure of the Bank of Upper Canada, led to a quiet but steady withdrawal of deposits, and the directors looked about for aid.

About the middle of September, L. H. Holton, who with Hugh Allan and others had recently taken hold of the Bank's affairs, sought out Galt to inquire whether the government could come to its assistance. Galt, who was himself a considerable shareholder, thought that it could not, on the ground both of doubt as to authority and of the danger of creating a precedent. He urged applying to the other banks for aid. At the desire of the directors and especially of the president, Richard Cartwright, Galt sought Cartier's and Macdonald's advice, but found them still more strongly of the same opinion. He then used his good offices with the Bank of Montreal to secure an advance of some $300,000 on a deposit of selected Commercial paper, and in the absence of Mr. King, the Montreal manager, R. B. Angus, readily agreed. Galt heard nothing further for a month, when Cartwright and Holton again sought him out. An examination of the Bank's affairs by Mr. Holton, Mr. Allan and Mr. Morris gave ground for believing that the embarrassment of the bank was only temporary, and that a limited advance would tide it over. This advance the Bank of Montreal declined to give. Galt then determined, in view of the imminent danger of a general panic, to recommend to the government to give assistance to the extent of half a million, and went to Ottawa to make the suggestion in person. Both Macdonald and Cartier still objected, and no meeting of Council was called. At their suggestion Galt returned to Montreal to see if assistance could be secured from the other banks. Representatives of the western banks came down to Montreal, and on October 21 a plan was worked out which it was believed would avert a crisis. Unfortunately the head officers of the western banks refused to sanction the plan. Galt then telegraphed Macdonald that all other efforts had failed, and desired a decision from the cabinet before morning. At two in the morning the answer arrived:

Ottawa, 21st Oct., 1867.

To Hon. A. T. Galt, –

Private. – Council met and considered your telegrams. Information as to condition of Bank, character of security offered, and reasons why other Banks declined to help, insufficient to warrant any action by Government.

JNO. A. MACDONALD.

On the morning of the 22nd, the Commercial Bank closed its doors. A serious run began on other western banks, and after a week's growing panic the government determined, if necessary, to come to their assistance. Fortunately nothing further was required than an assurance of readiness by the government, and, under pressure, by the Bank of Montreal, to accept all notes at par. The panic soon subsided. The liquidation of the Commercial Bank's assets confirmed the belief that timely assistance might have averted disaster. Eventually all depositors' and noteholders' claims were met in full, and the shareholders saved something from disaster by effecting a sale of the bank's remaining assets to the Merchants Bank on a basis of one Merchants share for three Commercial.

As the commercial storm died down, the political agitation increased. In consequence of the currency legislation of the previous session, neither Galt nor King was popular in Ontario banking circles. During the recent panic, a misconstruction of King's orders had led to a refusal by Bank of Montreal managers at several centres to receive the bills of one of the weaker banks, a course which seriously increased the danger. It was not surprising, then, that a popular rumour arose that the Commercial Bank had been driven to its doom by a conspiracy between King and Galt to remove one more rival from the path of the Bank of Montreal's unrestrained ambition. This preposterous cry was easily refuted, but Galt felt more keenly the failure of his own colleagues to stand by him.

Dealing with the first point, in a speech in the House on December 12, he declared:

I may add a word in regard to the extraordinary impression which seems to have prevailed in the public mind, in respect to the causes of that panic – an impression founded on the imputation that the Finance Minister of the country and the manager of the largest Bank in the country desired and deliberately attempted to bring about the ruin of one of the largest and most influential banking institutions in Canada, and to plunge the country into all the misery of a great commercial disaster. As far as the Finance Minister was concerned, I think he would have shown himself a fitting inmate for a lunatic asylum, if, a few days before the meeting of a new Parliament, he had put himself in the position of trying to bring about a violent disturbance of the financial and commercial relations of the country. To lay such an imputation upon one occupying the responsible position of Finance Minister, is, I think, extraordinary and preposterous – the very acme of absurdity. (Hear, hear.) Besides, Sir, to put it even on the low ground of personal interest, it is perhaps known to some honorable members that I am a shareholder in the Commercial Bank, and for me to have entertained a desire of the kind that has been imputed to me was equivalent to a wish deliberately to destroy my own property. So much for myself. With regard to the charge against the Bank of Montreal, I think that the banking institution which carries on the largest commercial transactions in the country must, ceteris paribus, be the largest loser in the event of a panic. Therefore I say that the impression that the Bank of Montreal and myself, as Finance Minister, entertained that design, was the most extraordinary delusion that ever took possession of this or any other country. (Hear, hear.) I hope that the explanations which I have just made will at any rate satisfy the House and the country, that whatever misconception may have taken place in regard to Mr. King and myself, certainly, as far as I was concerned, every effort that could have been made was made willingly by me to sustain the Commercial Bank, and, failing that, to prevent the disaster spreading to the other Banks.

As to the attitude of his colleagues, the same declaration makes his feelings clear:

I thought that the Government had placed the failure of the Bank in such a position that the matter would necessarily come before Parliament and the country in such a way as to make that event appear to be attributable to me, for not having given the Government full information and that the whole responsibility of not having obtained assistance, and of not averting any disaster that might occur, would fall upon my shoulders. The disappointment which I experienced was also increased by the feeling that I was placed in the painful position of being betrayed by my friends. Moreover, as Finance Minister, I had believed that I possessed the confidence of my colleagues, and that they would not have deserted me under such circumstances.

I had not recommended in my telegrams to Sir John that any assistance should be given to the Bank, because he was aware that I had been in Ottawa for the express purpose of recommending that assistance should be given. Therefore, I felt that I had been deserted by my friends, and that, as Finance Minister, looked to by the country for the maintenance of its credit and the averting of disaster, I was in the position of being supposed to have had power while I was impotent to save. Under these circumstances I felt that there was only one course for me to pursue, namely, to place my resignation in his Excellency's hands. I thought it necessary to address this answer to Sir John:

"Montreal, 22nd Oct., 1867.

"My dear Sir John, – At two a.m. I received the following telegram from you:

'Private. – Council met and considered your telegrams – information as to condition of Bank, character of security offered, and reasons why other banks declined to help, insufficient to warrant any action by Government.'

"The grounds stated for the refusal of the Government to act appear to me to imply both censure and want of confidence. As regards the alleged want of information, I must remind you that I went to Ottawa with Mr. Cartwright, the President of the Commercial Bank, on Thursday last, for the purpose of submitting the whole case to Council, and only at your express desire abstained from doing so. The whole state of facts was thus known to you, and also to other members of the Government. If you supposed any change had taken place, you could have sought and obtained this information by telegraph last night, before adopting the resolution you have communicated to me.

"Had the Government seen fit to rest their decision upon the want of proper authority, or the inconvenience of establishing a precedent, I might have consented to share the responsibility of this action; but I must decline to do so upon the grounds stated in your telegram.

"I have therefore only to place my resignation in your hands, and to request that you will submit the same to His Excellency the Governor-General.

Believe me, &c., &c.,

A. T. GALT."

On receiving this telegram, Macdonald took a special train to Montreal to induce him to withdraw his resignation, and

Cartier wrote strongly urging him to reconsider. Both insisted that the wording of the Council's telegram had been meant to hold open the door for further consideration, in the light of any information Galt might send. As eight hours had passed after Galt had telegraphed Macdonald, without any call for further data, and as the telegram sent at last did not suggest, much less make explicit, any such desire, the wording must, at best, be considered unfortunate. In any event the telegraph offices, which Galt had given orders to be kept open, had been closed on the agent's understanding that the government's message was final.

Galt's feeling at this juncture is made clear in a letter to Mrs. Galt:

Ottawa, 31st October, 1867.

My dearest Wife:

I have had any amount of anxiety and trouble the last two days, arising partly out of the financial crisis, and partly from the very unsatisfactory nature of the proceedings of the Government, which really is no Government at all.

I brought up in council yesterday their course towards me, and expressed myself very strongly, ending by saying that I would not again enter the council chamber unless they explained in writing what had been done. This of course caused a sensation, and to-day I have a letter from Macdonald disowning any desire to give me offense. So I went to council to-day, but the thing will not last long as Macdonald is not himself.

A Deputation was here to-day from Toronto about the Banks, and I think I have got them into a position when they must ask aid from the Government, which I told them we were ready to grant.

If it were not for the critical state of public matters, I would resign to-morrow on private grounds, but I am inclined to wait, as if the Banks ask aid, it will be a splendid justification of my policy.

But you may be assured of this, that the present Government is doomed, whatever may follow it.

Your loving husband,

A. T. GALT.

After full consideration, Galt determined to resign. His irritation against his colleagues' method of announcing their decision might not of itself have led him to take this course, but with the pressure of private affairs, it weighed down the scale, and on November 1 he gave up office, as it proved, for good and all. Two days later he wrote Macdonald confirming his decision:

(Confidential).   *Montreal, November 3, 1867.*
  My dear Macdonald,
      I have had the consultation of which I spoke, and I am confirmed in my decision to withdraw from official life until at least I have had the opportunity of putting my affairs in something like order. I will not dwell upon the subject, as it is excessively painful for me to take any step which may cause embarrassment to my colleagues; but feeling, as I do, that my matters have been seriously complicated by the C. Bank, I think my plain and paramount duty is to consider first what is due to my family.
      I shall be in Ottawa on Tuesday p.m., and will be most happy to give every assistance in my power to whoever may take my place. As, however, most of the work must stand over till after the New Year, I trust my resignation will not interfere with the intended course of public business.
      Pray, be so kind as to give a proper intimation to the press. I shall leave this in your hands.
                    Believe me, my dear Macdonald,
                        Yours faithfully,
                                    A. T. GALT.

A less formal explanation is given in the report to Sherbrooke:

                    Ottawa, 9th November, 1867.
My dearest Wife:
      You will no doubt have seen in the Montreal Gazette *the report of the explanation of my resignation which I yesterday gave. I had some difficulty in deciding on the exact line to take, as I could not with propriety allude to my extreme dissatisfaction with my colleagues, after having accepted their explanations. I therefore concluded to make but little of private affairs, and rather to let it be inferred that the reasons were withheld. The story has got circulated here that I had suffered very serious losses; this has, however, now been dispelled, and it is pretty well understood that I left the Government because I did not like it.*
      Among those who know the facts, much exasperation is felt against Macdonald, the more so on account of my resignation.

They say had he stood by the Bank as I did, it would have been saved, and this is true.

Tom has been here with me, very cross, because I would not go farther and attack the Government, but this would have been wholly wrong. The attack must come from those interested, not from me. He left for home this morning.

The impression seems to be general that the Government is rather tottery, and that my resignation will bear speedy fruit. I think so myself.

We had a capital set-to last night between Howe and Tupper. The former made his deliverance against Union, and enlarged on the woes of Nova Scotia. He speaks very well, but I do not judge him to be a very formidable antagonist. He is illogical and lacks point. Tupper replied very ably and had much the best of it. He is an earnest speaker, and puts his points forcibly; he really made a capital parliamentary speech. Mr. Fisher of New Brunswick, one of the late delegates and long a leading man there, spoke at length, but evidently will not come up to the standard of the two other men, who will be in the front rank of our speakers.

The Debate stands over till Monday and may last two nights.

Love to all at home.

Your loving husband,

A. T. GALT.

Relieved from the pressing cares of office, Galt now gave sorely needed attention to his own private affairs. Some copper mining ventures in the Eastern Townships and warehouse enterprises in Portland did not come up to his sanguine expectations, but from other quarters he soon recouped these losses. His old friends, Gzowski and Macpherson, pressed him to re-enter the railway field, and for a time he seriously considered it. "With you as the leader," Gzowski writes him, "keeping sharp lookout for good things and doing 'general tactics,' and Mac. on the nigh side labouring among the political altesse, and your humble servant to do the grubbing and digging, Holton's principles of division of labour will work admirably well. All joking aside, the only big thing left on this Confederated continent in the shape of railway enterprise, can, I am sure, if properly managed, be made to fall into our hands." It was to the same nebulous project that his friend C. J. Brydges, managing director of the Grand Trunk, and for many years one of the closest friends both of Galt and Macdonald, with whom, and with Langevin, he shared for some years prior to Confederation common quarters in Ottawa known as the "Quadrilateral," referred, in July, 1869:

> When in Toronto, I saw Ross and Cumberland, and we have talked over a North-West scheme which we want to discuss with you. . . . The idea has not gone beyond us three, and further participants must be settled when we meet you. The notion is to get a charter next session for a Company to build a railway through the Territory, getting if possible a bonus of £5,000 a mile and a large land grant, to enlist Hudson's Bay people in it, to take advantage of the political necessity in England just now of saving the N. W. from the Yankees, etc. etc. I think the scheme a feasible and profitable one, and it can do us no harm at any rate to talk it over quietly.

In spite of these alluring attractions, Galt held aloof from the plan and did not join Macpherson when he organized a Toronto company and fought bitterly against Sir Hugh Allan for the coveted charter. He did, however, lend his aid in drafting the very compelling memorials which Macpherson's company brought before the cabinet in the course of the controversy. He was more taken by a proposal of Sir Stafford Northcote, as representing the Hudson's Bay Company, to visit the West, Fort Garry and the Saskatchewan, in order to suggest a business policy for the Company under the new conditions created by the taking over of its old domains by the Dominion. "I am myself convinced," Northcote wrote, "that we have no officer capable of taking a really comprehensive view of the question, which is in truth one which will require a statesman to deal with, and which closely affects the interests not only of our company but of Canada likewise." It was, however, not found possible to undertake the mission.

Twenty years' activity in politics and ten years' experience of office had given Galt's interests now a political rather than a business bent, and, as his reorganized finances permitted, he began to give attention once more to current politics. He found it difficult to take any definite stand. The political situation had greatly changed. The coalition experiment had served to give Macdonald, for a time at least, overwhelming support from Ontario, and to make him less dependent than he had earlier been on the partnership and support of Cartier. Cartier himself was losing power; a quarrel with Bishop Bourget of Montreal had set the greater part of the Church against him, intrigues for local railway charters had undermined his position, and his health, but not his indomitable courage, was failing. Tilley, and later Tupper, had joined the cabinet, and the close alliance between Macdonald and Tupper took the place of the former close agreement among Macdonald, Cartier and Galt.

Between Galt and Macdonald a temporary political coolness developed. A succession of episodes contributed to it. In the autumn of 1866, D'Arcy McGee, with something less than his usual tact, had suggested to Macdonald that it would be well to let Galt take his place as Minister of Militia: the disorganization of the department, made evident during the Fenian raids of June, and the many financial questions involved, called for a man of executive and financial capacity. In view of the charges made in the press as to the reasons for the failure of the Militia department in the crisis, the subject was a delicate one, and doubtless McGee's well-meant suggestion caused irritation. On Galt's side "the double C.B." episodes rankled. His sensitiveness to criticism and his independence of thought made it difficult for him to run in party harness at any time. Now it was doubly difficult. The relations between Galt and Cartier grew still closer. They had from the beginning been close and devoted friends, and it was this friendship which had enabled Galt to enlist Cartier's powerful aid in the Confederation movement. For a time in 1868 and 1869, a Cartier-Galt-Langevin alliance seemed probable, but changing issues prevented.

On Cartier's motion an attempt was made to heal the breach and to regain Galt's services for the government. In March, 1868, it became necessary to take steps to counteract the vigorous campaign which Howe was leading in Nova Scotia. After sweeping the province in both federal and provincial elections, Howe had determined to carry the fight to London, and demand that the Imperial Parliament should reverse its action and set Nova Scotia free. Galt felt much alarmed over the agitation in Nova Scotia, which was rapidly assuming an annexationist tinge, and wrote Sir John on the question.

Sherbrooke, 10 Feb., 1868.
Private and confidential.
   My dear Macdonald:
   At the risk of your telling me that my advice is unasked for and unwelcome, I am compelled by the anxiety I feel to see the Confederation succeed, to write you about Nova Scotia. It

appears to me that matters there are assuming an alarming aspect, that Howe is rapidly approaching, if he has not reached, the point where he cannot control the movement, and that unless great prudence be observed, we shall have much difficulty in saving the ship.

So far as I can judge, their game appears to be to send their deputation home about the beginning of March, to keep their members back from attending at Ottawa, and to compel you to legislate on the Militia, Tariff, and other questions affecting Nova Scotia in their absence, thereby increasing the public irritation. The course which under these circumstances I would strongly advise you to take is to prorogue the House, and not meet on the 12th March, nor until the Deputation returns with their answer, when you will have it in your power to suggest to our Parliament whatever course may then appear to be wisest.

I will not trouble you with any argument on the course suggested, as you will readily perceive all that can be said pro and con. The crisis is, I think, a very serious one, as the failure to retain Nova Scotia voluntarily in the Union will not end with her secession, but practically paralyses all our efforts to build up a nationality independent of the U. S.

I leave this evening for Boston to be absent for two weeks.

Yours very sincerely,

A. T. G.

The government, while not deciding to take this course, felt equally strongly that Howe's campaign was too dangerous to ignore. They decided to send a rival mission to London to present the case for federation. In order not to make it appear that the government recognized officially the possibility of repeal and that it was prepared to negotiate, it was felt advisable to choose for the mission men not in office. Galt and Tupper were the men in mind. The following telegrams show Galt's attitude:

Ottawa, March 10, 1868,

To Hon. A. T. Galt:

Am authorized by Council to ask you if you will accept a mission to England as delegate on union question. It is proposed to associate Tupper with you if you have no objection. Please answer yes. If you see some objection or entertain doubt in your mind, don't give negative answer until we have discussed matter fully when you are here. Very important you should go. Thanks for your yesterday's telegram. Kind regards to Madame.

G. E. CARTIER.

Sherbrooke, 11 March, 1868.

To Hon G. E. Cartier, Ottawa.

If public interests will be served, I am disposed to accept mission, but consider it calculated to defeat object if Tupper goes, though personally this would be most agreeable to me. I think Archibald would be better. I will be in Ottawa Saturday morning to discuss matter.

A. T. G.

Ottawa, March 11, 1868.

To Hon. A. T. Galt:

Your telegram received. Thanks. Much pleased. Archibald's name was suggested. After discussion it was thought Tupper would do better. Messrs. Archibald and Kenny strongly think so. When you are here Saturday next we will explain reasons in which we hope you will concur. Answer.

G. E. CARTIER.

To G. E. Cartier.

Am very glad no absolute decision about Tupper has been arrived at. My reasons appear to me conclusive against his going, but will discuss on arrival. Shall be with you Saturday.

A. T. G.

The result of the conference was that Macdonald insisted that Tupper should go and Galt insisted that in this case he would not go.

Ottawa, March 16, 1868.

Dear Cartier:

I have given my best consideration to the proposal you have made to me on behalf of the Government, to undertake a mission to England on the subject of the Nova Scotia difficulty, in association with Dr. Tupper. While I would gladly put my services at the disposal of the Government in any way calculated to consolidate the Union, still I am obliged to consider how far the circumstances connected with the proposed mission bear upon the prospect of a useful result – and I must frankly say that I consider the selection of Dr. Tupper is calculated, in the present temper of Nova Scotia, so far to diminish the probability of success, that I do not believe I could myself be of any service. I beg therefore that you will express to the Council my acknowledgments for the proposal, at the same time that I feel obliged very respectfully to decline it.

Believe me, my dear Cartier,
Yours faithfully,
A. T. G.

It has been suggested that Galt's refusal to accept Tupper as a colleague was that he had been negotiating with Howe to form a political alliance. Writing to Macdonald from London, April 9, 1868, Tupper declared: "I think I have ascertained Mr. Galt's difficulty in coming with me. General Doyle tells me that Howe and his friends confidently relied upon Galt effecting with them the overthrow of your government, and I assume that Mr. Galt was too deeply committed to present himself in London with me to counteract Mr. Howe's efforts." Galt's papers give no indication of such an understanding or of any negotiations whatever. It is conceivable that an alliance was considered, but it could only come after Howe had given up his Repeal campaign and had definitely accepted Confederation. Under those circumstances there would be no more reason why Galt and Howe should not make terms than why Macdonald and Howe should not, as they eventually did. The obvious and sufficient reason for Galt's refusal to work with Tupper was his belief that in view of the bitter hostility felt toward Tupper by the anti-Confederate party, his going to London would be taken as an insult and would drive both Howe and his followers to extreme measures. As it turned out, Galt was wrong in this belief, and Macdonald and Tupper were right. Tupper went to London alone, and not only succeeded in his mission of stiffening the Imperial government's resistance to Nova Scotia's demands, but succeeded in coming to terms with Howe himself, and preparing the way for Howe's acceptance of Confederation, and of office, with better financial terms for Nova Scotia offered as an inducement. The fact was that Howe knew his game was nearly up, and Tupper knew that he knew it.

When Galt resigned the portfolio of Minister of Finance in 1867, John Rose was appointed in his place. Two years later Rose withdrew to accept a post in London as a partner of a New York banking house. Macdonald was hard put to find a successor. At Cartier's insistence, he offered the post again to Galt, who declined. At this moment Hincks returned to Canada after years of absence in colonial governorships. He was unquestionably an able financier, and nominally a Liberal. By appointing him Macdonald thought he could solve the Treasury's difficulties, and also do something to keep up what was fast becoming a mere pretence, the contention that the government was a coalition. The coup did not prove as successful as had been expected; Hincks, while adroit as ever, proved rash in some of his financial undertakings, and was found to carry less than no political weight.

One result of the appointment was to complete the estrangement of a rising young Conservative, Richard Cartwright. Cartwright, though young and comparatively inexperienced, had a just confidence in his own financial capacity, and considered that the post should have been offered to him. Two letters of the period show sufficiently the drift of political affairs; in writing the first, Cartwright was of course not aware that the post had been offered to Galt, and declined.

Kingston, Oct. 15th, 1869.

Dear Sir Alexander,

Excuse my asking if you are disposed to submit to Hincks' appointment. I am extremely dissatisfied with it and have formally notified Sir John to that effect, though I do not think it advisable to make any public protest till he has had an opportunity of making explanations. I quite understand that you may not feel at liberty to engage in any discussion on this subject and you, I have no doubt, will acquit me of any desire to pry into your views of the position, but it is a case in which a little concerted action may save much mischief in the long run. You will oblige in any event by keeping this entirely to yourself.

Yours very truly,

RICHARD J. CARTWRIGHT.

Kingston, Oct. 30th, 1869.

Dear Sir Alexander,

I have no idea of displaying my hand publicly before the House meets, but I have tolerably good reason for thinking that very prompt action will be advisable when it does. I have been approached, without any solicitation on my part, by several of our people and I am pretty sure that if any Ontario Conservative in good standing speaks out, at once, a considerable section must follow the lead, under penalties. — The feeling is quiet but deep-seated and I think only needs a proper exponent to make itself felt most seriously. . . . My wish is, as I assume yours is also, to preserve the present Liberal-Conservative party, in spite of all their leader is doing to destroy it. — To effect this it seems to me we must get and keep the initiative and neither give Sir John time to buy off the weaker brethren in detail nor let the regular opposition use us as cat's paws for their own special objects. . . .

I write, as you will perceive, unreservedly, and need hardly

*say that I have not hinted to anyone that I have opened com-
munications with you, though it is not unlikely it may be
guessed, as I have a kind of idea I have been put under surveil-
lance as a "suspicious character."*

Faithfully yours,

R. J. CARTWRIGHT.

*P.S. – I warned Sir John before Hincks' appointment as
well as after, so he knows what to expect from me.*

During the session of 1870 Galt came out openly against
the government. He was, however, unwilling to act with the
Liberal opposition, now rapidly gaining ground, especially in
Ontario. Though far from being a rigid party man, he could not
bring himself to break wholly with the past. The situation was
not a comfortable one, and he decided to retire from Parliament.
His leading Sherbrooke supporters strongly urged him to reconsider, but he insisted. In 1872 he withdrew from the House,
and did not again enter it. He was succeeded in the representation of Sherbrooke by his intimate friend, Edward T. Brooks.

In these years Galt's interest was, in fact, much more
absorbed by two great general questions affecting his country's
future than by personal and party issues. In the middle seventies,
as will be seen, he gave himself largely to the task of combatting
the aggressions of the ultramontane wing of the Roman Catholic Church; in the late sixties and early seventies the foremost
thought in his mind was the need of readjusting the relations
between Canada and the Mother Country and of preparing
the way for the independent position Canada must at some time
assume.

The independence movement of the seventies was distinctly
an outcome of the peculiar state of the relationship between
Great Britain and the United States, and of the reflex influences
which that relationship exerted on Canadian interests and feeling. The movement was short-lived, but it made a lasting
impression upon Canadian policy, even though that influence
was exerted in a form and a direction which was not expected
by either the advocates or the opponents of independence in
this period. . . .

~ By the early seventies, there was an opinion widely held in
Great Britain that the colonies would inevitably break away
from the Mother Country and go their separate ways. This
attitude was chiefly attributed to the Manchester School of

politicians, but had become accepted rather generally. A new surge of imperialism was to emerge late in the seventies, but in the meantime the dissolution of the Empire was assumed to be a very real possibility and one which was not unwelcome. It was becoming apparent to many that the advantage to be gained by the retention of the colonies was more than balanced by the heavy expense of maintaining an adequate defence of them. The Confederation of Canada in 1867 appeared to be an expression of a new nationalism which would surely lead to complete Canadian independence. ~

In Canada, the movement in favour of a more emphatic as-sertion of nationality had more than one root. In some measure it was, as in Great Britain, an outcome of the unsatisfactory international situation produced by the hostility between the Mother Country and the United States. It was seen that this situation was harmful and dangerous both to Canada and to Great Britain. Great Britain felt hampered in taking a strong course toward the United States because of military weakness in North America, while Canada on the other hand felt that it was continually being sacrificed on the altar of American good will. It would be easier for Canada to keep on good terms with the United States when it had ceased to be a hostage for the Mother Country's good behaviour and a temptation to every American prone to the national sport of twisting the lion's tail. When, in 1871, the British government withdrew the last of its regiments from the Dominion – Halifax retaining a small force as the fleet station – it was widely felt that the hint was plain.

But it was not merely this negative factor which stirred many Canadians to new aspirations. Confederation had aroused a new sense of nationality. McGee particularly had appealed to the sturdy self-reliance and ardent hopes of his hearers, holding before them the prospect of a more active and responsible part in the world's work than the provincial status had permitted. The glowing pride in the resources and possibilities of a nation which reached from the Atlantic to the Rockies, and soon, beyond, stirred many an ardent young mind to wish to throw off the leading strings of colonialism and assume the full responsibility and the full opportunity of nationhood.

It was not surprising that these new sentiments found their best exponent in Galt. He was more familiar than any other Canadian with the trend of opinion in Great Britain. Constant visits, and intimate relationship with official and commercial London, kept him closely in touch. It was at first with some surprise and much uneasiness that he noted the trend of this opinion. In conversation with Mr. Cardwell in 1865, he had emphasized the fact that "the desire and belief of Canada was, in seeking a union, not in any way to weaken the connection with the Mother Country, but rather to remove those causes which now afforded many parties in England arguments for asserting that the connection was mutually disadvantageous." Yet as he came more closely into touch with the men of all parties he was filled with forebodings; "they have treated us too much as ambassadors and on an equality. . . . It is very grievous to see half a continent slipping from the grasp of England with scarcely an effort to hold it." On the very eve of Confederation, we have seen, he was depressed by the evident desire to see the new Dominion strike out for itself. Later visits made these views familiar and convincing. He came to agree with the prevalent view in England that Canada was a source of weakness and of irritation in relation to the United States, and that both would be strengthened by separation.

Other reasons led him to take this stand. He was not in office or leader of a party, and therefore was free to take up any question in advance of public opinion. His cast of mind disposed him to take an interest in broad questions which more opportunist politicians left to ripen. While independent in judgment, he was peculiarly susceptible to new tendencies in thought, and the same disposition which later made him a pioneer on the imperial federation path now led him to take the independence tack. Further, he had always, Englishman-born though he was, been one of the stoutest defenders of Canadian self-government, and he was prepared to follow that principle wherever it might lead.

The new sentiment found expression in many quarters. In Toronto, the Canada First group, under W. A. Foster, pressed strongly for some solution which would open to Canadians a way out of colonial dependence. Whether this should take the form of independence or of imperial federation, its members differed, but they were agreed in feeling that it was impossible for a people occupying half a continent to remain forever a mere dependency. The two ablest young Ontario men who entered politics in these years, Charles A. Moss, afterwards Chief Justice of Ontario, and Edward Blake, sympathized strongly with these aspirations. "An organization which will draw the line between Canadians loyal to their soil and those who place their citizenship in a subordinate or secondary position," declared Foster, in a meeting supporting Moss' successful candidature for Parliament in 1873, "affords the surest means of cementing a confederation and securing political action in the interests of the whole Dominion." In the following year, Blake, in his famous Aurora speech, enigmatic as was his wont, appealed to national spirit, described Canadians as "four millions of Britons who are not free," and urged that by federation of the Empire or otherwise Canada should assert a voice in foreign policy. Howe was also insistent, in one of his last utterances, a speech made at Ottawa in February, 1872, that the time had come for a clearer understanding as to Canada's international status. . . . But it was chiefly in Montreal and in the English-speaking sections of Quebec that the most emphatic stand was taken. The *Quebec Chronicle* was a thick-and-thin advocate of independence, and George T. Lanigan of the *Montreal Star* one of its most ardent supporters. Lucius Huntington, member for Shefford from 1867 to 1882 carried on a campaign in the Eastern Townships in 1869 and 1870, and in Montreal a very influential group of businessmen advocated the same views.

At the same time, a movement in favour of annexation had developed, particularly in Nova Scotia, and it was with some difficulty that Galt and his friends, who were strongly opposed to that ignominious solution of Canada's difficulties, were kept busy warding off the charges of enemies that independence was only a first step to annexation and the desire of the annexation-ists themselves to annex the independence movement. In July, 1869, Lanigan wrote to Galt, urging a league, and referring to some dubious allies:

Montreal, 1st July, 1869.

Dear Sir:

Not having had the pleasure of seeing you in Montreal, I write briefly concerning the subject of Independence.

The feeling is, I judge, sufficiently strong just now to warrant the organization of a party tending in that direction. General Averell was considerably opposed to this, on the ground that the times were not yet ripe, and that were organized demonstration attempted, followed by failure, it would seriously damage the cause. I think we can raise a League here, put up pretty respectable figureheads, and by a subscription of $100 apiece raise $20,000 at once to put out speakers and educate the people a bit. . . . Our first aim, however, is to make a noise and wake up the people.

Galt lost no time in squelching this proposal.

Cacouna, 16 July, 1869.

Dear Sir:

Owing to my absence, your letter of 1st inst. only reached me yesterday.

My opinion is that such an organization as you speak of would be most objectionable, and depending, as I infer from your letter, on American sympathy and support, would be regarded as a movement in favor of annexation under the guise of independence.

So far from supporting any such scheme, it would prove most detrimental to the best interests of the country, and retard for years the peaceful solution of the question as to what is best for the future of the Dominion.

I am, dear Sir,
Your obedient servant,
A. T. GALT.

The movement found few supporters among active politicians. The leaders of both parties, Macdonald and Tupper, Mackenzie and Brown, set their faces against it. Though Galt had not in 1869 brought the question up in Parliament, he had made known his views in speeches outside, and it was to these expressions that Cartier referred in making the offer of the Finance Ministership already noted:

Ottawa, 13 Sept., 1869.

My dear Galt:

When I had the pleasure of seeing you in Montreal a few days ago, I expressed to you my individual opinion that I would like very much you should resume the office of Minister of Finance on the retirement of Rose from it. — Now, I am happy to say, I have the authority from Sir John A. Macdonald to make you the offer of joining the Government as Minister of Finance, so soon as Rose will cease to occupy his post. As you are aware, the question of "The Independence of Canada" is now being discussed in the public papers, and it is well I should mention that if it should be brought before the Houses of Parliament, it will be expected as a matter of course that the members of Government should be a unit in resisting any attempt or proceeding favorable to independence.

I regret very much that it is impossible for me to go near you, to commune freely with you on the offer now made to you,

*but if you should like to have a personal interview with Sir
John A. Macdonald or myself, I am enabled to say to you that
Sir John as well as myself will be very happy to see you here.*

Believe me, my dear Galt, as always,
Your devoted friend,
GEO. ET. CARTIER.

Montreal, 14 Sept., 1869.

My dear Cartier:

*I received your letter of 14th inst. last night, and have given
its contents my best consideration.*

*I thank Sir John and yourself for the desire you express that
I should again enter the Administration as Minister of Finance.
But my views of public duty compel me to decline.*

*I could have wished that you had not referred to the quota-
tion of Independence, as for other reasons I have no doubt my
reply would have been the same, but I suppose your reason in
doing so was lest it should be supposed that in inviting me to
enter the Cabinet you in any way countenanced my views on
this subject. I think this was needless as I am quite sure the
public would rather have supposed that I had receded from
my position than that Sir John's government had become so
progressive.*

*As you have introduced this subject, I must in all frankness
say that believing it is the policy aimed at by the Imperial
Government, and feeling confident that it would in many ways
benefit this country, I could not have consented to enter the
Cabinet under a pledge to oppose it in any form. On the contrary, I think our policy should be framed with reference to that
which appears to me to be inevitable – a separation of the
Dominion from Great Britain.*

Believe me,
Yours sincerely,
A. T. GALT.

The following year, February, 1870, brought out a vigorous
debate on the question in Parliament. In the course of the
discussion on the Speech from the Throne, both Tupper and
Hincks took occasion to make some references to Galt's views,
stigmatizing them as disloyal. In reply Galt made a frank and
vigorous defence and explanation of the stand he had taken.

Loyalty, he declared, was not the mere expression of sentiment. Loyalty meant a man giving of his best, giving his time

and his energy to the service and progress of his country. In this view Her Majesty's ministers evidently agreed with him, as would be made clear from a correspondence which had taken place during the past year and which he would ask leave to place before the public. Passing to the merits of the issue, Galt insisted that independence was the surest bulwark against annexation:

The effect upon the Canadian people of teaching them that they cannot exist unless they are holding on to the skirts of a great power for all time to come, will most surely, when the connection with Great Britain is severed, and the public mind is not educated to the point of believing that we can stand alone, be that annexation will ensue.

Let us look at this question with reference to the interests of the British Empire. Could any one look at the connection which exists between this country and Great Britain without perceiving it is a source of difficulty to her Statesmen, and at the same time of danger to ourselves? English Statesmen are teach- ing us — for their actions speak louder than their words — lessons of self-reliance. Every step that is taken is one in that direction. What does it all mean? Does it mean that they are teaching us that we are to continue for all time the connection, or does it not rather mean that they are gradually leading us up from depend- ency to an independent existence? The great interest of the British Empire at the present time I take to be the building up of a British Empire on this continent, independent of the United States. If she cannot succeed in that, then it is perfectly clear that these Provinces will be ultimately absorbed by the United States. The effect of that absorption would be to make that country the first Maritime Power of the globe. Therefore, I hold that the policy of England was a wise one. With a view to prevent this absorption the statesmen of England desire to teach us that we have a future of our own, and induce us to keep separate from that country, and thus preserve a balance of power. I believe that is the wisest and only policy for British statesmen to adopt, and in not accepting that policy and helping to carry it out as a matter of duty to the empire, we should be really doing more to imperil the empire, which we love, than by any other course we could take.

I have never proposed, nor do I now intend to take any action on the question of independence. It would not be wise to do so. I would vote against a motion for that purpose to-night if

it were brought up. I could not say when we would be prepared
for that future. If independence were to take place now it would
end in our drifting into the United States (hear, hear), but while
I hold that view, I believe that the day for independence will
come, and unless we were prepared for it, unless our legislation
be framed with that view, we will be found then in the same
position as now, and being unprepared for a separate political
existence, we will have no choice with regard to our future.
Confederation was an Act of Imperial as well as of Colonial
policy. The intention of that Act, I believe, was to secure by a
union of all the scattered British North American Colonies a
united country of sufficient power, population and wealth, to be
able to maintain itself alone. That policy was to a certain extent
carried out by the British North America Act, and my complaint
against the Government is that they have not made use of the
prestige which Confederation gave them, that they have not
been successful in their efforts to consolidate Confederation.

The reference to the correspondence with Lord Granville
makes it advisable to insert here the more important in the
series of letters exchanged upon the occasion of the offer of a
K.C.M.G. to Galt:

Ottawa, 15 May, 1869.
Dear Sir John [Young, Governor-General of Canada, 1868-72]*:*
I desire to offer my grateful acknowledgment to Earl Gran-
ville for the intimation which Your Excellency was good enough
to convey to me to-day, that Her Majesty's Government were
prepared to submit my name to the Queen for the distinction of
the second grade of the Order of St. Michael and St. George.
It will afford me the highest gratification to accept the offer
so graciously made. But as I have already verbally explained to
Your Excellency, I do not feel at liberty to do so without making
Her Majesty's Government aware of certain views which I hold
as to the political future of the Dominion, the knowledge of
which might possibly influence their decision.
I regard the Confederation of the British North American
provinces as a measure which must ultimately lead to their
separation from Great Britain.
The present connection is undoubtedly an embarrassment
to Great Britain in her relations to the United States, and a
source of uneasiness to the Dominion owing to the insecurity
which is felt to exist from the possibility of a rupture between
the two nations.

It cannot be the policy of England, and it is certainly not the desire of the people here, that Canada should be annexed to the United States, but I believe the best and indeed the only way to prevent this is to teach the Canadian people to look forward to an independent existence as a nation in the future as being desirable and possible. Unless such a spirit be cultivated, the idea will become ingrained in the public mind that failing the connection with Great Britain annexation must come.

I believe the existing relations would be safer if the future state were clearly recognized, and, if possible, a term fixed therefor. It is our interest and certainly my desire to postpone this event, and to avail ourselves of the moral and physical support of Great Britain as long as possible, meantime developing our own internal strength and resources.

I do not believe the advocacy of these views, as time and circumstances may warrant, ought to be offensive to Her Majesty's Government, or to be regarded as detracting from my duty as a subject of the Queen. But I cannot honourably accept the proposed distinction while holding opinions that may be regarded unfavourably, and that being known would have prevented the offer being made to me by Lord Granville.

I must beg Your Excellency to regard this note as confidential to all except Her Majesty's Government, as I do not wish to find myself openly committed to a policy now which events might later cause me to modify.

Should Her Majesty's Government, after this communication, still consider me worthy of the proposed distinction, I should accept it with much gratification. If not, I should still feel equally grateful for the goodness which has prompted the honour.

> Believe me, dear Sir John,
> Your Excellency's most obedient servant,
> A. T. GALT.

Ottawa, 17 May, 1869.
My dear Mr. Cardwell [Secretary of State for War, 1868-74]:
. . . I trust I will not be misunderstood in stating these impressions. I cannot help seeing that the United States regard our defenceless frontier as a source of weakness and possible humiliation to England, and I cannot doubt that the fear of exposing us to the horrors of invasion has a strong and restraining influence on the policy of England.

The knowledge of our position and consequent risk tends to

retard the progress of this country and to send emigrants from our shores.

I have always believed, in common with most thinking men, that at some period the Dominion would become detached from the Mother Country. But I now begin to fear the day is not distant, and the United States are determined to hurry it on. If that day should come while our people are taught and believe that they cannot exist without English support, we must drop at once into the United States. I therefore think the wisest policy will be to commence a discussion of our possible future as an independent country, so as to prepare for the time when the trial will have to be made.

Moreover, the responsibilities we are assuming in taking upon us the organization of the North-West are very great, and will entail burdens which, I think, will only be cheerfully borne under the idea that we are building up an Empire for ourselves. . . .

Lord Granville, in his reply to Sir John Young, declared that he had never been more pleased with any letter than that which Young had forwarded from Galt. His further opinions are indicated in the letter which he wrote later for publication, in response to Galt's reference to the correspondence in the 1870 debate.

Montreal, 25 Feb., 1870.

My dear Lord Granville:

I feel it my duty to offer some explanations to Your Lordship in reference to the remarks I have been compelled to make in the recent debate in our House on the Address.

For reasons which I cannot explain, except on the supposition that the charge would damage me in public estimation, the Government saw fit to give much prominence to my views on the question of independence, and then first indirectly through their supporter, Dr. Tupper, and afterwards directly through Sir F. Hincks, imputed disloyalty to me for holding such opinions.

In self-defence I was compelled to refer to my letter to Sir John Young when you were good enough to offer me the K.C.M.G., and generally to state the contents, pledging myself to produce the letter. I added that I was not at liberty to refer to the reply, but that it was followed by the distinction being conferred, and that therefore I did not consider myself more disloyal than Her Majesty's Ministers. I enclose report of my remarks.

The following day Sir Francis Hincks again returned to the subject and called on me to produce the reply to my letter. To which I rejoined that I would ask for permission to do so. This I have done by note to Sir John Young.

I beg Your Lordship to observe that I have not stated that Her Majesty's Government approved of my views, only that they did not treat them as disloyal.

I shall feel extremely sorry if this affair causes you any annoyance, but it was not brought on by me, as I have not said one word publicly about independence since the last session of our Parliament, and had no wish to give publicity to the corre- spondence with Sir John Young. The indiscretion, if such it be, rests with Her Majesty's advisers.

As the question has, however, now attracted a large amount of public attention, I venture to repeat the suggestion I offered in communication with Your Lordship, that the aims of the Government had better be plainly stated. It would be well to say that the Imperial Government must look forward at some future day to the independence of British North America, and that they consider we can but perform our duty to the Empire and the Queen by preparing for it.

Colonial Office, March 15/70.
Dear Sir Alexander:

I have to acknowledge the receipt of your letter of the 25th ultimo.

I have only one objection to authorizing you to publish a copy of my private letter to Sir John Young of the 19th of June. It would establish a precedent which might in other circum- stances be inconvenient if a liability be admitted to produce a private letter from the Secretary of State to the Governor because the latter had communicated it confidentially to a third person, as Sir John Young did to you, with perfect propriety in this case.

I had previously obtained the Queen's permission to offer you the K.C.M.G. with a view of paying a compliment to the Dominion, in the person of one of its most distinguished states- men. I was not then aware of the views which you entertained respecting the possible future of the Confederation. Sir John Young forwarded to me the letter in which, giving your reasons for it, you stated your opinion, that the confederation of the

*British North American Provinces must ultimately lead to their
separation from Great Britain, that it could not be the policy of
Great Britain, and was certainly not the desire of the people of
the Dominion, to become annexed to the United States, and that
the best course to avoid it was to encourage the Canadian people
to look forward to independence in the future, and you added
your belief that the existing relations would be safer and more
desirable if the future state were more clearly recognized, and if
possible a term fixed therefor, it being the interest of the
Canadians and your own desire to postpone the event, and to
avail yourselves of the moral and physical support of Great
Britain as long as possible.*

*You thought that these views ought not to be regarded as
detracting from your duty as a subject of the Queen, and you
did not like to accept the distinction, unless these opinions were
known to those who made the offer, and you asked that the
communication might be considered confidential, as you did not
wish to pledge yourself to a policy which events might cause you
to modify.*

*In reply I requested Sir John Young to inform you how
much pleased I was with the honorable spirit of your letter, and
to add that I did not consider your statement precluded a
Minister of the Crown from offering you a well deserved honor
from the Queen.*

Yours sincerely,

GRANVILLE.

*You will observe that I have not marked this letter
"private."*

In reply, Galt wrote thanking Lord Granville for his courtesy, and offering to resign the distinction if his retention of it
caused any embarrassment. Lord Granville once more took the
same position:

*16b Bruton Street, London, W.
May 18/70.*

Dear Sir Alexander:

*I have to thank you for your letter of last month. I fully
appreciate your honourable motives in offering to resign the
order of St. Michael and St. George.*

*When I first offered the distinction to you from the Queen,
I was not aware of the opinions you held respecting the future
of the Dominion.*

When informed by you confidentially of certain opinions

*which you held respecting the possible future of the Dominion
as a result of the confederation, I thought they constituted no
reason for recommending Her Majesty to withhold the honour
from a distinguished and loyal statesman like yourself.*

*I am not aware of anything which has since occurred which
should modify that opinion, or induce me to take the stronger
step of accepting your resignation of the honour.*

Yours sincerely,

GRANVILLE.

Galt consistently maintained that the time had not then
come for effecting independence. For the present, his sole
purpose was to endeavour to cultivate a stronger national spirit
and to accustom the people and the government to rely on their
own resources. In accordance with this view, he advocated, in
March, 1870, the acquisition of independent treaty-making
powers, so far as commercial agreements were concerned.
Huntington had brought forward a resolution to the same effect,
coupling it, however, with a demand for a Customs Union with
the United States, a policy which he defended by declaring,
without contradiction, that the government had sanctioned it by
agreeing, through Mr. Rose, to adopt a policy of free trade in
manufactures with the United States. Galt was not willing to
make any trade concessions to the United States which could
not also be extended to the Mother Country. He therefore
moved an amendment omitting all reference to the Customs
Union, and urging that powers should be obtained from the
imperial government to enable the Dominion government to
enter into direct negotiations with other British possessions and
foreign states to effect commercial agreements, subject to
ratification by the Crown. In reply, Macdonald, declaring that
"there could be no difference of opinion as to the advantage of
free trade with the United States and other nations," did not
agree that independent action could secure the boons desired.
"Why should we throw away the great advantage we now have
of the assistance of England in negotiating treaties?" he inquired. "How much better to have the powerful assistance of
Great Britain than to go with bated breath and humble tone
pleading *in forma pauperis* with foreign countries to make a
treaty with them. Their answer would be, 'We don't know you!
who are you?' 'A province of England.' 'Then send England to
us, and we will treat with her.' That would be the deserved
answer we would get. . . . Again, what guarantee would we have

that England would ratify the treaty of our making even if foreign nations were weak enough to enter into a treaty with us without having a previous guarantee that England would ratify it?"

The need of a sturdy assertion of Canadian nationalism is apparent when the premier of the country is found taking up a position of such apologetic and dependent colonialism as this. Fortunately, Macdonald's acts were better than his theories, and when an actual test came, a year later, no one could have upheld Canada's interests more sturdily than he did. His changed opinions of the "great advantage" of British assistance in negotiating treaties were the best justification of Galt's attitude in 1870.

Five years had passed since the close of the Civil War, and the disputes left as a legacy of that struggle were still unsettled. The United States demanded compensation from England for the depredations committed by the *Alabama* and other Confederate cruisers built in English ports. Canada countered with claims for the damages which an equally lax interpretation of the duties of a neutral state had permitted the lawless bands of Fenians to perpetrate. Reciprocity, in spite of negotiations by Rose in 1869, was still unattained. As a lever to secure trade privileges and in defence of her just rights, Canada was insisting upon a strict enforcement of her exclusive right to her inshore fisheries.

In 1870 the Dominion government suggested the appointment of a joint commission to settle the fishery dispute. In the later discussion between the British and United States authorities it was decided to appoint a commission, but to give it jurisdiction over all the questions at issue, whether between Great Britain and the United States or Canada and the United States. Canada was not consulted as to this linking up of the diverse issues, nor in framing the terms of reference. One concession was made, the offer to Macdonald of a place as one of the five British commissioners. With many doubts he consented to act, and made preparations to spend the spring of 1871 in Washington.

Galt at once demurred to this linking up of the *Alabama* claims with the Canadian issues. He feared that in order to pacify the United States on this question, the British commissioners would be prepared to sacrifice or overlook the interests of the Dominion. It would have been better, he contended, to negotiate separately, offering fishery in exchange for trade privileges, or to abstain from negotiations entirely, suffering whatever restrictions were in force rather than run the risk of worse arrangements. Had Canada insisted upon the right to be consulted in negotiations so directly concerning her, before they had taken a fixed form, this might have been kept in view. Now that the agreement for the joint commission had been made, the only course was to make the best of it, and to put the Parliament of the Dominion on record as insisting upon a vigilant guarding of her vital national interests.

On February 24, 1871, Galt, seconded by Cartwright, moved a series of resolutions, urging a sturdy assertion of these interests. In supporting these resolutions, Galt declared it was the duty of the House to strengthen the hands of the government in the approaching negotiations, in the unequal struggle in which the Canadian representative was about to be engaged. He regretted the mixing up of Canadian and British issues, not that the British authorities were capable of any action that was not wholly honourable, but that in view of their great anxiety to settle their outstanding difficulties with the United States they might be inclined to attach too little value to Canadian rights and interests. Our government had been entirely ignored since a period in 1870, and had had no share in determining the scope of the Commission's activities. He was doubtful whether the Fenian Raid claims could be brought before the Commission under the terms of reference, though certainly our rights to indemnification were stronger than the *Alabama* claims of the United States, and should have been pressed more firmly.

"We must guard our right," he continued, "and not be put in a position of inferiority to the United States. I wholly repudiate the idea that this country is in any way subordinate or ought to be subordinate to the policy of the United States. I desire to retain our connection with Great Britain so long as it can be maintained in the interest of both countries, but if the time ever comes that that connection will cease, I desire that the people of Canada should not be in a position of inferiority to the great republic. We must preserve in our own hands the great interests which would go hereafter to build up a great Empire on this continent and keep it intact for our posterity."

In the discussion which followed in the House and in the press, it was made clear that in these resolutions Galt had voiced a widespread opinion. Several leaders, however, including Macdonald, Blake and Mackenzie, took the stand that it would not strengthen the hands of the British negotiators to

pass a resolution which made clear a divergence of interests between Canada and Great Britain, and Galt agreed to withdraw
the resolution without a vote, as his main purpose had been
served by bringing on a discussion. In doing so, he declared that
whatever might be his differences of opinion with Sir John
Macdonald, he had no doubt he would uphold the interests of
Canada in his mission.

The proceedings at Washington confirmed every point of
Galt's contention, and showed that he knew both British and
United States statesmen better than Sir John. The oversight of
the British ambassador in framing the terms of the subjects
for discussion, and the sharp insistence of the United States
commissioners on the letter of these terms, resulted in ruling
Canada's Fenian Raid claims out of court. The *Alabama* claims
and the San Juan dispute were referred to arbitration. Macdonald's attempt to secure reciprocity in trade in return for the
concession of inshore fishing privileges came to nothing, and
after objecting strenuously to a calm proposal to purchase these
privileges in perpetuity for a million dollars, the best he could
do was to limit the concession of the fisheries to ten years, with
notice, and to have the question of the money compensation to
be made for their use referred to arbitration.

Macdonald now recognized "that Canada was not responsible for the commingling of the various subjects of difference
between the nations, and was prejudiced by it. The consequence
was that Canada was now called upon against her will to enter
into an arrangement which she considers in the highest degree
unsatisfactory to her people, in order to secure the settlement of
other matters in which England is more immediately interested."
He saw the advantage of having, had it been possible, a "minor
commission . . . to settle Canadian questions . . . to consist, on
our side, of two Canadians and Sir Edward Thornton," which
would "give Canada a far better chance than she has now, when
her pecuniary interests are considered as altogether secondary
to the present Imperial necessities." He told his fellow Commissioner, Lord de Grey, that it was out of the question "for
Canada to surrender, for all time to come, her fishery rights for
any compensation whatever; that we had no right to injure
posterity by depriving Canada *either as a dependency or as a
nation*, of her fisheries." As to his colleagues, he reported: "I
must say that I am greatly disappointed at the course taken by
the British Commissioners. They seem to have only one thing in
their minds — that is, to go home to England with a treaty in

their pockets, settling everything, no matter at what cost to Canada. . . . The U.S. Commissioners . . . found our English friends so squeezable in nature that their audacity has grown beyond all bounds."

As Macdonald anticipated, the announcement of these terms was met with a storm of denunciation in Canada. The other members of the government were in favour of withholding assent to the fishery articles which, by the terms of the treaty, were dependent upon ratification by the Canadian legislature as well as by the United States Senate for their validity, and for a time Macdonald himself was inclined to this course. After reflection, however, he came to the conclusion that now that the treaty had been framed, it would not be right for Canada to imperil the settlement of the vexed issues between the Mother Country and the United States and bring back the spectre of war. In a powerful speech he urged this course upon Parliament, and posterity, like that Parliament, has endorsed his stand.

With the settlement of the concrete international questions at issue by the Washington Treaty, the public, both in Canada and in Britain, ceased to take any strong interest in the topic of Canada's national status. In Great Britain, the belief that separation was inevitable and desirable lessened as the menace of war with the United States faded away. Provided that the large debit entry of military weakness was cancelled or diminished, the people of England were prepared to conclude that the prestige and potential profit of holding overseas possessions left a balance on the credit side of Empire. The reawakening of imperialist and protectionist sentiment occasioned by the Franco-Prussian War told in the same direction. In Canada, the same factors counted, lessening the irritation felt over the real or fancied surrender of Canadian rights and the concern over the military weakness of England's position involved in Canada's helplessness. The deep-seated love for the old land, the dependence born of generations of colonialism, the preoccupation of politicians with immediate personal or party issues, all made against any immediate action. Much of the nationalist feeling was turned into protectionist channels: the National Policy of Protection, which was brought forward soon afterward, professed to offer an economic Declaration of Independence more effective and more practical than any proclamation of political independence could be.

The discussion had not, however, been in vain. Galt and

those who with him urged Canada to take on the stature and responsibilities of nationhood did much to rouse the nation from contented colonialism. They emphasized one of the goals toward which Canada was steadily to strive: national autonomy. Later, Galt was to take a leading part in advocating a different means of securing the share in the world's affairs he had at heart – imperial federation. Posterity has not accepted either of the policies he urged in its entirety, but the ideal of the Empire as a partnership of equal and independent states which it has been the task and the achievement of these later years to work out, takes heed of both aims, reconciling them in a fashion that few in earlier days foresaw.

Galt was not in the House when the question of the ratification of the Fishery agreement came before it. He had, it has been seen, decided to retire at the expiration of the term of the first Parliament of federated Canada. Yet the turn of the political wheel soon brought insistent demands that he should re-enter the struggle, and take the leadership of a reconstructed Conservative party.

In the House elected in 1872, the position of the Conservatives was much less impregnable than in the earlier Parliament, though the Liberals were themselves weakened by the rivalry between Mackenzie and Blake for the leadership. Sir John Macdonald would have maintained his power unchallenged for another term, however, had not the revelations of the acceptance of huge campaign contributions from Sir Hugh Allan, one of the rival promoters of a Pacific railway scheme, driven him from office before an outburst of public indignation. There was still a Conservative majority in the House, and it was by no means inevitable that the Opposition leader would be called in to form the new ministry when Sir John resigned.

Galt was absent from the country at the time Parliament assembled in October, 1873, to consider the report of the Royal Commission which had been appointed to investigate the charges. He had been in Ottawa when the question of the procedure to be followed, inquiry by a committee of Parliament or by a royal commission, and the question of the prorogation of the House pending investigation by the latter body had been under discussion, and had been called on by Lord Dufferin for advice, as being the only Privy Councillor not involved in active party strife. This advice, after some hesitation, he had given. Having renounced any further parliamentary ambitions for himself, he had not cared to remain in the capital, waiting for something to turn up, and had gone to England on business.

"I have but little doubt," declared Sir Richard Cartwright in his *Reminiscences*, "that if Sir A. T. Galt had been in the House, or even in the country at that moment, he might easily have been sent for. . . . I thought at the time, and I found afterwards, that I was probably correct, that had Sir A. T. Galt been in Canada at the time he would have been asked to lead a joint party. You will observe that in the House, as it then stood, the regular Liberal party was in a minority, and the result of an appeal to the people was quite uncertain, while it was pretty clear that a large section of the Conservative party were not inclined at the time to have anything more to do with Sir John. These men would cheerfully have supported a Government presided over by Sir A. T. Galt, and failing him, a great many would have accepted Blake."

The soundness of his opinion is borne out by many indications. On Galt's return to Canada he was besieged by requests to take the field. A Conservative editor writes him shortly after his return:

Cobourg, Ont., Nov. 17, 1873.

Dear Sir Alexander:

I see a rumour in the papers to the effect that you have been asked to join the present government. If there is any prospect of your doing so, I would like to know it, so as to shape our political writings to suit the proposed change. Our six members would all support you, and you would have the strongest personal following of any member of the Cabinet.

If you take no action in the matter, but remain an independent, as heretofore, our members would continue to support Sir John. They don't like Mr. Cartwright, and won't support the present government on his account.

Yours truly,

H. J. RUTTAN.

A Quebec editor urges him in still stronger terms:

Quebec, January 5, 1874.

Why not come out now? Party knocked all to smash. We want a leader for Quebec. You were out of the Pacific mess.

S. B. FOOTE.

The shrewd Eastern Townships politician, J. H. Pope, who had of recent years been inclined to follow other leaders, now writes to urge him back:

Cookshire, Dec. 31st, 1873.

My dear Sir:

I have been wanting to see you about political matters for some time. You seem to me to be the man best able to advise, and, I think, best able to lead, of any man in the Province or in the Dominion. What do you say about the present position or about going into active political life? Webb wants to give up, I am told. You could carry the county easily. Would you do it?

Yours very truly,

J. H. POPE.

Still more significant was the appeal from Alexander Campbell, Sir John Macdonald's law partner:

Kingston, 6 January, 1874.

My dear Galt:

What of the coming elections? Shall you be a candidate? I hope so very earnestly. Your presence again in Parliament would be of essential service, I think, to the country and to our party. In Lower Canada especially, but extending all over Canada, almost everyone interested in public affairs and holding Conservative views, would hail your reappearance with infinite satisfaction, and in my opinion the time is coming when a large party in both Houses will be seeking in new alliances an outlet from dilemmas which trammel them now.

Brown, in the Senate, unless he is much changed, will soon assume the role of member and guide to the Ministry, and will push his influence until some of its members rebel. I do not look on Cartwright remaining very long with them, nor Albert Smith nor Scott.

What do you think of Cartwright as a Finance Minister? He is likely, I fear, to be tried by hard times and a tight money market, do you not think?

Come back to political life and we will pull together, and seek to put together all that may be found from all the provinces opposed to the present men.

Faithfully yours,

A. CAMPBELL.

In spite of these flattering appeals, and of his own interest in politics, Sir Alexander declined again to enter the arena. Requests to join forces with the Opposition were equally unavailing. His relations with the Liberals became more friendly than they had been when he first broke from his own party, but they did not go the length of alliance. He came to have a deep respect for Mackenzie, which was fully reciprocated. Later in 1873 the new premier sought his services in settling the unfortunate dispute with British Columbia in which rash promises, extravagant demands and hard times had involved the Dominion:

Ottawa, Dec. 25, '73.

My dear Mr. Galt:

I was very sorry that I missed seeing you on Tuesday in Montreal, as I wished very much to consult you about some matters of importance. We may have to try to effect some compromise with British Columbia regarding the railway terms of union as it is manifestly impossible for us to complete the Railway even on their soil within the time specified in the terms of Union. We have thought of sending some person to confer with them and endeavour to effect some other arrangement before the meeting of Parliament. If anyone is sent he must be one well known in the Dominion and possessed of influence and standing in the country.

Would it be possible for you to consent to be the plenipotentiary in the event of our deciding on such a course? In the event of your entertaining the proposition I will communicate fully with you regarding our plans and the present state of the proposed Railway. I have only mentioned to Blake and Cartwright my intention to write you with this request, but I know all the other members of the Cabinet would be delighted to know you could go on the proposed mission.

I am, My dear Sir,
Yours faithfully,
A. MACKENZIE.

Galt felt compelled to decline:

Montreal, 2 January, 1874.

My dear Mr. Mackenzie:

Unfortunately I went to Toronto the day after Xmas, and consequently did not receive your note of the 25th ult. till my return yesterday.

Allow me to thank you for the mark of your confidence contained in the proposed mission to British Columbia. I be-

*lieve your policy on the Pacific R.R. would have presented no
difficulty in the way of my accepting the trust. But unfortunately
my own personal engagements seem on reflection quite to preclude my acting and I have therefore no other course left but
to decline.*

Yours very faithfully,

A. T. GALT.

Somewhat later, it came to be widely believed that Galt
would re-enter politics on the Liberal side. In an open letter to
Senator Ferrier, September 3, 1875, he declared:

*While willing, if required, to re-enter Parliament, it would
not, according to my convictions of duty, be possible for me to
do so, either as a supporter of the present administration, or as
a member of the Opposition under Sir John A. Macdonald.*

*I continue to belong, with very many others, to that section
of the so-called Conservative party, which regretfully acquiesced in the condemnation passed by the country, upon the late
Administration. And I cannot blame those members of our
party who found it their duty to sustain Mr. Mackenzie's efforts
to carry on the government, which he would have been utterly
unable to do if dependent only on the support of his immediate
political friends. The exigency of the hour necessitated a breach
in the former party, and had I then been in Parliament Mr.
Mackenzie would have received from me all necessary support.
This necessity has now passed away, and the Administration
must henceforward be judged by its own merits, and not supported from any alleged fear that their resignation would absolutely restore Sir John A. Macdonald to power. My conviction
in reference to this latter contingency is that notwithstanding
the great and acknowledged public service by that gentleman, it
is impossible to ignore the circumstances that led to his defeat.
I regard his election as leader of the regular Opposition as a
grave mistake, which tends to perpetuate the breach in the party,
and will ultimately lead either to the formation of new party
lines, or to the final adherence of many of our friends to the
Liberals.*

Galt went on to attack the plan of immediate construction
of the Canadian Pacific, without relation to settlement, and to
set forth his views on the question of trade policy which was
then coming to stir the public mind. His views, he declared, had
ripened but not changed since he had arranged the tariff in 1859

and modified it in 1866; the policy of incidental protection or modified free trade, he still believed to be in the country's best interest. In applying that policy, however, regard would have to be paid to the change in conditions involved by the adoption by the United States of a high tariff. "For my part," he continued, "I am heartily tired of efforts at conciliating the United States commercially. We meet with no response from them. Our canals are open to their vessels, theirs are shut to ours. They trade on equal terms with us in our own waters, while our ships are excluded from theirs. I do not say that we should retaliate, but I affirm most strongly that henceforward the sole consideration as regards our trade relations with the United States should be the effect upon ourselves."

In an address in Toronto, in the following June, Galt repeated this position, and made the suggestion, which he was to urge repeatedly in future years, and which was to bear fruit twenty years later, that the products of the Mother Country should be given a tariff preference over those of the United States.

These and similar expressions of opinion made it clear that Galt was not prepared to side wholly with either party, or to make the sacrifice of personal opinions which a re-entry into politics would involve. If any further evidence of this attitude was required, it was supplied by the stand which he took on another question which was agitating the public mind, but which most politicians were keen to leave alone – the relations of Church and State in Quebec.

14: Church and State

The rise of ultramontanism; the movement in Canada; Galt takes the field; the triumph of moderation.

~ In the early nineteenth century many Roman Catholic priests were uneasy witnesses to the growing influence of scepticism, atheistic socialism, and other radical modern ideas which sprang from the enlightenment of the eighteenth century and threatened to undermine the foundations of the Church. In the latter half of the century, under the leadership of Pope Pius IX, the forces of reaction within the Church launched a massive counter-attack on modernism. A steady stream of encyclicals, letters and pronouncements condemning subversive ideas, and what was described as "political liberalism" poured forth from the Vatican. Finally, in 1864, Pope Pius published the *Syllabus of Errors* which listed eighty erroneous and sinful beliefs among which were included the ideas of church-state separation and secular education. In 1870 the Church, meeting in council at Rome, adopted the doctrine of Papal Infallibility and reasserted the claim that the Church was absolutely independent of secular control.

These developments caused a wave of consternation to sweep through the western world. Liberal Catholics, as well as Protestants, were alarmed at the prospect of a priesthood completely dominated by a Pope of such sternly reactionary views. In Bismarck's Germany the state and church authorities became locked in a vicious ideological conflict, aptly described as the *Kulturkampf*, and in England, Gladstone thundered against the pretensions of the Church in fiercely condemnatory pamphlets which enjoyed a tremendous sale.

Similarly in Canada, the Pope's pronouncements stirred a storm of controversy. Here the reactionary views of the Vatican were shared by a number of highly placed Catholic churchmen, most notably Bishop Bourget of Montreal. In his diocese the Jesuits, who were thought to have inspired the Pope's militant attitude, were accorded especially favoured treatment by the Bishop. When he undertook to build a cathedral in Montreal, he symbolically constructed a small replica of St. Peter's, and when the Pope appealed for financial help in defending Rome against Garibaldi in 1867, Bourget zealously went so far as to raise a contingent of volunteers to go to Italy.

Bourget was most concerned about the insidious spread of modernistic ideas among the youth of Quebec and he traced their source to the *Institut Canadien*, an organization whose members were noted for their radically advanced ideas on religion and politics. He went to extraordinary lengths in his efforts to combat the influence of the *Institut*. When one of its members, Joseph Guibord, died, the Bishop refused permission for burial in consecrated ground. This questionable decision was challenged and the case was eventually taken before the Privy Council in England. During the long drawn-out legal battle, the Bishop of Montreal became in many eyes the epitome of Roman Catholic conservatism. He attended the Ecumenical Council of 1870 in Rome, where his natural authoritarian inclination was reinforced, and he returned to Canada determined to renew the struggle against the forces of darkness with fresh vigour.

During the provincial election of 1871, Bourget attempted to throw the weight of the Church into the political arena. Hitherto the Church had generally supported the Conservatives who were considered to be most reliable in maintaining social stability and protecting the interests of the Church, particularly in education. Suddenly the Catholic electors were directed to vote only for those candidates, irrespective of party, who would guarantee to legislate in the interest of the Church. This open attempt to create a Catholic party in Quebec was repeated in the federal election of 1874 and the provincial contest of 1875.

Galt watched these developments with growing apprehension. In 1875 he wrote to Macdonald warning him of the ominous trend in the province and requesting an assurance that the Conservative party would never submit to dictatorial control by the Church. Macdonald replied in typical fashion by pointing out that both Bishop Bourget and Pope Pius were old men who must die soon and that it was likely they would be succeeded by men of more moderate views. Galt, who was never one to compromise with conviction, considered Macdonald's reply as something less than satisfactory and decided to express his fears in print. ~

In a pamphlet of some sixteen pages, *Civil Liberty in Lower Canada*, issued in February, 1876, Galt stated his uneasiness over the change in the attitude of the Roman Catholic hierarchy. The clergy, he insisted, whether Protestant or Catholic, must be forbidden to interfere with secular officers in any other charac-

ter than as ordinary citizens. "It is repugnant to all proper feeling," he continued, "that the tremendous weapons of religious
anathema should be lightly used in mere secular warfare, or
that the hold over the human conscience entrusted to the
Minister of God should be exercised for any other purposes
than those of piety and moral purity." It was not consistent with
the good government of the country that any portion of the
people should be held in such bondage as Bishop Bourget aimed
to ensure. He did not think it advisable to proceed on the lines
of the Protestant Defence Association, but rather to appeal to
men of all religions to range themselves on the side of freedom:
"With a plain and unmistakable declaration on the part of the
Protestants that they will, equally for their Roman Catholic
fellow-citizens, as for themselves, resist the encroachments of
the Church upon the State, it may be possible to arrest the
arrogant course of Bishop Bourget and his confrères."

This straightforward message had a wide influence. Many
of both races and creeds welcomed its plain speaking, though
others declared it inopportune. Few could question the serious-
ness of the situation in which the Roman Catholic citizens of
Quebec and the Dominion would be found if the ultramontane
wing of the hierarchy had its way, but it was urged that this was
not a matter that concerned the Protestants of the province, who
had been given the widest possible freedom in managing their
own affairs. Archbishop Lynch, of Toronto, after denying, like
Cardinal Manning in his reply to Mr. Gladstone's attack on the
Vatican Decrees, that the relations between Church and State
had in any way been changed thereby, insisted that Sir Alexander's fears were groundless, and that the Protestants of Quebec
enjoyed much greater privileges than the Roman Catholics of
Ontario. The *Nouveau Monde*, Bishop Bourget's special organ,
declared that the Church had a right to expect better of a man
who hitherto had only to felicitate himself on the liberality with
which he and his co-religionists had been treated by the Catholic
majority in the province; and then in the same issue proceeded
to illustrate its ideal of toleration by citing as a legitimate use
of the influence of the clergy instructions given by the Spanish
bishops of Catalonia on the eve of an election: "Freedom of
worship is forbidden in the Syllabus; no Catholic can vote for
that disastrous freedom or send as representative to the Cortes
those who have decided to establish it in Spain."

H. G. Joly de Lotbinière, the French-speaking Protestant
who led the Liberal party in the province, emphasized the fact

that in the past the English-speaking Protestants had thrown their weight in favour of the very party which the Protestant Defence Association was now attacking, and urged them in future to be a little less keen after the loaves and fishes, and a little more anxious to secure good government, that is, to support a party which would give equal rights and full liberty to all. The opinions of those Protestants who believed in a policy of neutrality were stated most forcefully in a pamphlet by Thomas White, the ablest and most promising of the younger leaders of the Conservative party in Quebec. White contended that there was no evidence of any change in the attitude of the majority toward the minority, that the situation was much the same as when Sir Alexander was a colleague of Cartier's and Upper Canada priest-baiters were denouncing both, and that the Liberals of Quebec were fully as submissive to the hierarchy as the Conservatives. He joined Sir Alexander in regretting that the school legislation of the previous session had placed Catholic education wholly under clerical control, but pointed out that this act had not been opposed on either side of the House, and that by the same measure Protestant education had been placed equally as fully under Protestant control. "The Protestant minority in the Province of Quebec," he concluded, "have had no reason up to this time to doubt the liberality and fairness of the majority in all matters affecting their interest. The guarantees which you secured for them at the time of Confederation remain to this day intact. No suggestion has ever been made looking to their abrogation. No request made by Protestants has ever been refused. . . . With the family quarrels of the majority they have nothing to do, and their best interest will be secured by preserving that position of neutrality which has hitherto marked their conduct."

The school legislation to which Mr. White referred, it may be noted here, afforded a very good instance of the power and policy of the hierarchy, and of the attitude of the Protestant minority, the wisdom of which Galt was calling in question. When the Province of Quebec had been formed in 1867, the premier, P. J. O. Chauveau, formerly superintendent of education, created and took for himself the portfolio of Education. Under the control of this department, Roman Catholic and Protestant committees were given a wide measure of autonomy in controlling their respective schools. The church authorities, however, were not content with an arrangement which admitted the supremacy of the state in matters of education. In 1875, under De Boucherville, a change was made whereby the port-folio of Minister of Education was abolished, and full control of Roman Catholic education was given to a committee consisting of the Bishops and of an equal number of laymen, with Protestant education similarly under the control of a Protestant committee. In this matter, and in connection with the administration of charities and other activities, the majority of the Protestants were prepared to purchase freedom for themselves by acquiescing in the control of the clergy over their fellow-citizens. They secured temporary advantage; whether the policy would be to their interest and to the interest of the state in the long run, Galt had come to doubt.

Galt replied in April to these and other criticisms, in a longer pamphlet, *Church and State*, dedicated to Mr. Gladstone.[1] His purpose, he declared, was to protest against the efforts now being made by the Roman Catholic hierarchy of Quebec to impose upon those belonging to their communion the extreme doctrines of the Italian ecclesiastical school. The treatment fell under three heads. First, had the attitude of the hierarchy changed since Confederation? The Vatican Decrees and their echo in the strife in France, Germany and Spain, showed the change in the general policy of the Church; – a policy, however, of extraordinary elasticity, exclusive, despotic and grasping where, as in Spain, it reigned supreme, but where, as in England, it lacked civil power, moderate and confined to its proper functions of teaching piety and morality. In Canada the same divergence was shown; Archbishops Lynch of Ontario and Connolly of Nova Scotia had followed a moderate and wise course, but the hierarchy of Quebec was seeking to rivet the most extreme pretensions of the Syllabus on the consciences of their people. This charge was driven home by quotations from official utterances showing that the Quebec hierarchy asserted the superiority of Church over State, the right to intervene in elections, the right to put the press under ban, and the extraordinary proposition that the Divine assistance claimed to be given the Pope descended with undiminished force to bishops, priests and curés. The provincial government was passing completely under the influence of the hierarchy. The assaults on free thought and speech in the *Institut Canadien* and Guibord cases, the ban on certain journals, the power given the bishops to divide the whole province into ecclesiastical parishes, the marginal note inserted to the statute referring to the erection of parishes, "decrees amended by our Holy Father the Pope are binding," were most ominous. "The clergy," he continued, "have also succeeded in drawing under their own control the expenditure of most of the public money voted for Charities, Reformatories, and Asylums, also for Colonization; and in the case of Education, have obtained, last session, the entire management of this most important subject, as regards Roman Catholics."

Next, had these changes affected the general rights of Protestants as citizens of Quebec, and especially weakened the Confederation guarantees? Protestant politicians, basking in the sunshine of episcopal favour, declared that all this affected Roman Catholics only; until we are assailed we should act with those who in the past were our friends and allies. The past, Sir Alexander went on, had disappeared. We would look in vain to the present leaders for that independence which characterized the former chieftains of Lower Canada. True, neither Rouge nor Bleu was free from clerical subserviency; he had not urged alliance with Catholic Liberals but with Liberal Catholics. Considering the solidarity of interest which necessarily existed between Protestant and Catholic in Canada, living together in the same country, enjoying equal rights, it followed that nothing could occur affecting the welfare of one without materially influencing the fortunes of all. The educational rights of Protestants, in important particulars, rested upon a provincial statute; the representation guarantees, prohibiting alteration of the boundaries of the Eastern Townships constituencies without their consent, illusory at best, were being brought to nothing by the repatriation campaign which was filling them with French-Canadian settlers. The only real security lay in the federal veto power. "If, then, nothing be heard but adulatory paeans to the hierarchy, to obtain their political support and influence, how can we expect to receive attention when we appeal to a government at Ottawa, almost all of whose supporters from Quebec owe their seats to the clergy?"

Is the issue thus raised, Galt concluded, religious or political? Wholly, he considered, political. Whether the existing relations between Church and State were to be changed, whether the priests were to be permitted to use at our elections an undue influence infinitely more powerful and more dangerous than that of gold or intemperance, whether they should dictate what the people might say or read or think and thus shackle all the energy and intelligence of the young Dominion, these were certainly civil and political issues. Let Catholics and Protestants, irrespective of creed, race or party, unite for the maintenance of the civil rights of the people, and "settle, for our day, at least, the proper and harmonious relations of Church and State."

Galt followed up this pamphlet by an address in Toronto in June along similar lines which did much to crystallize Ontario opinion on the issue. His protest did not stand alone. Within the Church and without, other voices called a halt upon the faction which sought to make another Spain in Canada. A few weeks after Galt's visit to Toronto, Archbishop Lynch delivered a comprehensive address on the relations of Church and State which set forth a much more prudent and statesmanlike conception of the attitude of the clergy to politics. In Quebec itself, Archbishop Taschereau, supported by the Seminary at Quebec and the University of Laval, opposed the extreme tactics of Bishops Bourget and Laflèche. The latter retorted bitterly, making charges of double dealing and of backstairs influences at Rome astounding in their frankness. The politicians, too, plucked up heart. The Liberals protested the election of several members, particularly of Hector Langevin in Charlevoix, on the ground of the undue influence exercised by the clergy. The facts were beyond dispute: curé after curé had declared it a mortal sin to vote for the Liberal candidate. Judge Routhier, one of the authors of the Programme, denied that the civil courts had any jurisdiction over ecclesiastics for acts done in their spiritual capacity, but the Supreme Court, in judgments delivered by Mr. Justice Taschereau, brother of the Archbishop, and Mr. Justice Ritchie, rejected the doctrine of clerical immunity and declared the election void. In a famous speech in June, 1877, a rising young Liberal, Wilfrid Laurier, laid down the creed of Political Liberalism, denying for his party any anti-clerical bias, admitting the right of priest and pastor to take part in politics like other citizens, but insisting that the right ceased when it encroached upon the elector's independence, and protesting strongly against the attempt to found a Catholic party.

Finally, Rome itself called upon its too zealous servants to halt. An Apostolic Delegate, Mgr. Conroy, sent to Canada in 1877 to inquire into the situation, condemned unreservedly clerical interference in politics. In condemning Liberalism, his instructions stated, the Church did not mean to condemn any political party. In a pastoral issued in October, 1877, the bishops of Quebec, while still insisting that their joint letter of September, 1875, contained the true doctrine of the Church, declared that they had never intended to authorize the priests to take part in the battle of political parties and denounce individual candidates. A year later, Pius IX died, at war with nearly every government in Europe. His successor, Leo XIII, as Macdonald had shrewdly foreseen, was of a more liberal and diplomatic temperament, and bent all his energies to healing the breaches which the intransigeant policy of the seventies had effected. His accession confirmed the victory of the moderate element in the Roman Catholic Church in Canada, but the victory had already been won.

The struggle for freedom of thought and speech was not ended, but the most audacious assault upon the common liberties of the people had been repulsed, and courage instilled into the defending ranks. That in future years the old tolerance and moderate policy in great measure revived was due in part, indeed, to the good sense of the leaders of the Church and the independence of a large section of the Roman Catholic laity, but it was due also in no small degree to the refusal of Galt and those who held with him to stand by in timid and time-serving neutrality when pretensions were put forward fatal to any breadth or freedom in public life.[2]

15: High Commissioner and Ambassador-at-Large

The Halifax Commission; the fisheries dispute; case and counter-case; the award and its reception; the French and Spanish mission; the High Commissionership; finding a footing in London; protection, preference and reciprocal trade; defence and imperial federation; wanted: an emigration policy; Galt's retirement.

~ Fisheries were a constant source of conflict between Canada and the United States in the nineteenth century. In 1854 a reasonably satisfactory agreement was arrived at when, in return for reciprocity, the United States was given the right to fish within the three-mile limit along the British North American coastline. Twelve years later, however, disappointed that Canada had initiated a protective trade policy and irritated by apparent Canadian support of the Confederacy during the Civil War, the American government terminated the agreement. The Canadian government retaliated by instituting a system of licences and began to seize American vessels caught fishing illegally within the three-mile limit. In one year the Canadian authorities detained as many as four hundred American vessels. New England fishing interests exerted strong pressure on the American government to negotiate a new settlement.

The fisheries question was included in the Washington Conference of 1871 which adopted a new agreement whereby the United States would be readmitted to the inshore fishery in return for a cash compensation.[1] The exact sum to be paid in compensation was left to be determined by an arbitration board consisting of three members: one representative to be appointed by the British government, one to be appointed by the American government, and a third to be chosen jointly. After considerable delay the Commissioners were duly selected. Galt was invited to represent Canada, and Ensign H. Kellogg acted for the United States. The selection of the neutral arbitrator, who was expected to have the deciding vote, proved to be difficult, but finally, in spite of the objections of the United States, the name of the Belgian ambassador in Washington, Maurice Delfosse, was agreed upon.

The Commissioners met in Halifax in 1877 to hear arguments. The Canadians argued for an award of fifteen million

dollars as fair compensation for the American fishing privileges.
The American estimate was about half a million dollars. The
Commission, with Kellogg dissenting, arrived at a figure of five
and a half million dollars but did not state publicly the reasoning
behind the decision.* The announcement of the award was
received with pained surprise in the United States, but the
American grudgingly agreed to pay. Galt was rewarded for his
service with the Grand Cross of St. Michael and St. George. ~

Galt had scarcely concluded his duties as Halifax Commissioner when he was called upon to represent Canada in
further ventures in controlling her own foreign relations. The
years from 1878 to 1883 were to be devoted mainly to diplomatic undertakings, admirably suited to Sir Alexander's capacity and temperament, and the more acceptable because they
meant putting into practice the principles he had long maintained as to Canadian autonomy in external affairs.

The commercial depression which affected Canada, in
common with the rest of the world, and especially the United
States, from 1873 to 1879 or 1880, made it more desirable than
ever before to seek new markets abroad for Canadian products.
The markets of the United Kingdom were already open wide.
Those of the United States were still barred, and the ascendancy
of protectionist views and the preoccupations of Washington
with currency questions made it certain that attempts to have
the bars lowered would be fruitless. If the government of Canada
was to secure increased facilities for export trade in any quarter,
it must be in Latin America or in the countries of Western
Europe.

Once before, on the eve of Confederation, the threatened

* Skelton implied that the award of the Halifax Commission was fair.
This opinion is not shared by others who have studied the fisheries
question. See C. C. Tansill, *Canadian-American Relations, 1875-
1911* (New Haven, 1943), p. 12; see also P. E. Corbett, *The Settlement of Canadian-American Disputes* (New Haven, 1937), pp. 33-34.
In the ten-year period from 1873 to 1882, the total cash value of
the fish caught by Americans inside the three-mile limit was
$598,429 or approximately what the Americans said it would be when
they appeared before the Commission. The Americans thus paid
about eight times as much as the fish catch was worth. While the
award of the Halifax Commission was generous, within the context
of long-range Canadian policy, it was irrelevant. The strategy of the
Canadians had been to use the fisheries as a lever to achieve renewal
of reciprocity. In this they had failed. See E. M. Saunders, *The Life
and Letters of the Right Honourable Sir Charles Tupper* (Toronto,
1916), I, 164-166.

loss of the American market had turned the attention of the northern provinces to the West Indies and the lands beyond. Nothing had come of the negotiations carried on by William McDougall and his fellow Commissioners, but hard times revived the project. Early in 1876 the premier, Alexander Mackenzie, wrote Sir Alexander suggesting that he should act on the government's behalf in a renewed effort. . . .

For a time Galt was inclined to undertake the commission and he was formally vested with the authority required. Upon reflection, however, he concluded that as sugar was the chief article of export which the islands would have to offer, and as the Mackenzie government was not prepared, in view of the complicated situation created by the bounty legislation of Europe and the countervailing duties adopted by the United States, to alter its fiscal policy in this particular at the moment, the undertaking would be of no avail. He therefore postponed action indefinitely.

Two years later the proposal was revived by the Macdonald government, shortly after its accession to power. Galt was again the man to whom the task was offered. His experience clearly marked him out for it, but notwithstanding this the offer would hardly have been made had not the intervening years done much to heal the breach which had arisen in personal and party relations between Macdonald and himself. On party issues, the growth of the protectionist movement brought Galt once more into harmony with his old colleagues. While his position, common in those days, of a free trader who believed in incidental protection, was a somewhat vague and flexible one, yet there had been a decided protectionist colour to his thought for twenty years. From 1862 to 1866, it is true, he had been in favour of lowering tariffs, but this was due to special circumstances abroad, to the free trade tendency in continental Europe and to the action of the United States in imposing high excise duties on liquors and thus making it possible for Canada to follow the same course and at the same time lower the rates on other goods. When these conditions had passed away, he once more reverted to his former attitude, and became a strong adherent of the National Policy proposals.

Galt's private relations with Sir John had been strained to the breaking point when he found it necessary not only to oppose the Pacific policy of his former chief, but to comment adversely, in his Ferrier letter of 1875, on Macdonald's continuing to act as leader of the Opposition. In October, 1876,

Galt took the initiative in seeking a reconciliation, by a letter addressed to his close friend, Colonel Bernard, Macdonald's former secretary and present brother-in-law. In reply, Macdonald stated it was the reference in the Ferrier letter which had pained him, the more so since he considered he had in the past stood by Galt to his own political hurt. "Enough of this," he concluded, "*liberavi animam meam*, and having done so, all I desire further to say is, that if Sir Alexander pleases we can meet in friendly intercourse and in society as before. The wound may be considered as healed over, but the scar will, I fear, remain for some time." Galt, in reply, declined to enter into a discussion of the past, or to revive episodes in which he considered he himself had been aggrieved; as to the Ferrier reference, that was unavoidable, since the circumstances of the invitation to stand for West Montreal made it imperative to state his position clearly. As to Cartier, he added, "I will only say, in brief, that it has always been a mystery to me, how either of them (knowing them as I did) ever got into the position they did. In conclusion, I will add, that I shall be heartily glad to meet Sir John on terms of friendly intercourse once more, and trust that the present soreness between us may disappear, under the influence of a wish, I hope, on both sides, that the past should be forgotten as well as forgiven."

Friendly relations were resumed, and soon became intimate and confidential once more, though the scar did, indeed, remain. Neither could ever sympathize wholly with a man of the other's temperament. Macdonald, a practical politician, careful never to take up a cause until it was ripe for action, could not understand Galt's interest in broad issues which would not for years, if ever, become subjects of actual legislation, and was prone to consider his openness to new ideas and his sensitiveness on all points involving his honour as qualities synonymous with instability, interfering with the working of a well regulated party. Galt, on the other hand, while appreciating highly Macdonald's practical capacity and his fundamental devotion to his country, was not prepared to condone corruption because it aided a party, or to consider every issue in the light of its immediate effects on party fortunes. Yet, with all these divergences, the friendship revived, as the scores of intimate letters interchanged in the years that followed make clear.

The general elections, which resulted in a sweeping victory for protection and for the Conservative party as its champion, took place in September, 1878. In October, Sir John formed his cabinet, and a month later Galt was called upon to take up again the negotiations for West Indian trade, especially with reference to the islands of Cuba and Puerto Rico. It had already been made known that in the Spanish empire, at all events, the old ideas of the due subordination of colonies to the home government still held sway, and that the negotiations must be carried on at Madrid, not at Havana. Accordingly Sir Alexander sailed to England, and there arrangements were made with the Colonial and Foreign Offices to secure their sanction and the co-operation of the British Minister at Madrid, Sir Lionel Sackville-West, in the discussion.

Before Galt had left London for Madrid, a further diplomatic task was assigned him. The commercial relations of France had lately been in a state of flux. The Franco-Prussian war of 1870, like the Civil War in the United States, had halted the trend toward free trade. The passions engendered in the struggle, the desire to build up a self-contained country, and the necessities of the revenue, had led to a stiffening of tariff rates alike in France and in Germany. As an incident in this protectionist reaction, the government of France, in 1873, had raised the duties on Canadian-built wooden ships to prohibitive rates. The general tariff duty was forty francs per ton; by the Cobden Treaty of 1860 this rate had been reduced to two francs on English ships, and by the informal understanding arranged in 1861 through the French consul-general in Canada, this reduction had been extended to Canada. Standing on the letter of the treaty, the French government withdrew this concession, and in 1874 the Canadian government retaliated by raising its duties on French wines. It was now desired to settle this dispute, and if possible to secure access to France on favourable terms for Canadian agricultural implements and similar manufactures. Mr. Tilley, as Minister of Finance, had expected to carry on the negotiations himself while in England in the winter of 1878, but being compelled to return to Canada, he arranged to have Galt undertake this second mission, with Colonel Bernard as Assistant Commissioner.

The machinery of negotiations was complicated. First it was necessary for the Canadian government to communicate its desire to the Colonial Office; the Colonial Office requested the Foreign Office to act; the Foreign Office instructed the minister at Paris or Madrid to put Sir Alexander into communication with the French government, and the discussions began. "The formal negotiations between the governments of this

country and of France on the subject," continued Lord Salisbury, then Foreign Secretary, in his instructions to Lord Lyons,
Ambassador at Paris, "should be conducted by Your Excellency,
the settlement of the details of the arrangement being dealt with
by Sir Alexander Galt."*

Neither in Paris nor in Madrid were the times favourable
for the immediate success of the negotiations. In France, a
general tariff was being framed, and the ministry were reluctant
to bind themselves to any reciprocal concessions before it was
completed. After several interchanges between Sir Alexander
and the Minister of Commerce, M. de Bort, an agreement was
arranged by the end of December to reduce the duties on wines
and ships to the former levels. At the last moment, however, the
basis of the agreement was upset by the action of Austria in
terminating the commercial treaty with France, a clause in
which had served as the starting point for the concession of the
two franc rate to other countries, under the most favoured
nation policy. Automatically, therefore, the conventional tariff
of 20 per cent took effect on all ships, English as well as
Canadian, and could not be altered except by legislative action.
A month later, a change of ministry having meanwhile occurred
in Paris, the revival of the Franco-Austrian treaty appeared to
offer an opportunity for reopening the discussion, and Galt
returned to Paris. The new government proved equally favourable, but an attempt to include a clause giving Canada the
concessions desired in the Austrian Treaty bill met with such

* Later researches have revealed that the arrangement here described
was even more complicated than Skelton suspected. Galt's official
reports to the government contain no hints as to the adequacy of the
procedures and are mostly accounts of interviews and correspondence
with British and French officials. In private letters to Macdonald,
however, Galt described the early difficulties he encountered in Paris.
He arrived there with letters from the Foreign Office but the English
ambassador, Lord Lyons, who had no sympathy for colonial
diplomats, completely ignored him. Galt impatiently wrote to the
Foreign Office with, as he described it, "wonderful effect." Lord
Lyons hastened to invite him to dinner and energetically arranged
interviews with French officials. It was not surprising, therefore, that
Galt's reception by the British Ambassador to Spain should have
been extremely cordial and co-operative. Galt recognized that the
failure of his mission had little to do with the attitude of the British
diplomats, but his experience was a clear indication that more efficient procedures must be adopted if Canadian negotiations with
foreign powers on commercial matters were to be successful in the
future. See Glazebrook, A History of Canadian External Relations
(Carleton Library, 1966), pp. 135-36.

opposition in the Chamber that it was withdrawn, and the negotiations were once more postponed until a more fitting season.

In Madrid, the same partial measure of success was attained. With the co-operation of Sir Lionel Sackville-West, the British Minister, Galt soon came to terms with the Spanish cabinet of the hour. The premier, Señor Canovas, in fact, suggested that the scope of the negotiations should be widened to include Spain itself as well as the colonies, and Galt, after seeking an extension of power from Ottawa, cordially assented, as it was advisable to have France and Spain competing for favourable terms for their wines. The fact that the British government was itself negotiating a new treaty of commerce with Spain made the British minister unwilling to have the Canadian negotiations as to Spain itself pushed ahead for the present. Canovas, moreover, stated that it would be necessary to await the coming of the Cuban member of the Cortes before a definite arrangement on the West India phases could be framed. Before that day came, a change of ministry, of a somewhat more sweeping character than usual, suspended the negotiations.

Towards the end of February, 1879, Galt reported to the Canadian government that no immediate action was possible, but expressed his belief that the favour shown to his proposals by the cabinets both in Paris and Madrid foreshadowed an agreement at a more fortunate conjuncture. The experience had served to give the amateur diplomats some idea of the cross currents and uncertainties of negotiations in the chancelleries of Europe, and had familiarized European statesmen with the newcomer among the nations.

Galt returned to Canada early in March. Four months later, on July 26, in company with Macdonald, he sailed once more for England, where Tupper and Tilley joined them. Their stay was brief, as Sir Alexander and Sir John sailed for home on September 11, but in those few weeks many matters of importance had been discussed with the British government, and the way prepared for another striking advance in Canada's national status.

The most pressing question which came up for discussion was the financing of the Canadian Pacific Railway. The new government had continued the policy of the Mackenzie cabinet in attempting to build the road as a government work, and at the same time to confine the expenditure within modest limits.

The results were not encouraging, and accordingly the government devised a new plan which would, it was hoped, provide
ample funds, without imposing further burdens on the people.
The proposal was to set aside one hundred million acres of the
best land in the West, to be sold eventually at a price which
would more than meet the railway outlay, and in the meantime
to raise funds by the sale of bonds secured by these lands, as
well as by a mortgage on the road itself. To strengthen the
security still further, and to obtain a lower rate of interest, the
British government was requested to guarantee the loan.

Disraeli was then in power, for the last time, with Sir
Stafford Northcote at the Exchequer and Sir Michael Hicks-
Beach as Colonial Secretary. They were personally very cordial
to the Canadian visitors, but declined politely to accede to the
request for a guarantee. While, however, the immediate object
of the mission was not attained, an informal agreement was
reached for the establishment in London of a permanent representative of the Canadian government, who, it was hoped,
would in time be able to secure this and similar concessions.*

The proposal to establish the office known later as that of
High Commissioner for Canada was based both on specific
needs and on general considerations of the changing relations
between Canada and the Mother Country. So long as Canada
was a colony, subordinate to the British authorities, the only
possible channels of communication between the two governments were the Colonial Office and the Governor-General. Now
that the Dominion was feeling its way toward partnership and
full equality of status, it was fitting and necessary that some
quasi-diplomatic official should be appointed to represent the
views of Her Majesty's Government at Ottawa to Her Majesty's
Government at London.[2]

In a very effective memorandum signed by Macdonald,
Tupper and Tilley, and submitted to the British government in
August, 1879, the purpose and necessity of the proposed ap-

---

* Skelton neglects to mention that a form of Canadian representation
had already been established in London. In 1869 Sir John Rose had
been accredited to Her Majesty's Government "as a gentleman
possessing the confidence of the Canadian Government with whom
Her Majesty's Government may properly communicate on Canadian
affairs." Rose proved to be a useful intermediary on such questions
as the transfer of Hudson's Bay territory, the formation of the Joint
High Commission in 1871, and the financing of the Canadian Pacific
Railway. See M. H. Long, "Sir John Rose and the Informal Begin-
nings of the Canadian High Commissionership," *Canadian Historical
Review*, XII (March, 1931), pp. 23-43.

pointment were clearly stated. Experience was daily proving, they declared, the necessity of providing means of constant and confidential communication to supplement the formal correspondence carried on through the Governor-General. "Canada," they continued, "has ceased to occupy the position of an ordinary possession of the Crown. . . . Her Central Government is becoming even more responsible than the Imperial Government for the maintenance of international relations towards the United States, a subject which will yearly require greater prudence and care, as the populations of the two countries extend along and mingle across the vast frontier line three thousand miles in length. The Canadian government has, in short, become the trustee for the Empire at large, of half the continent of North America."

It was essential to secure full interchange of views and harmony of policy, and to prevent the idea becoming established that the connection of Canada with the British Empire was only temporary. Many questions were constantly arising which could only be dealt with by personal discussion, and if the ministers themselves had to go over constantly, this involved serious inconvenience. Further, the need of direct negotiations with foreign powers for the proper protection of Canadian trade interests had now been recognized. In negotiating treaties of commerce with foreign countries, the British government had considered only their effect on the United Kingdom; the divergence of views on fiscal policy between Great Britain and Canada created a further difficulty in the way of having the former become responsible for the representations to be made. "The Canadian Government therefore submit," the memorandum continued, "that when occasion requires such negotiations to be undertaken, Her Majesty's Government should advise Her Majesty to accredit the representative of Canada to the foreign court, by association, for the special object, with the resident minister or other Imperial negotiator."

To carry out these suggestions, the Canadian government proposed to appoint a representative, selected from the Queen's Privy Council for Canada, who would occupy "a quasi-diplomatic position at the Court of St. James, with the social advantages of such a rank and position." He would have the supervision of all the political and financial interests of Canada in England, and, when so requested, might be duly accredited to foreign courts.

The programme thus outlined was a logical development

of Galt's insistence in 1870 upon Canada's right to the controlling voice in determining her foreign commercial relations. It proposed a recognition of Canada's full autonomy which embodied all that was essential in his former independence views, now that the military danger from the United States had disappeared. It was now beginning to be apparent that the independence desired could be obtained in great measure within the Empire, without any formal separation. Sir Alexander's views had thus been modified by the teaching of events, but in essence they were embodied in the policy to which his former colleagues had now felt their way.*

The new doctrine of colonial equality thus foreshadowed, was, however, too strong meat as yet for English consumption. Sir Michael Hicks-Beach, in expressing his sense of the advantage which would result from the appointment of such a representative, hastened to add that his position could hardly be said to be of diplomatic character, but would be "more analogous to that of an officer in the home service." As to the foreign activities proposed, it would rest with the Foreign Secretary to determine in what capacity his services might be utilized, whether he should remain in London and advise with Her Majesty's

* There is some mild difference of opinion concerning the extent to
which the High Commissioner's office, in its final form, embodied the
views of Galt in 1880. In a memorandum to Macdonald and in his
speech in Montreal on the eve of his departure for England, Galt
outlined his views as to the functions of the High Commissioner. He
interpreted the responsibilities of the office very broadly, listing
finance, immigration and diplomacy as the main areas of activity. He
was particularly anxious that the last of these should be a vital part
of the High Commissioner's work and mentioned Imperial defence
and preferential commercial arrangements within the Empire as illustrations of the subjects with which the High Commissioner should
properly be concerned. Apparently he saw the office as a significant
step toward closer Imperial unity and, by implication at least, a move
toward some form of political federation of the Empire. However,
the official instructions to the High Commissioner, as drawn up by
the Canadian cabinet after prolonged discussion with the British
government, made no reference to a grand political alliance between
the colonies and Great Britain, specifying instead that the High
Commissioner should merely concern himself with financial matters,
immigration and liaison with the Colonial and Foreign Offices. There
was no specific mention of an Imperial preferential tariff. The official
functions of the High Commissioner have been described as "the
palest reflection of Galt's scheme" (Glazebrook, *A History of Canadian External Relations*, p. 134), but the instructions may be more
properly described as a blending of the views of Galt, Macdonald,
the Colonial Office and the Foreign Office. See Farr, *The Colonial
Office and Canada, 1867- 1887* (Toronto, 1955), p. 267.

government there, or assist Her Majesty's representative abroad.

In reply to this polite snub, the Canadian government, in a Council minute of December 22, intimated in effect that there was now more than one Government of Her Majesty:

"The Committee recognize the fact," they declared, "that Canada cannot, as an integral portion of the Empire, maintain relations of a strictly diplomatic character. But they respectfully submit that while this is true as respects foreign nations, it does not accurately represent the actual state of facts in regard to the United Kingdom. Her Majesty's Government is unquestionably the supreme governing power of the Empire, but, under the British North America Act, self-governing powers have been conferred upon Canada in many most important respects, and Her Majesty's Government may on these points be more correctly defined as representing the United Kingdom than the Empire at large. In considering many questions of the highest importance, such as the commercial and fiscal policy of the Dominion as affecting the United Kingdom, the promotion of Imperial interests in the administration and settlement of the interior of the Continent, and on many other subjects, indeed on all matters of internal concern, the Imperial Government and Parliament have so far transferred to Canada an independent control that their discussion and settlement have become subjects for mutual assent and concert, and thereby have, it is thought, assumed a quasi-diplomatic character as between Her Majesty's Government representing the United Kingdom per se and the Dominion, without in any manner derogating from their general authority as rulers of the entire Empire."

In their dealings with foreign powers they did not desire to be placed in the position of independent negotiators, as they recognized the value of the support of the carefully trained British diplomatic service. They concluded by proposing that the new official, to mark the distinctive character of the post, should be termed the "High Commissioner of Canada in London," to which the Colonial Secretary in due time agreed.

In these formal statements of their purpose, the Canadian ministers had not made explicit all that was in their minds. In the background loomed up the project of reviving the old system of imperial tariff preferences. Both in Canada and in the United Kingdom events had occurred which made it seem possible to resurrect this buried policy. In Canada, the continued failure of the attempt to secure entrance to the United States market revived memories of the day when a preference for certain Canadian raw materials had been enjoyed in the United Kingdom. This was not all. The resentment felt in the Mother Country against the Canadian system of protection, revived by the material increase in tariff rates which had followed the success of the National Policy campaign in 1878, led some of the Canadian Conservative leaders to seek an antidote. Obviously, if the United Kingdom could be brought to adopt protection, with incidental preference, it would no longer be able to throw stones at the glass houses in which Canadian industries were being nursed.

Could the United Kingdom be brought to make this sweeping change? It had long appeared rooted in its free trade faith, but new movements were developing which led sanguine observers to foretell a speedy conversion to protection once more. The manufacturing depression of the later seventies, accentuated by contrast with the prosperous years that neutral England had enjoyed when France and Prussia were at grips, produced discontent, in which protection found its opportunity. The competition of American foodstuffs was now being felt acutely by British farmers. The revival of protection on the Continent, already noted, naturally was echoed in Great Britain. Those who led the reaction did not go so far as to demand the full restoration of protection; they urged rather a policy of Reciprocity or Fair Trade, of tariffs for bargaining purposes, or for offsetting the artificial handicaps of duties or bounties.

With this policy some of the Conservative leaders in Great Britain showed increasing sympathy. Lord Beaconsfield would have none of it: "reciprocity is dead," he insisted, and Sir Stafford Northcote held to his free trade faith, but Lord Salisbury, as well as several lesser lights, showed strong Fair Trade leanings. It was not surprising, therefore, that the Canadian ministers conceived the hope of a rapid development of a policy which would give a preferred market for Canadian goods and would make it possible to reconcile protection and loyalty.

On the first of April, 1880, Sir John Macdonald brought down the correspondence as to the establishment of the office, and moved the appointment of Sir Alexander Galt as first High Commissioner. Two days earlier Galt had sailed for England. On the eve of sailing, a great banquet had been given him in Montreal, widely attended by public men. He took this occasion to survey the duties of his new post. The financial tasks came first; the time had come when the Dominion should undertake its own financial work in London, floating loans and making payments, rather than entrust the work to agents. Emigration would be an important subject. Canada had the largest area of undeveloped fertile land in the world; it was to the interest of the Empire that the swarms that left Britain's shores should be directed to these lands rather than be lost to an alien flag. The diplomatic duties were growing with the increased control of Canada over its tariff relations. Under the new arrangement with Great Britain Canada was securing all that could be achieved in any way. What could Canada gain by any more formal position of independence? It was to her interest to avail herself of Britain's diplomatic machinery and experience rather than to stand alone, among the small powers of the earth. Defence would call for consideration; possibly naval stations might be established for instructing Canadian soldiers, in connection with the naval reserve. And as to trade, he would like to emphasize the possibility that the Empire might be made self-sufficient; those who thought England would never impose a tax on foodstuffs had not considered the situation which would arise when the North-West was equipped to supply all her needs.

With Lady Galt and all his family except his eldest son, Elliott, who had entered the government service in the Department of the Interior, and John, who was on the staff of the Bank of Montreal, Sir Alexander reached London early in April. He found a suitable house, at 66 Lancaster Gate, Hyde Park, and was soon settled and ready for the new tasks that faced him.

While Galt was on the ocean, the situation had materially changed. In the general election of 1880, Gladstone had roused the country against Beaconsfield's jingoism and especially his pro-Turkish policy, and had been returned with a sweeping majority. As many of the sanguine expectations of the Canadian ministers had been based upon the continuance in office of the English leaders with whom they had formed relations of personal intimacy, this was a serious blow. "The result of the elections," Galt wrote Tilley immediately after his arrival, "has been a great disappointment to me, and must be so to you all. We can scarcely hope to have as friendly a government to deal with as that which is about to pass away."

This disappointment coloured all the early dealings between Galt and the new government. The ministers with whom he had most to do were Lord Kimberley, Colonial Secretary, Hon. W. E. Forster, Secretary for Ireland, Lord Granville, Foreign Secretary, and the Under Secretary in the same department, Sir

Charles Dilke. With Dilke, Galt was soon on very friendly terms, and Forster he felt was sympathetic, but he repeatedly complained of Kimberley's coldness and of the failure of Gladstone himself and the other leaders to take any interest in Canada's affairs or the Canadian representative. Writing to Macdonald in June, he stated: "I had a most unsatisfactory interview with Lord K. on Monday. The fact is, it could not be worse, and he went on displaying such indifference to our interests that it ended in my asking him to explain to me what possible advantage there was in maintaining the connection if they cared nothing for us and would just as soon see their emigrants go to the United States rather than Canada. This rather startled him, and he somewhat harked back." Sir William Harcourt, however, and Lord Rosebery, to whom he referred as "a very able man who will go far," were very cordial.

Some measure of aloofness was not surprising. The Canadian ministers had made no secret of their sympathy with the English Conservatives, and Galt was at still less pains to conceal his likes and dislikes. The reference in his Montreal speech to the possibility of protection and preference reviving in England had been widely quoted, and in private circles in London he had made his preferences equally clear, even joining the Tory Club, the Carlton. Quite aside from the inherent merits or demerits of the plans brought forward, it was not to be wondered at that some of the Liberal ministers managed to restrain their enthusiasm. Kimberley's coldness was more a question of manners and temperament than of principle. Even so, further intercourse removed any ground for complaint, and before the close of Galt's term the relations with the ministry were quite friendly.

One episode at the outset rather complicated matters. The Governor-General, Lord Lorne, had been extremely cordial in discussing with Galt the possibilities of the new office, and had done all that could be done to smoothe his path by friendly introductions to men high at Court and in politics. Yet he was not unnaturally desirous to prevent the new policy resulting in lessening still further the role of the Governor-General as the connecting link between the British and Canadian governments. Macdonald, writing to Galt on June 3, 1880, notes:

There was some delay in finally settling the instructions, as the G. G. left Ottawa before they could be submitted to him. He was very anxious that his position should not be ignored and made sundry suggestions from Quebec, which of course we agreed to. He is evidently jealous lest things should be done without his knowledge or intervention, and I had to assure him he would be fully informed. It was necessary to keep him with us and with you, or you might be balked some morning by Lord K. informing you that he had not been advised by the G. G. on the subject. Every one of your official letters is copied and sent him, and I have read to him or made extracts and sent him such portions of your notes to me as I thought would please him and do good to you. Lord Lorne is a right good fellow and a good Canadian, and it is important to identify him as much as possible with your mission.

Unconsciously, the Governor-General upset the carefully laid plans to lead the unsuspecting British government on from aid to emigration to the more ticklish ground. Writing to Macdonald on May 26, 1880, Galt reports:

You will see that I have absolutely avoided raising any question about aid to the C.P.R., or, in fact, any doubtful question, with the new men. And, of course, I shall not suggest a Zollverein to them, for the present! If I can get them committed to aid Emigration, it will be the thin edge of the wedge.

A little later, he finds that the new men know the thick edge in store for them; he writes to Macdonald on June 10:

By the way, Lord K. astonished me to-day by saying that I need not read to him the paragraphs about the treaties, because he had a copy of my instructions! I fear this will prove rather an indiscretion on the G. G.'s part, as it shows Lord K. all my hand. My intention was to get the government committed to Emigration, as it must involve the Railway and administrative questions afterward. If you look at your instructions, you will see how evident are your future intentions. Of course, this cannot now be helped, but in future it is well we should know that the Colonial Office knows all you say to me.

In determining the footing upon which the Canadian representative was to be received, Galt had several interviews with the Colonial Office. The late government had declined to accede to the Canadian request that the new official should be given "a quasi-diplomatic position at the Court of St. James, with the social advantages of such a rank and position." The new government was not any more eager to grant it. Galt wrote Macdonald on May 4:

*I had my first interview with Lord Kimberley yesterday. . . .
I then inquired what had been decided on the question of
'status.' To which he replied that he had ascertained that this
point had been settled by the late Lord Chamberlain at the
request of his predecessor, and that the High Commissioner was
to take precedence, by the Queen's command, in the Royal
Palace only, immediately after the Privy Councillors. He added
that it was impossible to put this in the London Gazette, as there
were many protests of precedence that would be interfered with,
and would create difficulties. He said the precedence had to be
given to me personally, but would no doubt be extended to my
successors.*

*I then inquired as to my presentation to the Queen, which
he said he would be prepared to do at the Levee or Drawing-
room. I suggested that on previous occasions, by the Queen's
pleasure, we had more than once been honoured by a private
audience, and that I had hoped for it now, as a suitable recognition of the importance the government attached to the office.
But this he declined, on the ground that it might excite the
jealousy of the other Colonies, to which I replied that none were
in the same position, the result being that he adhered to his
decision.*

To anticipate a little, it may be noted here that when, early
in January, 1883, Lord Kimberley was promoted from the
Colonial to the India Office, Galt seized the occasion to get his
successor, Lord Derby, started on the right lines. He arranged
that a deputation consisting of the Agents-general of the Aus-
tralasian and South African colonies should wait upon Lord
Derby and formally welcome him to his new task. Acting as
spokesman, Sir Alexander, after conveying their good wishes,
referred to the growing appreciation of the importance of the
colonies and the need of a greater formal recognition of their
place in the imperial system.

When the presentation at Court was arranged, a somewhat
embarrassing situation arose. The law of England did not yet
recognize the legality of marriage with a deceased wife's sister,
and the Court officials therefore declared that Lady Galt could
not be presented. Sir Alexander at once declared that if that
decision were adhered to, he would not be presented either, and
would immediately return to Canada. Fortunately the Prince of
Wales, who was strongly in favour of having the British government follow the colonial example on this question, and who had

in fact moved in the House of Lords the passing of a law to that effect, intervened. The Prince had been forewarned by Lord Lorne that some difficulty might arise. He, therefore, sought a private interview with the Queen and succeeded in having the edict reversed, much to Sir Alexander's relief and gratitude.

Once these various preliminary questions of status and terms of intercourse with the ministers were determined, Galt turned to the specific objects of his mission.

As to the task of converting the British government to protection, he soon realized that headway would be slow. "I do not fail to observe," he wrote Macdonald on April 21, "that with all the people I meet the Liberal victory is regarded as a reindorsement of the existing form of Free Trade." The only Liberal quarter in which he found any sympathy was in his interviews with Dilke; he writes Macdonald:

8 May, 1880.

I met Sir Charles Dilke last night at the Prince of Wales, and he asked me to see him to-day about our French business. I said I must proceed through Lord Kimberley, but as he was present, that was soon arranged. . . .

We then discussed generally the prospect of treaties, of which he was not sanguine, as England had nothing to give. Strange as it may seem, I found he leaned to the Reciprocity heresy. I am quite sure before he has finished the negotiations with France, he will see that it is the only true basis for negotiations. He quite laughed, however, at the idea of Gladstone consenting to anything of the kind, and I greatly fear foreign nations will take advantage of this and that England will have her hands tied for next to nothing.

Galt was at first more hopeful about the Conservatives. "If things commercially go badly, as I believe they will," he wrote Macdonald in May, "the Conservatives will next go to the country, if not as Protectionists, certainly as Reciprocitarians, as they call those who, like yourself and myself, retaliate on foreigners." A year later, on May 26, 1881, he wrote Tilley that the Conservatives were going in for protection as their only chance, being greatly impressed by the success of a protectionist campaign in the bye-election at Preston. He continued:

I met last night at the State Ball, W. H. Smith and Sir R. Cross, both members of the late government. They quite recog-

nize me as sharing their views, and told me that the Conserva-
tives would now fight every vacant seat. I pressed upon them
that their true policy was to fight the Liberals in the boroughs
on the trade question, and I think they will ultimately, and
indeed soon, take this line. Sir Stafford is altogether too timid
a man to initiate and carry out a new policy and this is what the
Conservatives want. Poor old Dizzy represented the brains of
the party.

Yet as time passed, and trade revived, or Irish or foreign issues
diverted interest, Galt was forced to recognize that the hopes
of his Canadian colleagues and himself were at least premature,
and that the task of making the people of England see the error
of their ways would be a long and uphill fight.

In the trade negotiations with France and Spain which were
carried on fitfully during his term of office, Galt was influenced
by his desire for a tariff agreement with the United Kingdom.
He was averse to seeing either the United Kingdom or Canada
tie its hands by treaties with foreign countries. As he wrote to
Dilke in December, 1881: "I will not conceal from you that the
policy I would like to see adopted is that of getting as near free
exchange as we can with our own colonies, and a renewal of
engagements with France makes this more remote." He was
anxious, also, acting on instructions from Tilley, to avoid being
hampered in later negotiations with other foreign powers by
having promised France or Spain to accord them automatically
most favoured nation treatment.

Little progress was made with either France or Spain in the
first years of his mission. The United Kingdom was negotiating
with both countries, and the Foreign Office desired to have the
right of way. Protectionist sentiment in France was still strong,
and after 1881, the ill-feeling over Britain's occupation of
Egypt caused much friction. In the case of Spain, the unpopu-
larity of the British ambassador, Sir Robert Morier, proved a
handicap, and Galt preferred to negotiate through the Spanish
Minister at London, with whom he was on very good terms.
These negotiations had just been begun when he resigned; they
were carried through to success by Sir Charles Tupper. Speaking
some years later in the House of Commons, Sir Charles threw
light on some of the difficulties which his predecessor had faced
and which on Sir Alexander's advice had been overcome in
future arrangements with the Colonial and Foreign Offices:
"When I had the honour of succeeding Sir Alexander Galt in

the office of High Commissioner, he left for my information and perusal a document in which he said that he found himself greatly hampered in discharging the duties imposed upon him by the government of Canada, because he only stood in the position of a commercial commissioner, and it was necessary that all negotiations with the government of Spain should be filtered through Her Majesty's Minister at the Court of Madrid."

Not the least important object of Galt's endeavours was to secure the abrogation of the clauses in the treaties between the United Kingdom and Belgium and the German *Zollverein*, assuring these countries any tariff privileges granted by a British colony to the United Kingdom or a sister colony. These privileges would automatically extend to other countries having most favoured nation relations with the United Kingdom, and thus it was practically impossible to set up any exclusive preference within the Empire. Sir Charles Dilke expressed great sympathy with this object, but upon inquiry both countries expressed unwillingness to alter this clause alone, and the attempt to secure freedom of action was postponed.

Neither the subject of imperial preference nor the denunciation of the Belgian and German treaties as a necessary preliminary step became a practical issue again during the later period of Sir Alexander's term of office. They did not pass from his mind, however, and nearly a decade later, when the question of unrestricted reciprocity with the United States was being hotly debated in Canada, he endeavoured once more to turn men's thoughts into the channel of inter-imperial preference.

But in the eighties these and still more notable developments were still in the future. During his tenure of office as High Commissioner, Galt was almost equally interested in other phases of imperial relationship, defence in some measure, and especially the question of the reorganization of the political machinery of the Empire.

The defence of the Empire and Canada's relation to it, had ceased to be a burning issue with the rapid return of the United States to a civilian footing and the settlement of the disputes outstanding with that country. The revival of colonial ambitions on the part of Continental European powers was just beginning to affect naval and military policy, but as yet the mad rivalry of a generation later was only in the germ. Even so, some stirrings of national spirit led to a sporadic discussion in Canada of means of taking part in naval as well as military defence.

In 1881, the government decided to establish a training-school for naval officers, and to assist in carrying out this plan the British government offered a gunboat just returned from the China station, the *Charybdis*, as a free gift. Unfortunately, the old tub was hardly in shape for service. Writing to Tilley in July, 1881, Galt declares: "You will want all your surplus if you are favoured with many more presents from the British Government. Your last favour is the *Charybdis*. To-day I have an official report condemning the boilers, and saying she must be laid up till spring. I have cabled Pope about his ship, adding my recommendations that she had better be returned with thanks. . . . Every blessed thing was taken out of her down to the tin cups of the crew. . . . If the rotten hull of a wooden ship constitutes a man-of-war, then you have got a splendid commencement of a navy." The Canadian government decided not to accept the proffered gift, and the training-school idea came to nothing.

Much more spectacular were the projects which came to birth in this period for the political reorganization of the Empire. The belief prevalent in the United Kingdom a few years earlier that separation was inevitable, had died away with the passing of the danger from the United States, the growing realization of the potentialities of the colonies, and the new international rivalry for privileged trade areas which had followed the consolidation of the nationalities of Western Europe. Many in the colonies who had shared the same views came to believe that the share in the shaping of foreign policy which independence was designed to secure might be attained more effectively by some form of imperial federation, now that the changing temper of British public men made it practical at last to discuss such a plan.[3]

With his usual interest in broad questions, and his responsiveness to the changing currents of thought, Sir Alexander became one of the foremost advocates of the new policy. He discussed it on various occasions, but the most notable were two addresses delivered by invitation in Edinburgh and Greenock, in January, 1881, and reprinted in pamphlet form as *The Relations of the Colonies to the Empire: Present and Future*.

After reviewing the progress and sketching the possibilities of the colonies, Sir Alexander declared that it was not likely that the millions of intelligent, energetic men in the self-governing colonies would long be content with the position they at present enjoyed in the British Empire. What was the remedy? Separation? This was neither desirable nor necessary. For the United Kingdom it would mean a loss of prestige, of trade opportunities and naval strength. For the colonies it would mean an insignificant position in the world, a position like that of a South American republic, or one of the minor nations, which exercised no influence on human affairs and were the very playthings of the powerful nations of the earth. What then? The difficulty in Ireland pointed the way. It was impossible that the distress and discontent there would end until some form of Home Rule had come. The disaffection which existed in Ireland was not so much that England misgoverned Ireland but that she governed Ireland at all. It was a realization of this situation, a situation that had very direct consequences for Canada in the Fenian raids, which had lately led the Canadian Parliament to send its much criticized address, petitioning the Queen to give her assent to a measure for the self-government of Ireland. Canada's experiences of federation pointed the remedy – the extension of the principle of federation to the whole self-governing Empire, with the general interests which concerned all consolidated under the general legislature, and with local interests entrusted to the legislatures of England, Scotland, Ireland, Canada and Australia. The British Empire, he concluded, had grown beyond its political system. He hoped that whatever changes came would be in a direction which would give vitality and permanence to the Empire: "I cannot believe that the statesmen who have built up this great empire have not bequeathed ability and talent enough to their successors to hold it together."

In these and similar utterances Galt developed one phase of the policy of empire which was eventually to take shape by the reconciling of opposing but complimentary principles. Neither the imperial federation plan which he, and soon afterwards, so many others advocated, nor the independence which he had defended a decade earlier, was to commend itself wholly to the generation which followed, but each policy contributed an essential element to the new connection of the Empire as an alliance of independent states which in our own times has come to prevail in doctrine and in practice.

His colleagues in Canada were now more nationalist than he. Sir Charles Tupper wrote him in March, 1883: "I read with

great interest your speeches at Edinburgh, Greenock, and Liverpool, and need not tell you that they showed your usual ability.
Of course, you know that I do not agree with you on the
question of Imperial Federation, believing as I do that we will
for many years find ample work in consolidating our existing
constitution and developing out material resources." Macdonald, writing on February 2, was equally opposed to any plans
for submerging Canada in a London parliament: "We are
informed by telegraph of your speech at Edinburgh, and I
await with some little anxiety its arrival in extenso. I hope you
have not committed yourself too much to the project of Imperial
Federation, which, in my humble opinion, can never be worked
out."

It was not, however, in these essays in high policy that the
time and energy of the High Commissioner were chiefly concerned. The pressing and practical task before him was to
promote emigration from the British Isles to Canada. At great
cost the Dominion was opening the North West to settlement,
and unless emigrants could be found in large numbers, the rails
of the Canadian Pacific would rust and the country be saddled
with a vast and useless expenditure. The need of men from
overseas was the greater because of the constant drain, "the
exodus," from Canada itself to the United States, though the
very fact of this migration, exaggerated by United States agen-
cies, was the greatest stumbling-block in the path of success in
the United Kingdom.

The Dominion had already several emigration agents in the
United Kingdom, but dry rot had set in. "So far as I can judge,"
Galt wrote to Pope, who, as Minister of Agriculture, was in
charge of immigration, shortly after his arrival in England, "the
whole establishment here is a complete sham and waste of
money. Dyke at Liverpool is a really good man, but the rest are
simply obstructions." He effected a thoroughgoing shake-up in
the staff, and secured the adoption of more business-like
methods. Some improvements were made in the pamphlets and
settlers' and delegates' reports prepared for distribution, though
characteristically the freedom of action of the man on the spot
was hampered herein by the necessity of having all the appropriation for printing spent in Canada as an incident in the
patronage system. Galt took every occasion to cultivate friendly
relations with the press, and by his speeches and other activities
endeavoured to keep Canada in the mind of the public.

He felt, however, that some policy more striking and comprehensive than these routine methods should be adopted, wholesale rather than retail measures. The agricultural depression in Great Britain, and still more the distress and famine in Ireland, for the relief of which the Canadian Parliament had the year before voted $100,000, appeared to offer the opportunity and the need for a scheme of emigration on an unprecedented scale. In season and out he sought to enlist the sympathy and aid of the government, and later of private associations, in such a plan. He urged that it was the only effective way of draining the swamp of misery in Ireland: with an appropriate Irish bull, he declared in one of his letters to Macdonald, that "in the end Kimberley and Forster must discover that there is no other way of making the west of Ireland support its 600,000 souls than to take half of them away." And if they were to leave, there was no question that it was to the interest of the whole Empire that they should go to Canada rather than be lost to the flag. If left to themselves, it would be to the United States they would go. There the first tide had flowed, and as three out of four new emigrants had their passage paid by friends on the other side, the start of the United States was hard to overcome.

In debating ways and means of promoting emigration on a large scale, Galt considered the advisability of reviving once more the land company plan. The chief shareholders of the Canada Company in London were approached, and showed some interest. The homestead and preemption system which had been adopted in the North-West was found, however, to preclude the activities of a company organized on a commercial basis, and Galt turned once more to the government for aid. He drew up a plan for joint action between the British and Canadian governments which enlisted the sympathy of Forster, the more cautious approval of Kimberley, and the endorsation of the Canadian cabinet. It was manifest, Galt premised, that it was only by the removal of entire families that any sensible relief could be secured; provision would have to be made not only for their transport but for their maintenance until a crop had been secured. He proposed, therefore, that ready-made farms should be prepared in the North-West, a small dwelling built and about eight acres of land broken and prepared for a crop, the first settlers being employed to do this work for the later comers. Forty pounds would be required for transportation and the same amount to prepare the land. The Canadian government would give a free homestead with preemption rights; a

Commission or National Emigration Association, to which the British government should advance funds at a low rate of interest, would organize and carry out the work, the outlay being made a first charge on each settler's land, to be paid off in annual instalments. One of Galt's later letters put his estimate of the cost of the plan as it should be carried out at £10,000,000 – rather a large sum for Victorian days. . . .

~ Galt reported that W. E. Forster, the Secretary for Ireland, approved of the scheme but that Gladstone opposed it in cabinet as too expensive and likely to alienate influential Irishmen who were attempting to stop the flow of immigrants to North America. ~

Systematic plans of emigration were at a discount in Ireland. The Land League movement was at its height; the people had determined that "their America was here or nowhere," and the Nationalist leaders looked upon emigration as a device for draining the country of the most enterprising men and for blocking the reform in the land system which was long overdue. They wanted to attack the cause, not the symptoms of the disease. Hence Galt fared little better when he turned to the Irish landlords, with many of whom, particularly Lord Lansdowne, he entered into detailed discussion. The visit of Archbishop Lynch, of Toronto, to Ireland in 1882, and letters written by other Canadian prelates, at the government's suggestion, had somewhat more effect. A little earlier Galt had discussed plans of co-operation in emigration with the directors of the Canadian Pacific. One outcome was seen when in 1883 the Company made the British government an offer to settle 10,000 Irish families upon stocked and equipped farms in Manitoba, provided the government lent them £1,000,000 without interest for ten years. The British authorities sought a guarantee of the loan from the Canadian government, and when it declined, the plan fell through. It was announced that the British government would itself back a similar plan in the spring of 1884, but violent opposition by the Nationalists ended any such idea.

Seeking elsewhere for men, Galt discussed emigration in every promising quarter from Highland landlords to Russian Jews' relief committees. No systematic policy was adopted by any of the bodies approached, but individual emigration increased notably, for a time. The boom in the North-West gave a fillip to emigration, but it died down as soon as depression came. Not till Canadians themselves had proved the land, and not until the free land of the United States had practically vanished, was the great west to attract the settlers it cried for and could so amply reward.

One legacy of these activities was the responsibility which Sir Alexander assumed upon his return to Canada of looking after a colony of Russian Jews settled near Moosomin, a task of no little magnitude which for many years kept him in close communication with the Montagus, Rothschilds, and other leaders of the Jewish community in London.

Throughout these and other activities, Sir Alexander had been distracted by the desire to return to Canada. His health, which had hitherto been robust, had suffered. "There is either something in the air of London," he wrote Macdonald, in March, 1882, "which does not agree with me, or the confinement and regular office work tell injuriously on me. I have not had two days of thorough health since the first of December, and you and I both know that at our age such monitions must not be neglected." "There is no use my continuing constantly feeling poorly," he wrote again, "and unfit for work, while I have the conviction that a return home will make me well. 'At my time of life,' as poor old Hincks said, I cannot afford to waste my remaining strength, and I have much to do in Canada before my final disappearance, I hope."

It was not, however, his ill-health alone which led Galt to think of returning to Canada. Canada's first diplomat was experiencing the difficulty which has faced every democracy in the conduct of diplomacy. As the game has been played, the diplomats who wished to maintain the dignity of their office and their country, to meet on an equal footing the personages in society and finance who in the past have guided the destinies of nations behind the scenes, have considered that they were compelled to spend generously. Yet there was nothing democracies were less willing to do than to provide adequately for their servants in these and other similar high places. The United States had starved its embassies, and in Canada one of the first acts of the Parliament which met after Confederation was to attempt to cut down the Governor-General's salary. A government might with impunity waste millions in inefficient administration, but it dared not spend a few thousands in paying officials salaries materially higher than the income of the average voter.

In the case of the High Commissioner, the salary had been fixed at $10,000, with $4,000 for dwelling and contingencies, a sum which fell very far short of meeting what Galt considered the necessary outlay. Had his private finances been in the condition of earlier years, he would gladly have borne the added expense out of his own pocket, but during the depression in Canada his estate had been seriously encumbered, and for the time the net income had materially fallen. He put the case frankly before Macdonald a year after taking office:

13 March, 1881.

You recommend me to hold on, cut down expenses, and suspend hospitalities, etc. All this I have done to the fullest extent possible, but it does not fit in with my ideal of usefuless. Let us consider the position. . . .

. . . As I told you when in London, my early expenditure was £150 a month more than my salary, and even this would not have been enough. I then clearly saw that the thing was impracticable; you could not help me, and I could not help myself. However, having then adopted the course you now suggest, and having luckily got something more out of my own estate, I have at last a sense of freedom, and shall not trouble you any more. I have systematically abstained from making calls and accepting invitations, which I cannot return, and generally placed myself under close reefed topsails. But this is neither pleasant nor is it the course the High Commissioner of Canada should take.

To succeed in influencing public opinion and the government in favour of Canada, both as a field for emigration, and also looking to a change in trade policy, it is essential that one should meet in society the large landlords, the leaders of the Conservative Party and generally members of both Houses. This cannot be done by staying at home. It means frequenting the clubs (of which I have plenty), going to the House, appearing at dinners and receptions, in short, keeping myself before the Public. You can get a hundred men quite as good as I am, to sit in my office and write letters, but if you ever expected real service from me, it could only be in the personal influence I could exercise in the circles referred to. Circumstances render it impossible for me to do what you have a right to expect, and what I consider imperative.

Let me now ask you as an old friend, and not as Premier of

Canada, to reflect that if I have duties to my country, and possibly ambitions for myself (though the latter are pretty well extinguished), that I have still more serious responsibilities, as the father of eleven children, eight of whom are daughters, and that I am sixty-four years old. My coming here at all I now see was a most serious error, and I cannot again resume the place I had in Canada, without serious loss and difficulty, but this far better than to attempt the impossible task of remaining. Return-ing, I shall have a good hope of taking advantage of the evident return of prosperity and speculation to extricate my estate, and to avail myself of some one of the many openings which must arise in connection with the North West. . . .

I have no other definite plans in view, only wishing to see my way out of my present false position.

I think you should insist now on your Representative being recognized as a member of the Corps Diplomatique. It is really the only proper definition of his rank, and the only way to en-sure proper respect here. As a Colonial these "arrogant insulars" turn up their noses at us all. It strikes me I shall make this confidentially *but officially the real ground of my resignation....*

A little earlier he had written to Sir Charles Tupper:

. . . With my large family I cannot live here as I consider I ought to do without spending £1,500 a year of my own, and this is in the first place inconvenient, and secondly, paying too dear for the honour of representing Canada.

Of course, circumstances may alter the situation, and it may appear my duty to remain, but at present I do not see it. . . . You mentioned while you were here that you would yourself rather like this English mission. I confess I am heartily tired of it, and the post is quite at your service. I should prefer going back to Parliament or helping to do my part particularly in the colonization of the North-West.

Upon the strong urging of Macdonald and Tilley, Galt agreed to stay on. A year later, with failing health added to his other reasons, he put in a formal resignation, but was again prevailed upon to withdraw it for the time. It was only for the time, however, and on June 1, 1883, he definitely retired from office, Sir Charles Tupper succeeding him.

In the nearly six years which he had given to the diplomatic service of his country, Sir Alexander Galt had not carried through all the projects his fertile imagination had conceived, but he had done a great deal to help bring Canada before the world. The government and the general public in the United Kingdom, and the statesmen of Western Europe had been made in great measure familiar with the possibilities and ambitions of the new power among the nations, and the foundations had been well and soundly laid for the development of the inter-imperial interest and the international relations which were to be the outstanding feature of the succeeding generation.*

---

* Not all scholars have been as charitable as Skelton in judging Galt's accomplishments as High Commissioner: "He had failed to obtain diplomatic status for the new Canadian envoy, he had made little headway in his discussions with France and Spain on commercial questions, he had been unable to interest the British government in subsidizing emigration to North America, and he had been quite unsuccessful in attempting to convert the Imperial authorities to a system of tariff preferences. . . . To the masterful Galt it was a disappointing experience. . . ." (Farr, *The Colonial Office and Canada*, p. 268). In part his failure was due to circumstances over which he had little or no control, but it was also attributable in large measure to a personality which was ill-suited to diplomacy. Macdonald was devastatingly critical of Galt's shortcomings as a spokesman for Canada in London. See Donald Creighton, *John A. Macdonald*, Vol. II, *The Old Chieftain* (Toronto, 1955), 290, 311, 334, 343, 349-350.

16: Closing Years

~ During his stay in London as High Commissioner, Galt became interested in schemes to develop the Canadian North-West. One of his sons, Elliott, had joined the Department of the Interior and was posted to Regina as Assistant Indian Commissioner. In the course of his duties, the younger Galt travelled widely through the western territories and learned of a coalfield in what is now southern Alberta, on the site of the future city of Lethbridge. He informed his father of the find and urged him to develop it. Impressed by his son's reports, Galt persuaded several acquaintances in London, including the heads of two publishing firms, W. H. Smith and William Lethbridge, to join him in a mining syndicate. Following a personal survey of the area, Galt formed the Northwestern Coal and Navigation Company in 1882.

The Company encountered serious obstacles to development almost immediately. Transportation presented the first problem. The Canadian Pacific Railway extended only six hundred miles west of Winnipeg and it became necessary to move equipment for the operation by wagon from the rail-head in Montana. Once production started, there still remained the problem of shipping the coal for sale. After abortive attempts to transport the coal via the Belly and Bow rivers to the South Saskatchewan and thence to Medicine Hat, which was the nearest point on the advancing Canadian Pacific, Galt and his associates concluded that they must build a railway from the mines to Dunsmore, a point near Medicine Hat. The one hundred and ten miles of track were completed in 1885. In the meantime, the company had undertaken construction of Mounted Police posts at Fort MacLeod, Medicine Hat and Maple Creek, and, in addition, operated ferries and stage coaches at various points in the territory. When it was discovered that Canadian markets for coal were inadequate, the company decided to build another railway to join the Great Northern Line in Montana and thus provide a market in the United States.

These expanded operations led to the formation of a new company, the Alberta Railway and Coal Company, which absorbed the original firm in 1889. As railways were built, the company acquired the rights to large tracts of land through which the lines ran and consequently became as much involved in land development as in coal mining. Through his efforts to provide a sufficient water supply to soil which was compara- tively fertile but subject to a low annual rainfall and periodic drought, Galt incidentally became a pioneer in large scale irrigation projects.

When Galt died, his son Elliott took over the management of the company until it was sold to the Canadian Pacific in 1910. ~

The ten years which followed Sir Alexander's first western undertaking were years of stress and strain. The task of financ- ing the ever expanding Alberta enterprises, in face of stagnation at home and doubt abroad, was one that wore down his strong body if not his optimistic soul. Even so, he found time to con- tinue his interest in other business relations, acting as director or president of several financial corporations with which he had long been associated. His interest in political affairs continued unabated, and he considered the possibility of returning to the Canadian Parliament in 1887 or of seeking an English seat in 1886, but the unescapable duties of the Alberta undertakings soon put any such diversions of energy out of the question.

In an earlier chapter, reference has been made to the inter- est which Galt took in the question of closer trade relations within the Empire, during his term as High Commissioner. This interest remained with him, and the agitation in Canada for unrestricted reciprocity with the United States led him to bring forward the imperial alternative. One of his steps was to write to Mr. Gladstone, while in England:

26 February, 1891.

Dear Mr. Gladstone:

When appointed High Commissioner for Canada in 1880- 84, I received such valuable support from your Government in my negotiations with France and Spain, that I venture to send you the enclosed letter on the relation of Canada to the United States.

My earnest desire is that you may feel warranted in pressing upon the present Government the importance of early and decided action. . . .

The important issues involved in the present political con- test in Canada, induce me, after much reflection, to address myself to you, believing that your position enables you alone to secure acceptance of that policy, which will immediately and

*permanently counteract the McKinley Tariff, and the political
ends which Mr. Blaine is seeking to promote through its agency.*

*This Tariff, though primarily and directly aimed at the
exclusion of British manufactures from the United States, has
also avowedly for its object to create a state of feeling in Canada
hostile to the maintenance of the Colonial connection, while the
Reciprocal Treaties of Commerce proposed with South America
point to most serious interference with British Trade there.*

*I need not enlarge on these points, as they cannot fail to
have occurred to your own mind. The American Tariff is
therefore a hostile measure – an act of commercial war – and
goes far beyond those measures of mere customs duties, which
in this country are regarded as only injurious to those adopting
them.*

*Retaliation is the only argument applicable in the present
case, and the United States are so peculiarly vulnerable, that its
effect would be immediate, and would necessitate negotiations
probably resulting in a great and permanent amelioration in
their fiscal system, while the "object lesson" might not be lost
upon France and the other European Nations.*

*The imposition of the former British duties on grain and
agricultural produce, limited strictly to the United States, and
removable on the conclusion of a Treaty of Commerce, would
instantly array the whole farming community of the United
States against the McKinley Tariff, and would seriously affect
their commercial and railway interests, while the price of food
in this country would not be much enhanced, as the markets of
the rest of the world would remain available.*

*Such a measure of retaliation is not really a departure from
Free Trade principles, but an act designed to give them greater
expansion, and I do not believe that such a departure could be
even suggested when adopted by you, whose record on these
questions is absolutely unimpeachable.*

*As a Canadian, I may have no right to express an opinion
on British politics, but I venture to think, that in their present
chaotic condition, much good would arise by the introduction
of a new subject of supreme importance, not only to the manufacturing and trading classes, who have been seriously injured
by the McKinley Tariff, but also to the agricultural interests,
who would welcome a measure in this direction, while in Canada
the announcement before the General Election on 5th March
would scatter the political objects sought by Mr. Blaine to
the winds.*

I shall not trouble you to reply to this somewhat lengthy letter. If the idea presents itself attractively to you, I should be happy to wait on you if so desired.

To Sir John Macdonald he wrote suggesting that an address should be sent to the Queen by the Canadian Parliament, urging the denunciation of the Belgian and German treaties and the gradual creation of a tariff-cemented, self-contained Empire. Sir John, then very near his end, wrote by his secretary:

> *Earnscliffe, Ottawa,*
> *14th May, 1891.*
>
> My dear Galt:
> *I have yours of the 12th inst. I have been a little out of sorts and have not been able to attend to many matters but I shall take an early opportunity of bringing up your suggestion as to an address to the Queen before my colleagues.*
> *My present impression is that no action on the part of Canada would be of any value until after the next General Elections when, if Lord Salisbury carried the Country, we ought to make a strong push for the Imperial notion.*
> *Believe me,*
> *Yours faithfully,*
> JOHN A. MACDONALD.

Following up his policy, Sir Alexander next communicated to his old friend, Sir John's successor, Sir J. J. C. Abbott, the result of his sounding of English statesmen on the question:

> *Montreal, 23rd July, 1891.*
> Confidential.
> My dear Abbott:
> *As requested by you I now write the purport of two important interviews which I had in London early in April last.*
> *Owing to the issues raised at the recent election, in reference to our commercial relations with the United States, and their bearing on our position as a portion of the British Empire, I thought it desirable before my return to Canada in April, to endeavour to have the views of leading men in regard to promoting inter-Imperial trade and counteracting the effect of the McKinley Tariff.*
> *My personal relations enabled me to discuss these subjects fully with one of the most influential members of the [Salisbury] Government, and while guarding himself against being supposed to commit his colleagues in any way, he expressed the opinion*

that the effect of the McKinley Tariff, and the threatened increase of duties by France and other countries, was rapidly developing a feeling in England that the existing policy of Free Imports without discrimination could not much longer be maintained, and that the advocates of different treatment towards our own colonies, were gaining ground daily. I asked him whether action by the Canadian Government and Parliament would be favorably received by Salisbury's Government. To this he replied that he must refer me to Lord Salisbury's own speeches, adding the very important declaration that he believed they would be glad to have – "a pressure put upon them" – not only as regards the existing Commercial Treaties, but also the wisdom of suggesting to the United States that discrimination against them might become necessary to meet their attack upon Canadian and British interests.

I do not think you require me to mention the arguments I advanced, as I presume you are more concerned to know how they were received.

At the conclusion of a long interview, I asked him whether he would permit me to mention to Sir John Macdonald, confidentially, what had passed between us, and he at once assented to my doing so.

On parting I further enquired whether I might mention to the gentleman, who is perhaps the most influential supporter of the Government in the Commons, the fact of my interview with himself, and its support, to which he replied, that he would be pleased if I did so.

I thereupon waited upon the statesman referred to, with whom I had already on previous occasions discussed these subjects, and after a long discussion in which I found he fully shared the opinions I have briefly recapitulated, I put the question plainly to him – what do you think would be the effect in England of an Address to the Queen by the Canadian Parliament, embodying these views, and offering substantial discrimination in the tariff in favour of British industries on condition of the adoption of a policy by Great Britain favourable to the colonies in future treaties with foreign Powers, and especially towards the United States? To this question my friend said most emphatically that he thought that such an Address would meet an immediate and warm reception in England, and that he himself "would stump the country upon it." This statement coming from a prominent Free Trader, I welcomed as evidence that the time for action by Canada had come.

The foregoing is the substance of the interview which I mentioned to you, and with your permission I would say I am convinced that this country is ripe for a policy which would squarely meet your political opponents — by putting inter-Imperial Trade against Unrestricted Reciprocity with the United States. Canada should lead the way, as her interests are more materially affected by the tariff legislation of the United States.

The time is propitious, as the Treaties of Commerce all expire next year — and with the action of the United States, and that indicated by France, a bold policy of fostering British industry may not be an unlikely card for the English Ministry to play at the coming General Election — which will probably take place very soon, especially if the reports be confirmed of Mr. Gladstone's probable retirement from public life.

If I may, without offence, say so, I would remark, that the best way to neutralize the effect on the public of the wretched scandals now disseminated at Ottawa, is to place some subject of supreme importance in the foreground, and to choose such subject as your political opponents can scarcely venture to oppose — nor to adopt — after the line they took at the last election.

You are aware that on my arrival in Canada in April, I placed these points before Sir John Macdonald, and his private letters, which I have given you, indicate that, had he lived, the subject would have been brought by him before the Council.

Yours very faithfully,

A. T. GALT.

This led to the introduction of a resolution praying the denunciation of the Belgian and German treaties, which was passed unanimously by both Houses at Ottawa. For the time, no heed was given. It was not until a new policy had been adopted by the Liberals in 1897, by giving a preference on British goods without asking for return concessions, that popular opinion in England was stirred to the point of requiring the abrogation of the objectionable treaties. Without the pioneer work of Galt and his colleagues, however, this result would not have been attained.

One of his last important public services was to act as Chairman of a Royal Commission appointed by the Dominion Government in 1888 to consider the question of state regulation of railways. The establishment of the Interstate Commerce Commission in the United States in 1886 had brought to a head the demands from Canadian shippers for more effective supervision. The commissioners in their report noted the existence of many grievances for which they suggested specific remedies. As to the wider question, they recommended that until the British and American attempts at government regulation had had time to prove their worth or their weaknesses, it would be better to extend the powers of the Railway Committee of the Privy Council or Cabinet, rather than to establish an independent commission. When, eventually, a commission was established, the benefit of waiting was seen in the much more adequate powers and scope given it than the British or United States bodies enjoyed.

After 1890, his health began to fail rapidly. After an illness of many months, the end came on September 19, 1893, at his home on Mountain Street, Montreal. To a friend, Dr. Potts, who sat beside him a few weeks before the end, he wrote on the flyleaf of a book: "I have much to be thankful for, a long life with many blessings, and I try to accept God's will as my most supreme comfort. No one could have had greater blessings in his family than myself. I do not pray God to prolong my life, but only to support and strengthen me and to let my departure be tranquil."

Sir Alexander was survived by Lady Galt and by three sons and eight daughters: Elliott Galt, of Montreal; John Galt, of Winnipeg; Alexander Galt; the Misses Kate and Selina and Muriel Galt, Mrs. Robert Grant, Mrs. A. R. Springett, Mrs. C. A. Magrath, Mrs. A. D. Durnford, and Mrs. W. Harvey Smith.

It was a year of deep depression, of world-shaking business failures, and of national doubt and despondency. Yet the turn of the tide was near, and before the century had ended, the abounding prosperity of the country, west and east, and the growth of a strong sense of national unity and national consciousness had justified the faith that he and his fellow-builders had held alike through good and through ill report.

To his friends he left a warm and lasting memory. He was not a man who could easily unbend in public life; of the hand-shaking arts of the lesser politician he had few. In private intercourse, however, he was a rarely genial and delightful companion. His courtly manners were no conventional and external acquirement, but the expression of a wide and genuine sympathy and a kindly considerateness that paid no heed to rank or place. It was significant that alike in his middle and in his later years, young men were among his closest friends.

To the wider public he left a tradition of good work well done. Alexander Tilloch Galt had given nearly sixty years to his adopted country. They were years of momentous change, years which saw the scattered, struggling, backwoods provinces grow into a nation. In this development he had taken a distinctive and essential part, a part marked by untiring effort, a high and sensitive honour, and a constructive vision which was never content to let chance and drift settle the affairs of state. The name of Galt will not soon pass from the memory of the country he served.

NOTES

(Footnotes which appeared in the original edition are denoted by an asterisk.)

CHAPTER 1:

The British American Land Company
(pp. 1-15)

[1] A few of John Galt's books continue to occupy a respectable place in English, and more particularly, Scottish literature. Four of his novels, *The Ayrshire Legatees* (1821), *Annals of the Parish* (1821), *The Entail* (1823), and *The Provost* (1824), have given him, in the words of one critic, "a safe niche in literature" (A. C. Ward, *Illustrated History of English Literature* [London, 1955], III, 151). In the use of imaginative autobiography, the literary form which he employed most successfully, he has been described as "approaching greatness" (Ian Jack, *English Literature, 1815-1832* [Oxford, 1963], p. 235; see also David Daiches, *A Critical History of English Literature* [London, 1960], II, 854).

In two of his novels Galt drew on his Canadian experience. *Laurie Todd* (1830) and *Bogle Corbet* (1831) are not among his best works but are not without merit. C. F. Klinck has said of them: "Observation, ingenuity, humour, the right tone, reliable detail, and general applicability made these novels popular, though only for a few decades" (C. F. Klinck, "Literary Activity in the Canadas, 1812-1841," *Literary History of Canada* [Toronto, 1965], p. 142).

[2] For a general survey of immigration and land settlement, with particular references to the Canada Company, see W. A. Carrothers, *Emigration from the British Isles* (London, 1929), pp. 144*ff*; Norman Macdonald, *Canada, 1763-1841: Immigration and Settlement* (London, 1939), pp. 265-285; Helen I. Cowan, *British Emigration to British North America* (Toronto, 1961), pp. 132-135; G. M. Craig, *Upper Canada, The Formative Years, 1784-1841* (Toronto, 1963), pp. 135-138.

[3] For further information on the British American Land Company, see Macdonald, *op. cit.*, pp. 286-301; Cowan, *op. cit.*, pp. 135-139; and D. G. Creighton, *The Commercial Empire of the St. Lawrence, 1760-1850* (Toronto, 1937), pp. 276-278.

CHAPTER 2:

Galt and the Coming of the Railway
(pp. 16-26)

[1] For a comprehensive description of the first railway era in British North America, see G. P. deT. Glazebrook, *A History of Transportation in Canada* (Carleton Library, 1964), I, 140-179; G. R. Stevens, *Canadian National Railways* (Toronto, 1960), pp. 52-89.

CHAPTER 3:

The Building of the Grand Trunk
(pp. 27-48)

1 The definitive study of the Grand Trunk Railway is A. W. Currie, *The Grand Trunk Railway of Canada* (Toronto, 1957). For the part of the story told in this chapter see Currie, *op. cit.*, pp. 3-70; also Glazebrook, *op. cit.*, I, 140-179.

CHAPTER 4:

Canada Under the Union:
The Coming of Responsible Government
(pp. 49-62)

1 The most convenient edition is G. M. Craig, (ed.) *Lord Durham's Report* (Carleton Library, 1963).

CHAPTER 5:

The Aftermath of Responsible Government
(pp. 63-70)

1 For a full discussion of the background to the annexation movement within the context of the broader continental trade pattern, see D. G. Creighton, *The Commercial Empire of the St. Lawrence*, pp. 349-385; C. D. Allin and G. M. Jones, *Annexation, Preferential Trade, and Reciprocity* (Toronto, 1911), esp. pp. 99-207; G. N. Tucker, *The Canadian Commercial Revolution, 1845-1851* (Carleton Library, 1964).

*2 "My prejudices were altogether against the annexation movement," [Galt] writes to Alexander Gillespie, Governor of the Land Company, in October, 1849, "but my very situation here has probably given me as good an opportunity of judging of the effect of the measure as any one in the province possesses, and I am thoroughly convinced it is the only cure for our manifold ills. . . . All the plans for ameliorating our condition now before the country are based upon reciprocity with the United States, and are therefore only adopting one of the advantages which would flow from annexation." O. D. Skelton, *Life and Times of Sir Alexander Tilloch Galt* (Toronto, 1920), p. 153.

*3 "If Lord Stanley were to get into office," he writes again, early in 1850, "some attempt might be made to restore Protection, but I fear it would do us more harm than good to have a *partial* revival of the old system. Could Great Britain retrace her steps and establish a proper colonial system, this country might remain a flourishing dependency for years, but it is, I fancy, quite absurd even to dream of such a thing. The hour has passed for erecting a great Colonial Empire and now we poor provincials must struggle upward as we best may." *Ibid.*

CHAPTER 7:

Sectional Conflict and the Way Out: 1854-1856
(pp. 77-82)

[*1] "I would now move that the House resolve themselves into Committee of the Whole to consider the following resolutions:

1. That in view of the rapid development of the population and resources of Western Canada, irreconcilable difficulties present themselves to the maintenance of that equality which formed the basis of the Union of Upper and Lower Canada, and require this House to consider the means whereby the progress which has so happily characterized this province may not be arrested through the occurrence of sectional jealousies and dissensions. It is, therefore, the opinion of this House that the union of Upper and Lower Canada should be changed from a Legislative to a Federative Union by the subdivision of the province into two or more divisions, each governing itself in local and sectional matters, with a general legislative government for subjects of national and common interest; and that a Commission of nine members be now named to report on the best means and mode of effecting such constitutional changes.

2. That considering the claims possessed by this province on the Northwestern and Hudson's Bay territories and the necessity of making provision for the government of the said districts, it is the opinion of this House that in the adoption of a federative constitution for Canada means should be provided for the local government of the said territories under the general government until population and settlement may from time to time enable them to be admitted into the Canadian Confederation.

3. That a general Confederation of the provinces of New Brunswick, Nova Scotia, Newfoundland and Prince Edward Island with Canada and the Western territories is most desirable and calculated to promote their several and united interests by preserving to each province the uncontrolled management of its peculiar institutions and of those internal affairs respecting which differences of opinion might arise with other members of the Confederation, while it will increase that identity of feeling which pervades the possessions of the British Crown in North America; and by the adoption of a uniform policy for the development of the vast and varied resources of these immense territories will greatly add to their national power and consideration; and that a Committee of nine members be appointed to report on the steps to be taken for ascertaining without delay the sentiments of the inhabitants of the Lower Provinces and of the Imperial Government on this most important subject." Skelton, *Galt*, pp. 219-221.

CHAPTER 8:

Party Changes and the Federation Proposals
(pp. 83-106)

[1] Galt bitterly resented Brown's inept inquisition. For further light on the decisive episode, and subsequent events as seen from two different viewpoints, see J. M. S. Careless, *Brown of the Globe*, Vol. I, *The Voice of Upper Canada, 1818-1859* (Toronto, 1959), p. 240; and Donald Creighton, *John A. Macdonald*, Vol. I, *The Young Politician* (Toronto, 1952), pp. 251-252.

[*2] The comments of the *Globe* are of interest (Aug. 9th, 1858): "The Game of Thimble-rig: One day the Galt thimble hid the pea, on the next the Cartier-Galt contrivance covered the prize, and twenty-four hours more placed the coveted article under the identical thimble which stood first upon the table when the Macdonald-Cartier compact feigned an abandonment of their position.

"The accession of Mr. Galt as Inspector-General is, however, the great future of the new arrangement. No one will deny to him greater skill and resources than his predecessor, but as to honesty, economy or desire to bring the finances of the country into proper condition, we believe he is even worse than Mr. Cayley. He will be far more dexterous in his treatment of figures, far more clever in humbugging the House, but as to economy he is incapable of it. He has not the courage of a mouse, nor has he the sense of right and desire for the people's good necessary to induce him to apply the pruning knife to the expenses of the country. He is a jobber at heart; the benefit of the people is his last thought in considering a public question." Skelton, *Galt*, p. 237.

CHAPTER 10:

Canada and the United States
(pp. 127-134)

[1] Skelton also noted, without going into great detail, that I. D. Andrews, the United States Consul at Saint John, played an important part in the achievement of reciprocity. Further light on Andrews' contribution has been provided in a recent article. See Irene W. D. Hecht, "Israel D. Andrews and the Reciprocity Treaty of 1854: A Reappraisal," *Canadian Historical Review*, XLIV (December, 1963), 313-329.

[2] Recent studies have considerably supplemented Skelton's description of Canadian-American relations during this period. For an excellent, concise summary of the background of the reciprocity question, see W. T. Easterbrook and Hugh G. J. Aitken, *Canadian Economic History* (Toronto, 1956), pp. 361-74. More detailed discussions will be found in L. B. Shippee, *Canadian-American Relations, 1849-1874* (New Haven, 1939); D. C. Masters, *The Reciprocity Treaty of 1854* (Carleton Library, 1963); C. C. Tansill, *The Canadian Reciprocity*

Treaty of 1854 (Baltimore, 1922); J. B. Brebner, *North Atlantic Triangle* (New Haven, 1945, and reprinted in the Carleton Library, 1966).

3 The problem of Canadian public opinion concerning the Civil War, and more particularly the attitude of Canadians toward the North, has been the subject of a recent exhaustive study. See Robin W. Winks, *Canada and the United States: The Civil War Years* (Baltimore, 1960), pp. 1-21, 205-243.

CHAPTER 11:

Canada and the Mother Country
(pp. 135-144)

1 Skelton's judgment of the fighting potential of the militia was not quite so extreme as this. For a detailed examination of the military situation in Canada during the Civil War, see C. P. Stacey, *Canada and the British Army, 1846-1871* (Toronto, rev. ed., 1963), pp. 117-78.

CHAPTER 12:

The Coming of Confederation
(pp. 145-194)

1 For an account of the events described in this chapter see Donald Creighton, *The Road to Confederation, The Emergence of Canada: 1863-1867* (Toronto, 1964). Fascinating sidelights on the politics, people and press of the same period may be found in P. B. Waite, *The Life and Times of Confederation, 1864-1867* (Toronto, 1962).

2 For a description of the Galt-Brown clash over reciprocity, which more generously evaluates Brown's motives, see Careless, *Brown of the Globe*, II, 213-217.

CHAPTER 14:

Church and State
(pp. 237-244)

*1 Mr. Gladstone had thus acknowledged the receipt of a copy of the earlier pamphlet, *Civil Liberty in Lower Canada*:

4 Carlton Gardens, S.W.,
March 23, 1876.

My Dear Sir:
I have read your Pamphlet with much interest and I am very glad that you intend to play a manful part in the contest with Ultramon-

tanism, as that formidable power has selected your quarter for one of its present points of attack upon human liberty.

My own action in this warfare is, I hope, completed, but I watch the struggle everywhere with great interest.

Most cordially do I agree in the sense of your concluding paragraph [opposing the policy of the Protestant Defence Association]. It is folly, it is almost madness, to mix this question with the Protestant Propaganda, in this country at least, so I read with deep concern an account of a recent exhibition in Canada by a late R. C. priest which I hope was not true, for if true his conduct was, as far as I could judge, profane.

Such conduct serves the purpose of the Court of Rome far better than any other conceivable line of action, or than the most servile obedience.

Believe me,

Faithfully yours,

W. GLADSTONE.

Skelton, *Galt*, p. 488.

---

[2] For a description of the religious controversy in Quebec, which gives a useful picture of the opposition to Bishop Bourget's policy within the Church itself, see Mason Wade, *The French Canadians, 1760-1945* (London, 1955), pp. 339-370; J. S. Willison, *Sir Wilfrid Laurier and the Liberal Party* (Toronto, 1903), I, 27-76, 253-314. The moderation displayed by Archbishop Taschereau and the Bishops of Rimouski and St. Hyacinthe was far more influential than Galt's fulminations in the defeat of the "audacious assault upon the common liberties of the people."

CHAPTER 15:

High Commissioner and Ambassador-at-Large
(pp. 245-272)

[1] For the Treaty of Washington (1871) and the fisheries settlement, see L. B. Shippee, *Canadian-American Relations, 1848-1874*, pp. 348-425. For the Halifax Commission, see C. C. Tansill, *Canadian-American Relations, 1875-1911* (New Haven, 1943), pp. 10-12.

[2] Skelton's description of the origins of the office of High Commissioner has been largely complemented by a definitive study of the relations between the Colonial Office and Canada. See David M. L. Farr, *The Colonial Office and Canada, 1867-1887* (Toronto, 1955).

[3] The standard work on the movement for imperial unity and the Imperial Federation League is J. E. Tyler, *The Struggle for Imperial Unity, 1868-1895* (London, 1938). See also Seymour Cheng, *Schemes for the Federation of the British Empire* (New York, 1931), and A. L. Burt, *Imperial Architects* (Toronto, 1913). Galt became a member of the Council of the Imperial Federation League, a pressure group advocating a federal union of the various parts of the Empire, but he was never very active in the movement.

SUGGESTIONS FOR
FURTHER READING

The historical literature devoted to Galt is not extensive. However, those readers who will want to deepen their knowledge and understanding of the man and his times should round out Skelton's portrait by reading the biographies of two of Galt's contemporaries. A staunch political ally, John A. Macdonald often relied on Galt's counsel, but this did not deter him from incisive judgments on his character. These are found in DONALD CREIGHTON, *John A. Macdonald* (Toronto, 2 vols., 1952, 1955). One catches glimpses of Galt's motives as seen by a persistent foe and less charitable critic, George Brown, in *Brown of the Globe* (Toronto, 2 vols., 1959, 1963) by J. M. S. CARELESS. A more recent work by D. G. CREIGHTON, *The Road to Confederation, The Emergence of Canada: 1863-1867* (Toronto, 1964) emphasizes Galt's remarkable statesmanship at the Charlottetown Conference in 1864.

One cannot fully appreciate Galt's achievements as a brilliantly imaginative financier without reading such standard works on Canadian transportation and economic history as G. P. deT. GLAZEBROOK, *A History of Transportation in Canada* (Carleton Library, 2 vols., 1964), and W. T. EASTERBROOK and HUGH G. J. AITKEN, *Canadian Economic History* (Toronto, 1956).

Galt's work as High Commissioner in London is described in G. P. deT. GLAZEBROOK, *A History of Canadian External Relations* (Carleton Library, 1966) and in DAVID M. L. FARR, *The Colonial Office and Canada, 1867-1887* (Toronto, 1955). Galt's views on the economic policy of the colonies will be found in the two articles by D. C. MASTERS cited in the note on p. 140 of this volume.

NOTE ON THE AUTHOR

Oscar Douglas Skelton, author, teacher, and public servant, was born in Orangeville, Ontario, in 1878. He was educated at Queen's University and the University of Chicago. For seventeen years he was Professor of Political and Economic Science at Queen's where he wrote prolifically on history, politics and political thought. Among his most important works are: *Socialism: A Critical Analysis* (1911); "General Economic History, 1867-1912," in volume IX of *Canada and Its Provinces* (1914); *The Day of Sir Wilfrid Laurier* (1916); *The Canadian Dominion* (1919); *Life and Times of Sir Alexander Tilloch Galt* (1920) and *Life and Letters of Sir Wilfrid Laurier* (1921).

In 1924 Skelton joined the Department of External Affairs and became Under-Secretary a year later, a post he held until his death in 1941. The trusted adviser of three prime ministers, he played a key role in the formation of Canadian foreign policy and the creation of the Common-wealth.

THE CARLETON LIBRARY